KB066841

한국 경제성장에서 박태준 리더십의 역할과 개발도상국 적용방안에 대한 연구

A Study on the Role of TJP Leadership
in the Korea Economic Development
and Application to the Developing Economies

청암 박태준 연구서 8

한국 경제성장에서 박태준 리더십의 역할과 개발도상국 적용방안에 대한 연구

A Study on the Role of TJP Leadership in the Korea Economic Development and Application to the Developing Economies

김동헌
Dong Heon Kim

아시아

청암 박태준 연구서를 펴내며

2011년 12월 13일 청암 박태준은 위업을 남기고 향년 84세로 눈을 감았다. 그의 부음을 알리는 한국의 모든 언론들과 해외의 많은 언론들이 일제히 헌화하듯이 그의 이름 앞에 영웅·거인·거목이란 말을 놓았다. 시대의 고난을 돌파하여 공동체의 행복을 창조한 그의 인생에 동시대가 선물한 최후의 빛나는 영예였다. 그러나 어쩌면 그것이 망각의 늪으로 빠지는 함정일지 모른다. 영웅이란 헌사야말로 후세가 간단히 공적으로만 그를 기억하게 만들 수 있는 것이다.

영웅의 죽음은 곧잘 공적의 표상으로 되살아난다. 이것이 인간사회의 오랜 관습이다. 세상을 떠난 영웅에게는 또 하나의 피할 수 없는 운명으로 강요된다. 여기서 그는 우상처럼 통속으로 전락하기 쉽고, 후세는 그의 정신을 망각하기 쉽다. 다만 그것을 막아낼 길목에 튼튼하고 깐깐한 바리케이드를 설치할 수는 있다. 인물연구와 전기문학의 몫이다.

인물연구와 전기문학은 다른 장르이다. 하지만 존재의 성격과 목적은 유사하다. 어느 쪽이든 주인공이 감당한 시대적 조건 속에서 그를 인간의 이름으로 읽어내야 한다. 작업을 진행하는 과정은, 그의 얼굴과 체온과 내면이 다시 살아나고 당대의 초상이 다시 그려지는 부활의 시간이다. 이 부활은 잊어버린 질문의 복구이기도 하다. 어떤 악조건 속에서 어떻게 위업을 이룩할 수 있었는가? 이것은 관문의 열쇠이다. 그 문을 열고 천천히 안으로 들어가야 비로소 그의 신념, 그의 고뇌, 그의 투쟁, 그의 상처가 숨을 쉬는 특정한 시대의 특수한 시공時空과 만날 수 있으며 드디어 그의 감정을 느끼는 가운데 그와 대화를 나누는 방에 이르게 된다.

거대한 짐을 짊어지고 흐트러짐 없이 필생을 완주하는 동안에 시대의 새 지평을 개척하면서 만인을 위하여 헌신한 영웅에 대해 공적으로만 그를 기억하는 것은 후세의 큰 결례이며 위대한 정신 유산을 잃어버리는 사회적 손실이 아닐 수 없다. 짧은 인생을 영원 조국에, 이 신념의 나침반을 따라 한 치 어긋남 없이 헤쳐 나아간 박태준의 일생은 철저한 선공후사와 솔선수범, 그리고 순애殉愛의 헌신으로 제철보국 교육보국을 실현하는 길이었다. 그것은 위업을 창조했다. 제철보국은 무無의 불모지에 포스코를 세워 세계 일류 철강기업으로 성장시킴으로써 조국근대화의 견인차가 되고, 교육보국은 유치원·초·중·고 14개교를 세워 한국 최고 배움의 전당으로 만들었을 뿐만 아니라 마침내 한국 최초 연구중심대학 포스텍을 세워 세계적 명문대학으로 육성함으로써 이 나라 교육의 새로운 개척자가 되었다. 더구나 모든 일들이 오직 일류국가의 이상과 염원을 향해 나아가는 실천이었다.

그러므로 후세는 박태준의 위업에 내재된 그의 정신을 기억하고 무형의 사회적 자산으로 활용할 수 있어야 한다. 그의 생애와 사상에 대한 학문적 연구를 체계화한 『청암 박태준 연구서』는 그러한 목적에 이바지하려는 책들로서, 앞으로 전개될 박태준 연구에 대한 선행연구의 역할을 맡는 가운데 기존 '박태준 전기문학'과 함께 언젠가 그를 공적의 표상으로만 기억하게 될지 모르는 그 위험한 '길목'도 지켜줄 것이다.

박태준미래전략연구소

일러두기

1. '청암 박태준 연구'의 기본 텍스트는 국판 편집으로 일만 쪽에 이르는 '박태준 어록', 포스코의 사사(社史)와 사보(私報), 포스코에 대한 기존 연구 논문들, 포스텍(포항방사광가속기연구소 포함)의 교사(校史), 포스코교육재단과 학교들의 교사(校史), 포항산업과학연구원(RIST)의 사사(社史), 박태준에 대한 전기문학과 저서들, 신문과 잡지 등이다.

2. 박태준의 기록 육성과 녹음 육성의 디지털화 작업은 포스코경영연구소가 주관해 2009년에 완료하였으며, 그의 생각과 감정을 생생히 담은 그것은 마치 사초를 쓰듯이 기록하고 보관한 '포스코 기록 문화'의 귀중한 선물이라 할 수 있다. 현재 '박태준 어록'은 포항공과대학교(POSTECH) 부설 박태준미래전략연구소 홈페이지와 연결되어 있다.

3. 이 연구서들에 엮은 모든 논문에 대해서는 학문적 객관성 담보를 위하여 '학술진흥재단 등재지 또는 등재 후보지' 게재를 원칙으로 삼았으며, 그에 따라 게재를 마친 논문이 다수이고 다른 매체에 게재한 논문도 있다.

4. 각 권의 제목은 논문들을 주제별로 분류한 뒤 편찬 회의에서 정한 것이다.

5. 앞으로 전개될 '박태준 연구'의 결과물이나 포스텍의 박태준미래전략연구소가 주관한 다양한 연구 논문들도 꾸준히 이 연구서로 발간할 계획이다.

차 례

표 · 그림 차례

한국 경제성장에서 박태준 리더십의 역할과 개발도상국 적용방안에 대한 연구

김동헌

김동헌

학력
고려대학교 경제학과 학사
고려대학교 대학원 석사
미국 캘리포니아주립대 (샌디에고) 경제학 박사

주요 경력
영국 맨체스터대학교 경제학과 조교수, 부교수
미국 캘리포니아주립대(샌디에고) 교환교수
기획재정부 공공기관장 평가단 위원 및 팀장
《Manchester School》 공동편집위원장
현 고려대학교 경제학과 교수

주요 논문
"A Re-examination of the Predictability of Economic Activity Using the Yield Spread" (JMCB, 2002)
"Nonlinearity in the Fed's Monetary Policy Rule" (JAE, 2005)
"The New Keynesian Phillips Curve: from Sticky Inflation to Sticky Prices" (JMCB, 2008)
"Observed Inflation Forecasts and the New Keynesian Phillips Curve" (OBES, 2008)
"What is an oil shock? Panel Data Evidence" (EE, 2012)
"The Evolution of Monetary Policy Regimes in the U.S." (EE, 2012)
「한국의 일별 콜금리 분석」 (2008), 「금리준칙에서 통화의 역할」 (2010), 「미국 금융시장 여건 변화가 한국금융시장에 미치는 영향 분석: FCI를 중심으로」 (2013), 「노동력의 고령화는 노동생산성을 저하시키는가?: 한국 사례에 대한 실증분석」 (2014), 「거시건전성 정책수단 설계 및 적용방법론」 (2014)

요 약

　한국은 특별한 부존자원이 없고 산업기반이 거의 전무한 세계 최빈 국 상황에서 공업화 및 경제자유화를 일구어 왔으며, 이는 2011년 기 준 경제규모 세계 12위, 무역규모 세계 9위라는 세계적으로 유례없는 경제발전의 성공사례로 평가되고 있다. 한국이 1950년 한국전쟁 이후 60년이라는 짧은 기간 동안 연평균 4.5%를 상회하는 경제성장률을 달 성하면서 성공적인 경제발전을 이룩할 수 있었던 핵심 요인은 무엇인 가? 특히 박정희 정부의 강력한 지원 하에 1968년 창립된 포항제철주 식회사(2002년부터 포스코로 명칭 변경)는 국내 제조업체에 저렴하면서도 양 질의 철강 제품을 공급함으로써 조선, 자동차, 기계, 전자 및 건설 산업 등의 수출경쟁력을 강화하고 이들 산업의 성장 발판을 마련하여 1970 년대 이후 중화학공업화를 통한 한국경제 발전에 중추적인 역할을 담

15

당하였다. 한마디로 포스코 성장의 역사는 한국경제 성장의 역사와 맞닿아 있다고 볼 수 있다.

포스코 기업 차원의 노력과 국가적 지원이 포스코 성공사례를 만들어 낸 것으로 볼 수 있겠지만, 보다 핵심적인 포스코 성공 요인은 창립자 박태준 회장(이하 TJP)의 리더십이다. 박태준 회장은 1968년 포스코 창립 당시부터 초대 사장을 맡아 1992년까지 포항제철소 1-4기, 광양제철소 1-4기 공장을 완공하여 1992년 포스코를 연간 조강생산능력 2,050만톤을 갖춘 세계 3위 제철소로 만들었다. 또한 박태준 회장은 재임기간 동안 연평균 매출증가율 34%, 순이익증가율 71.3%, 그리고 1992년 한국경제 GDP 대비 포스코 매출액 비중이 2.3%에 달하는 경이로운 경영성과를 이룩하였다. 1인당 조강생산량으로 측정한 1인당 노동생산성증가율은 연평균 15%에 달하였고 1992년 기준 국내철강생산량 중 포스코 생산량은 71.3% 그리고 생산설비 국산화 비율은 63.1%를 이룩하였다.

오늘날 한국경제는 고도성장에 힘입어 국제사회에서 그 위상이 점차 높아지고 있으며 이에 따라 세계경제에 대한 한 차원 격상된 기여가 요구되고 있는 실정이다. 개발도상국의 입장에서 한국경제 성장 경험으로부터 가장 절실히 요구되는 것은 무엇일까? 그 출발점은 경제발전 초기단계에서 중추적 역할을 담당하는 산업기반 조성과 국제 경쟁력을 견인하는 초일류 기업 육성 전략의 학습이다. 이러한 관점에서 한국경제는 어떻게 산업기반을 조성하였으며 포스코, 삼성전자, 현대자동차 등과 같은 초일류 국제적 기업들을 육성할 수 있었을까?

본 연구는 지난 40년간 한국경제가 성취한 고도성장의 배경과 그 핵심 성장 동력으로서 포스코의 역할을 심도 있게 분석하여 포스코형 성장 모형의 실질적 프레임워크를 개발하고 베트남, 인도 등 아시아를 중심으로 한 개발도상국들이 자국의 경제성장 전략을 추진하는 과정에서 중요한 도구로 활용할 수 있는 방안을 모색하고자 한다. 특히 국가 기간산업 확립의 근간이 되었던 철강회사 포스코의 한국경제 발전에 대한 기여와 포스코 초일류기업 육성에 지대한 공헌을 한 TJP 리더십의 핵심적 요소는 무엇이며 이러한 요소들이 어떻게 작용하여 한국경제발전을 선도하였는지를 집중적으로 조명한다. 나아가 TJP 리더십을 중심으로 한 포스코 성장모델을 정형화하여 경제개발을 기획하고 있는 개발도상국에게 한국과 같이 효율적인 경제개발을 추진할 수 있는 전략을 전수하는 방안을 연구한다.

한국경제 고도성장의 핵심적 요인은 다음 4가지 관점으로 요약할 수 있다. 첫째, 제조업의 성장과 대외지향적 무역정책이다. 둘째, 경제발전 전략 수립 및 추진 과정에서 정부의 강력한 리더십과 역할이다. 셋째, 경제발전 단계에 따라 효율적 시장경제 체제를 정착시켰고 효율적 자원배분 전략을 지속적으로 추진한 것이다. 넷째, 높은 교육열을 바탕으로 교육과 경제의 선순환 구조를 형성하여 최적의 인적자본을 축적하였고 기술개발 및 경영혁신 등을 통해 높은 생산성을 달성하여 지속적이면서 고도의 경제성장을 달성하였다. 위의 4가지 핵심요인 중 가장 중요한 두 가지 요소는 정부의 강력한 리더십과 인적자본의 축적으로 압축할 수 있다.

포스코는 한국경제 성장의 4가지 핵심 요소들의 관점에서 어떠한 기여를 하였는가?

첫째, 포스코는 산업발전 기여를 통해 중화학공업 및 제조업 성장을 견인하는 중추적인 역할을 담당하였다. 철강은 산업화의 쌀이고 철강산업은 규모가 큰 장치산업으로서 타 기업의 많은 제품을 수요하고 다른 주요산업들에게 철강제품을 중간재로 공급하기 때문에 타 산업과 연관효과가 매우 크다. 포스코는 타 산업에 대한 기여도를 평가하는 산업연관분석에서 상위 1-2위의 전후방 연관효과를 보여줌으로써 한국경제 산업화에 기여했고 이는 제조업 성장에 크게 공헌한 것으로 평가된다.

둘째, 포스코는 시장지향적 국영기업을 통하여 국가주도 산업화에 기여했다. 경제발전 초기의 자본축적이 빈약하고 사회 인프라가 미약한 상황에서 민간 주도에 의한 성장전략은 효과적인 경제성장을 견인할 수 없다. 포스코는 대한민국 정부의 시대적 사명을 실현하기 위하여 제철보국이라는 경제적 이념으로 중화학공업화의 선봉이 되어 국가주도 산업화를 견인했고 세계 초일류 철강기업이 되기 위해 국제경쟁력을 추구하는 시장적 국가기업의 역할을 충실히 감당한 것이다.

셋째, 포스코는 기술개발, 연구개발 투자, 산학연 협동 및 기업복지를 통해 국가 생산성 향상 및 인적자본 형성에 기여했다. 포스코는 제철보국을 실현하면서 국가의 미래 산업을 선도할 인재육성이라는 박태준 회장의 교육보국 정신을 실천하기 위해 기술개발 및 혁신, 연구개발 투자, 산학연 협동연구 및 산업 현장인력 양성, 전사적 자주관리를 통한 현장혁신, 기업복지발전과 흑자경영의 선순환 구조, 포스코 성공의 학습 및 확산을 통한 국가 산업화에 외부효과 창출 등을 만들어내면서 국가경제의 생산성 제고 및 인적자본 축적을 도모하여 한국 경제성장에 기여했다.

포스코의 성공과 한국경제 성장 간 실증분석 결과, 포스코 매출액 증가율은 제조업성장률에 긍정적인 영향을 끼쳤다. 특히 포스코가 제철소 확장 준공을 펼친 연도에는 제조업 성장률이 다른 기간에 비해 훨씬 높은 것을 확인하였다. 또한 포스코 생산성 증가율은 국가 생산성 증가율에 3년의 시차를 두고 긍정적인 영향을 끼치는 것으로 분석되었다.

한국경제 성장을 견인한 모범적 기업사례로서 포스코 성공의 핵심 요인은 무엇인가? 많은 기존 연구들은 포스코 성장의 핵심적 요소로서 TJP 리더십을 강조한다. 본 연구에서는 TJP의 선도적 리더십 ⇒ 포스코의 성공 ⇒ 한국경제의 성장이라는 메커니즘을 전제로 TJP 리더십의 특성들을 종합하여 한국경제 성장에 결정적 기여를 한 TJP 리더십의 핵심을 분석한다.

첫째, 태준이즘과 제철보국 구현을 통해 제조업 성장 및 급속한 산업화에 기여한 점이다. 박태준은 한국 현대사의 비극을 극복하는 길이 산업화를 통한 부국강병이라 믿고 이를 위해 산업화의 쌀인 철강산업을 육성하는 데 자신의 전 생애를 바친 혼신의 리더십을 보여주었다. 박태준 회장은 소신껏, 청렴하게, 사심 없이 그리고 온갖 반대와 장애를 뚫는 절대적 절망은 없는 자세를 견지하면서 결사적 조국애와 순교자적 희생정신으로 포스코 건설을 추진하였고 용혼경영사상을 통해 포스코 성장을 주도하였다. 포스코 성장의 대성취를 통해 한국경제 성장에 이바지한 박태준 리더십의 포괄적 종합체계는 태준이즘이고 이는 제철보국의 종합적 정신 동력이다.

둘째, 박태준은 초일류 기업추구를 통한 대외지향적 정책에 기여했다. 박태준은 포스코의 국가적 사명을 깊이 절감하고 제철보국을 구현하기 위해 글로벌 초일류 철강기업 건설을 꿈꾸었다. 포스코가 세계 초일류 철강기업이 되기위해서는 국제경쟁력이 확보되어야 하고 이를 위해 박태준 회장은 생산비 절감, 품질 개선, 효율적 경영, 그리고 지속적 성장을 위한 기술개발 등 다각적인 노력을 펼쳤다. 초일류 철강기업 실현을 위한 TJP의 선도적인 리더십은 포스코의 선봉적 역할을 통하여 한국 정부가 주도하는 대외지향적 수출위주 성장정책을 펼치는 데 주요한 공헌을 한 것이다.

셋째, 박태준은 시장지향적 공기업 추구를 통해 정부주도 경제발전을 이룩하는 데 선봉장의 역할을 감당하였다. 박태준은 포스코 창립부터 국가경제에서 포스코가 갖는 중차대한 의미를 전사적으로 공유하고 제조업 및 국가 산업화를 선도하는 국영기업으로서 책무를 다했다. 또한 포스코 제품의 품질 향상과 생산비 절감을 통해 국제 경쟁력을 높이기 위해 한 발 앞선 신기술 도입, 연구개발, 과학기술분야 확장, 산학협력 등 시장지향적 경영활동을 추진하여 포스코 기업을 국내적으로 중화학공업화를 추진하는 데 핵심적 역할을 도모하여 국가주도 산업화를 선도하고 국외적으로 정부주도 수출위주의 대외지향적 경제정책을 펼쳐 경제발전을 추구하는 전략 실천의 선봉장 역할을 감당하게 한 것이다.

넷째, 박태준은 기술혁신, 경영혁신, 교육보국, 선진적 기업문화 추구를 통해 생산성 향상 및 인적자본 축적에 기여했다. 박태준은 산업 및 국가발전을 위한 교육의 필요성을 인식하여 교육보국 의지가 투철하였다. 현장인력의 양성, 산학연 연구협력체 구축 등을 통해 산업인력 양성과 고급두뇌 인력양성에 전력을 다하였다. 박태준은 기술개발 및 기술혁신, 경영혁신, 자주관리 및 현장혁신, 선진적 기업복지 등을 통해 포스코 생산성을 지속적으로 향상시켜 국가경제 생산성 향상에 기여했다. TJP 리더십이 포스코 경영성과에 미친 실증분석 결과, TJP의 적극적인 경영제언 리더십은 포스코 경영성과와 생산성에 긍정적인 영향을 미친 것으로 분석되었다.

박태준 리더십, 포스코 성공, 그리고 한국경제 발전 간 핵심적 인과관계 분석 결과, 본 연구는 개발도상국에 적용하기 위해 다음을 제안한다.

첫째, 포스코형 성장모형의 학습이다. 포스코형 성장모형의 핵심은 ①시장지향적 국가기업을 육성하여 정부주도 경제발전을 추진하는 것, ②대외지향적 경제발전 전략을 견인하기 위해 초일류 국가기업을 육성하는 것, ③산업화와 근대화를 위해 기반이 되는 선도적 기업을 육성하는 것, ④기술혁신, 경영혁신, R&D, 산학연 협력체 구축 등 생산성 향상과 인적자본 축적에 지속적인 노력을 경주하는 것, ⑤결사적 애국심, 시장지향적이고 합리적인 태도, 용혼경영사상을 추구하는 CEO를 육성하는 것이다.

둘째, 포스코는 박태준리더십센터 건립을 통해 리더십 학습, 교육, 그리고 연구를 지속적으로 추진하고 개도국의 잠재적 리더들을 발굴하여 리더십 연수를 주최하고 개도국에 장학금과 연구비 지원을 통해 잠재적 지도자 육성에 기여하며 개도국 정책결정자를 위한 리더십 프로그램을 운영할 필요가 있다. 또한 포스코의 사회적 책임을 다할 수 있는 프로그램을 개발하여 개도국 사회공헌활동을 지원하고 박태준리더십 프로그램 운영에 적극적인 지원을 펼칠 필요가 있다.

셋째, 개발도상국 정부는 포스코와 협력관계 프로그램을 개발하여 박태준 리더십, 포스코 경영, 포스코 기업문화를 학습할 수 있는 연수 프로그램을 기획하고 포스코가 지원하는 리더십 프로그램을 유치하며 장학금과 연구지원비를 유치하여 잠재적 지도자 육성에 전력하고 한국 정부 및 포스코와 유기적인 협력관계를 구축할 필요가 있다.

본 연구는 TJP 핵심 리더십이 개발도상국에 효과적으로 전수되어 이들 국가의 경제발전 전략 수립 및 추진에 이바지하는 것을 목표로 한다. 또한 현재 제2의 도약을 꿈꾸고 있는 포스코의 신성장 모형을 한국경제의 중장기적 플랜과 새롭게 접목시켜, 포스코 및 한국경제의 중장기적 발전 간 지속적 연계성을 확보하는 중요한 연구 자료로서 활용되길 기대한다.

I. 연구목적

한국은 특별한 부존자원이 없으며 산업기반이 거의 전무한 상태에서 공업화 및 경제자유화를 일구어 왔다. 이러한 경제발전의 성과는 세계적으로 유례가 없는 성공사례로 꼽히고 있다. 한국이 1950년 한국전쟁 후 60년이라고 하는 짧은 기간 동안 성공적인 경제발전을 달성할 수 있었던 배경에는 개도국 무역에 우호적인 세계무역환경이 조성된 것을 바탕으로 한국이 수출주도형이면서 대외지향적인 산업발전전략을 택했던 점, 경제발전 초기에 철강 및 조선 산업 등을 중심으로 핵심 산업을 적기에 육성했던 점, 교육인프라 조성을 통한 풍부한 인적자본을 축적했던 점, 경제발전 단계에 따른 정부의 적극적인 경제정책이 추진되었던 점 등을 꼽을 수 있다.

특히 박정희 대통령의 강력한 지원 하에 1968년에 창립된 포항제철주식회사(2002년부터 포스코로 명칭 변경)는 국내 제조업체에 저렴하면서도 양질의 철강 제품을 공급함에 따라 조선, 자동차, 기계, 전자 및 건설 산업 등의 수출경쟁력 강화와 이들 산업의 성장에 발판을 마련함으로써 1970년대 이후 한국 경제 발전에 중추적인 역할을 담당하였다. 한 마디로 포스코 성장의 역사는 한국 경제 성장의 역사와 맞닿아 있다고 볼 수 있다(김병연 최상오 2011). 2012년 현재, 포스코는 세계 철강제품 시장에서 2.6%의 점유율 및 연 3,990만 톤 철강생산을 갖는 세계 5대 철강회사로 인정받고 있다. 철강산업은 대규모 자본집약적 장치산업으로서 규모의 경제가 큰 산업이며 주요 산업에 필요한 기초 소재를 제공하는 국가 기간산업인데(최동용 2007) 한국의 경제개발 초기에 포스코의 성공적 설립과 경쟁력 있는 철강산업 육성은 한국경제성장을 견인하는 데 주요한 역할을 담당한 것이다(곽상경 외 1992, 김상규 외 1998).

그러면 무엇이 포스코의 성공적 신화를 만들었고 궁극적으로 한국 경제발전을 일구어냈는가? 기업차원의 성장사와 국가개발론적 관점에서 보면 포스코의 기업차원의 노력과 정부의 역할이 성공사례를 만들어 낸 것으로 볼 수 있겠지만(류상영 2001) 보다 핵심적인 포스코 성공요인은 단연코 포스코 창립자인 박태준 전 회장(이하 TJP)의 역할이다. TJP는 제철소 건설 초기단계에서부터 인력개발에 초점을 맞추고 건설현장의 근로자들과 대부분의 시간을 함께 일하면서 제철보국의 의지를 불태웠으며 일본으로부터 자본과 기술을 지원받아 제철공장 건설에 지대한 공헌을 하였다. 이후 포스코의 신화적인 발전과 포스코 고유의 시민의식이 투철한 기업문화를 정착시키는 데 핵심적인 역할을 담당하였다. 결국 TJP의 선도적 리더십이 포스코의 신화적 성공을 불러 일으켰고 포스코의 위대한 성공이 국제적 철강산업을 육성하는 데 초석이 됨에 따라 한국경제 성장을 견인하는 데 주요한 역할을 한 것으로 추론할 수 있다.

오늘날 한국은 고도성장에 힘입어 국제사회에서 위상이 점차 높아지고 있으며 이에 따라 세계경제에 대한 한국경제의 한 차원 격상된 기여가 요구되고 있는 실정이다. 이에 부응하여 한국정부는 국제사회에서 한국의 주도적 역할을 확보하고자 부단히 노력하고 있으며 특히 2010년에는 개발도상국 최초로 G20 정상회의를 개최한 바 있다. 이러한 가운데 세계경제 속에서 한국경제의 위상을 더욱 강화시키고 확보하기 위한 실질적 방안으로서 경제개발에 박차를 가하고 있는 개발도상국에게 한국경제의 절대적 우위를 전수하기 위한 한국경제 성장모형의 수립 및 적용 필요성이 더욱 부각되고 있다.

개발도상국의 입장에서 한국경제 성장 경험으로부터 가장 절실히 요구되는 것은 무엇일까? 본 질문에 대한 답변의 출발점은 경제발전 초기단계에서 중요한 역할을 담당하는 산업기반 조성과 국제 경쟁력을 견인하는 초일류 기업의 육성이다. 이런 관점에서 한국경제는 어떻게 산업기반을 조성하였고 포스코, 삼성전자, 현대 자동차 등과 같은 초일류 글로벌 기업들을 육성할 수 있었을까?

본 연구에서는 지난 40여년 간 한국경제가 성취한 고도성장의 배경과 그 성장 동력으로서 핵심에 있었던 포스코의 역할을 심도 있게 연구하여 한국경제 성장 모형의 실질적 프레임워크를 개발하고 베트남 및 인도 등 아시아를 중심으로 한 개발도상국들이 자국의 경제성장 전략을 추진하는 데 중요한 경제정책 전략으로 활용할 수 있는 방안을 연구하려고 한다. 특히 국가 기간산업의 근간이 되었던 철강회사 포스코의 한국경제발전 기여와 포스코 초일류기업 육성에 지대한 공헌을 한 TJP 리더십의 핵심적 요소는 무엇이고 이러한 요소들이 어떻게 작용하여 한국경제발전을 선도하였는지를 집중적으로 조명해 볼 것이다. 나아가 TJP 리더십을 중심으로 한 포스코 모델을 정형화하여 경제개발을 기획하고 있는 개발도상국에게 한국경제 발전과 같이 효율적인 경제개발을 견인하는 전략을 전수할 수 있는 방안을 연구해 볼 것이다.

본 연구를 통한 기대효과는 크게 두 가지로 요약된다. 첫째, 한국경제 발전에서 포스코의 역할과 포스코를 초일류기업으로 육성하는 데 결정적 기여를 한 TJP의 리더십을 집중적으로 조명하여 포스코형 경제성장모델을 개발하는 것이다. 둘째, 이러한 모형을 개발도상국에 효과적으로 전수하여 이들 국가 경제발전 전략 수립에 기여하여 궁극적으로 개도국의 경제발전에 이바지하는 것이다. 더불어, 한국과 개도국간 경제협력을 촉진하여 한국경제의 지속적인 성장 터전을 확보하는 것이다. 본 연구는 현재 제2의 도약을 꿈꾸고 있는 포스코의 신성장 모형을 한국경제의 중장기적 플랜과 새로이 접목시켜 포스코 중장기적 발전과 한국경제 발전의 연계성을 지속적으로 견인하는 데 중요한 연구자료로 활용될 것으로 기대한다.

II. 연구내용 및 범위

본 연구는 크게 3가지 부문으로 나누어서 진행될 예정이다.

첫째, 한국경제 발전의 핵심 원동력이 무엇인지를 파악하고 그 핵심을 중심으로 한국 철강산업의 아이콘인 포스코의 역할을 분석한다. 이러한 과정에서 실증적 분석방법을 이용하여 포스코 기업차원의 성장사와 한국경제 발전의 인과적 관계를 살펴봄으로써 포스코의 성공이 한국경제 발전에 지대한 역할을 했는지 재조명해 볼 것이다.

둘째, 포스코의 성공요인과 TJP 리더십의 역할을 살펴보는 것이다. 1968년 포스코 창립부터 국제적 철강 기업으로 우뚝 서게 된 1992년까지 TJP는 포스코 회장으로 혼신의 리더십을 발휘하였고 결국 이러한 리더십이 포스코의 성공과 나아가 한국경제 성장을 이끌었다는 것을 가설적으로 추론해볼 때 TJP 리더십의 핵심 동인은 무엇이고 이러한 리더십이 포스코 발전과정에 어떻게 기여하였는지 서지적 관점에서 뿐만 아니라 계량경제학적 분석 방법을 이용하여 살펴보려고 한다. 이러한 과정을 통해 TJP 리더십이 결국 한국경제 성장에 주요한 역할을 하였다는 것을 직·간접적으로 보여줄 것이다.

셋째, 궁극적으로 TJP 리더십이 포스코 성공신화를 통해 한국경제 성장에 지대한 역할을 하였다는 상기 연구결과를 바탕으로 포스코형 경제성장모형을 완성하고 이를 개발도상국 경제발전에 적용하기 위해 포스코와 개도국 정부의 역할은 무엇인지를 살펴본다. 이러한 과정을 통해 TJP 리더십의 핵심 요소를 전파하고 궁극적으로 TJP형 리더를 체계적으로 양성할 수 있는 방안에 대해서도 심도 있게 연구할 것이다.

1. 한국경제 성장과 포스코의 역할

한국경제는 빈약한 부존자원, 일제의 압제로부터 해방, 전쟁의 상흔을 극복하고 지난 40년 동안 세계적으로 유례가 없는 기적적인 경제적 성과를 달성하였다. 한국은 2차 세계대전의 종료와 함께 일제 식민지배 아래서 독립을 쟁취하였으나 민족분단을 경험하게 되었고 곧이어 1950~53년 동안 민족상쟁의 한국전쟁을 겪게 되었다. 휴전 이후 한국은 전쟁의 복구와 함께 세계 최빈국 농업국가의 반열에 있었다. 그러나 1962년 역사적인 제1차 경제개발 5개년 계획을 시작으로 대외지향정책을 일관되게 추구하여 압축형 공업화를 달성하였다. 즉, 한국은 대외통상환경의 변화에 기민하게 대응하면서 수출주도형 경제발전전략과 대외개방정책을 상호상승 효과가 발생하도록 배합하여 세계은행이 지칭한 동아시아 경제 기적(East Asian Miracle : World Bank, 1996)의 주역이 되었다. 그 결과 한국은 40년 전 세계최빈국에서 2010년에는 경제규모에 있어서 세계 13위권에 이르고 통상 규모에 있어서 세계 10위권에 육박하는 경제대국으로 발전하였다.

본 연구부문에서는 기적의 역사를 일군 한국경제 40여년 간의 경제개발 정책과 성과를 신고전학파 및 내생적 경제성장이론 뿐만 아니라 경제사적 관점에서 객관적으로 분석하고 평가함으로써 한국경제 성장의 원동력을 분석한다.

상기에서 개발된 한국경제 성장 이론에서 포스코의 역할을 분석한다. 초일류기업의 성장이 국가경제 성장을 어떻게 견인하는지 이론적 관점에서 살펴보고 실제 포스코 발전이 이론에서 보여주는 역할을 성공적으로 수행하였는지를 분석한다. 한국경제 발전에 대한 포스코의 기여도를 분석하기 위하여 회귀분석 등을 활용하여 수량적 증거들을 확보할 계획이다. 궁극적으로 한국경제 발전에서 포스코의 역할을 학문적인 관점에서 조명함으로써 기업형 한국경제 성장모형을 도출할 것이다.

2. 포스코의 성공과 TJP 리더십

포스코는 1968년에 설립되어 국가기간산업의 근간을 이루었고 1970년대 중화학공업을 육성시켜 나가는 데 중추적인 역할을 수행하였다. 포스코는 지속적인 설비효율화와 생산성 향상을 통해 1990년대 후반 세계적인 철강회사로 발돋움하였으며 현재는 글로벌 기술리더십과 포스코 고유 기업문화를 정착하여 글로벌 초일류 기업으로 발돋움하였다. 오늘날 글로벌 초일류 기업의 초석을 다지는 데 결정적인 공헌을 한 것은 TJP의 리더십이다(백기복 외 2012, 김명언 외 2012, 배종태 외 2012).

본 연구 부문에서는 포스코 성장과정에서 TJP 리더십이 어떻게 작용하여 포스코의 성장을 유도하였는지를 서지적 관점에서 간략히 살펴보고 좀 더 핵심적으로 계량경제학적 분석을 이용하여 수량적인 시사점을 찾아볼 것이다. 이 과정에서 TJP 리더십을 지수화시키는 방안을 연구하고 본 지수를 이용하여 포스코 성장에 대한 기여도를 분석할 것이다.

3. TJP 리더십과 포스코형 성장모형 개도국 적용방안

TJP 리더십이 포스코 성장에 지대한 공헌을 하였고 포스코 성장이 한국경제 발전에 상당한 역할을 하였다면 궁극적으로 TJP 리더십이 한국경제 성장에 지대한 공헌을 한 것을 유추할 수 있다. 본 연구는 이러한 추론을 바탕으로 한국경제성장에 지대한 공헌을 한 포스코형 성장모형을 정형화시키는 것이다. 특히 포스코형 성장모형을 일목요연하게 제시함으로써 개도국 경제발전 전략 수립에 필요한 핵심적 요소를 모색해 본다.

궁극적으로 본 연구는 개도국들이 경제발전 전략을 수립함에 있어서 포스코형 성장모형을 어떻게 활용할 수 있는지 그 방안을 모색해 볼 것이다. 특히, 이를 위해 포스코, 한국정부 그리고 개도국 정부의 역할은 무엇인지 살펴본다.

포스코는 본 연구 결과를 고려하여 개도국 및 여타 국가들과 경제협력 방안을 전반적으로 검토하고 이를 바탕으로 제2의 도약을 기획하며 나아가 한국 경제발전을 지속적으로 견인할 수 있는 신성장전략 구축을 모색해야 할 것이다.

III. 한국경제 성장과 포스코의 역할

1950년 한국전쟁 전후만 하더라도 한국경제는 세계 최빈국 중의 하나였다. 그러나 1962년 제1차 경제개발 5개년 계획을 시작으로 정부 주도형 대외지향정책을 추구하고 중화학공업 육성을 통한 공업화 전략과 열정적인 교육의지를 기반으로 하는 인적자본 축적은 2010년 한국을 세계 경제규모 13위권에 진입하게 하였다. 그 결과 한국은 대만, 홍콩, 싱가포르와 더불어 동아시아 네 마리 호랑이(East Asian Four Tigers)로서 세계 경제성장 기적의 주인공으로 등장하였고 개도국의 성공적인 발전모델로 평가받게 되었다.

본 장에서는 고도성장을 경험한 국가들의 정형화된 사실이 무엇인지를 간략히 살펴보고 이런 맥락에서 한국경제성장의 핵심적 요소들을 도출할 것이다. 다음으로 대규모 자본집약적 장치산업인 철강산업의 대표 기업인 포스코가 한국경제 성장의 핵심적 요소에 어떻게 공헌하였는지를 살펴봄으로써 한국경제 발전에서 포스코의 핵심적 역할을 파악한다. 특히 계량적 실증분석을 시도하여 포스코 역할에 대한 수량적 증거들을 제시할 것이다.

1. 고도성장 국가들의 정형화된 사실

경제성장 결정요인에 대한 많은 기존 연구들에서는 장기적 경제성장에 영향을 미치는 주요 요인들 중 하나가 조세정책을 포함한 경제정책을 들고 있다(김동헌 외 2011). 콜리어 및 달러(Collier and Dollar 2001)는 경제정책 개혁이 국가빈곤율 감소에 크게 기여하는 것을 보여주고 있고 에스털리(Easterly 2005)는 조세정책을 중심으로 경제정책 변화가 경제성장에 얼마나 중요한지를 이론적으로 보여주고 있다. 김동헌 외(2011)는 신고전학파의 외생적 성장모형을 이용하여 정부정책의 변화가 경제성장에 커다란 영향을 미치는 것을 보여주고 있다. 이와 같이 국가 경제 발전단계에 따라 정부정책의 적절한 변화는 국가경제의 지속적 성장에 매우 중요함을 시사하고 있다.

그렇다면 저소득 경제가 선진국의 소득수준으로 진입해 가는 과정에서 국가경제 발전단계에 따라 정부정책 변화에 대하여 공통적으로 관측되는 현상들은 무엇인가? 김동헌 외(2011)는 로드릭(Rodrik 2003)을 중심으로 지난 40여년간 주요국의 경제성장 정책 경험들을 중심으로 정책입안자 측면에서 현실적으로 가장 적절한 경제성장 전략이 무엇인지를 분석하고 있다. 로드릭(Rodrik 2003)에 따르면 1950년 이후 주요국들의 경제개발 정책은 1950-1960년대 수입대체정책, 1970년대 시장지향적 정책을 중시한 강력한 대외지향적 정책, 1980년대 윌리암슨(Williamson 1990)이 최적의 정책 틀에 대하여 명명한 워싱턴합의 (Washington Consensus), 1990년대 워싱턴 합의에 덧붙여 정부 및 기업의 거버넌스 문제를 보완하는 제도적 측면으로 전개되었다.

그러나 일관된 경제정책을 추진해오면서 높은 경제성장률을 달성한 동아시아지역 국가들의 경제성장 정책이 상기 워싱턴 합의에 부합되는 정도는 높지 않고 중국, 인도, 남미국가들, 아프리카 국가들의 사례들은 경제개발을 위한 제도적 정책적 환경의 정비가 곧 경제성장으로 이어지는 것은 아니며 또한 모든 국가에 공통적으로 적용될 수 있는 성공적인 경제성장 전략은 존재하지 않을 수 있다. 즉, 저개발국 또는 개발도상국들이 경제개발 정책을 수립하고 집행하는데 있어 오직 유일한 최선의 방법이 존재하지 않고 해당 국가의 정치적, 경제적, 사회적 여건에 따라 다양한 정책이 가능할 수 있다는 것이다.

그럼에도 불구하고 김동헌 외(2011)는 과거 40년간 고도 성장을 달성하였던 국가들로부터 관측된 정형화된 사실을 다음 4가지로 요약하고 있다.

첫째, 고도성장 시발점은 대부분 전면적인 제도개혁이 아닌 부분적인 제도 개혁이라는 것이다. 예컨대 한국의 경우 1962년 이전 0.6% 경제성장률에서 연평균 7%대 높은 성장률을 촉발시킨 시발점은 정부의 강력한 성장우선정책 의지와 함께 시행된 환율절하 및 금리인상이었다. 이는 개발도상국의 경제발전은 광범위한 제도적 개혁을 시행하는 것보다 정부의 뚜렷한 성장에 대한 목표의식 아래 작은 정책 및 제도의 변화로부터 고도성장을 달성할 수 있음을 시사한다.

둘째, 고도성장과 관련된 정책 및 제도개혁은 정통적인 요소와 비정통적인 요소의 결합으로 이루어졌다는 것이다. 재산권, 시장중심의 인센티브, 안정적 물가관리, 재정건전성 확보 등 정통적 요소에 대한 최소한의 경제성장 여건의 마련없이는 고도경제성장이 어렵다는 것이다. 그러나 정통적 요소가 잘 갖추었다고 해서 고도성장을 가져오는 것은 아니며 금융규제 시스템, 선별적 수출보조 정책 또는 산업정책 등 워싱턴 합의에서 벗어나는 비정통적 요소도 고도성장에 주요한 기여를 할 수 있다는 것이다.

셋째, 국가별로 고도성장과 관련한 정책패키지를 살펴보면 유사점보다 상당히 상이한 접근을 취하고 있다. 예컨대, 한국과 대만의 보호무역주의와 싱가포르의 개방무역주의는 상반되며 한국과 대만의 보호무역주의도 그 내면에는 신용공급과 세제혜택이라는 상이한 방법을 통해 추진되었다. 이는 성공적인 경제성장을 이룩한 국가들의 일방적인 정책모방은 경제정책의 실패로 끝날 수 있다는 것이다.

넷째, 지속적인 경제성장은 성장의 시발보다 훨씬 더 어렵고 보다 광범위한 제도적 개혁을 필요로 한다는 것이다. 한국, 대만, 홍콩, 싱가포르 등 동아시아 일부 국가를 제외하고는 지속적인 성장을 경험하면서 선진국 소득 수준으로 수렴한 국가는 드물었다. 즉, 잠시 동안 고도성장을 달성한 대부분의 국가들이 얼마 지나지 않아 성장동력을 상실하면서 성장률 둔화를 경험하는 것이다. 이는 단 중기 일시적 성장률 상승이 장기 안정적 성장으로 항상 이어지는 것은 아니며 궁극적으로 지속적 성장을 이어나가기 위해서는 초기개혁 단계부터 시장경제의 제도적 체제를 군건하게 다지면서 생산활력의 유지와 외부충격에 대한 탄력적 대응을 추진할 수 있는 제도 정비가 매우 중요함을 시사하고 있다.

2. 한국의 경제성장 모델

1) 한국경제의 성장과 위상

한국의 연도별 실질GDP를 살펴보면 1960년 27조원(2010년 기준), 1970년 68조원, 1980년 163조원, 1990년 420조원, 2000년 821조원, 2010년 1,265조원 등 60년대 후반부터 급속한 성장과 오랜 기간 성장을 지속해왔다. 연평균 경제성장률은 60년대 8.72%, 70년대 9.37%, 80년대 7.77%, 90년대 6.14%, 2000년대 3.67% 등 70년대 후반 오일쇼크 시기와 IMF 구제금융시기(1997-98)를 제외하면 성장률의 급락 없이 연평균 6%를 상회하는 경이적인 성장률을 달성해왔다. 다만 최근 한국경제는 저출산, 고령화사회에 직면하면서 성장률이 현저히 저하되고 있는 상황이다.

1960년-2000년간 개도국의 1인당 GDP 연평균 성장률은 2.3%, 선진국들의 연평균 성장률은 2.7%임에 비하여 동기간 동안 한국의 연평균 성장률은 4.5%를 상회하였다. 참으로 한국경제는 세계경제 역사상 경이로운 경제발전을 이룩한 것이다. 2011년 기준, 한국의 경제규모는 세계 12위이고 통상규모는 세계 9위이다. 한국은 G20과 OECD 회원국으로서 세계경제에서 그 위상은 날로 커지고 있다. 그렇다면 지난 40년 동안 무엇이 세계경제사 속에서 찾아보기 힘든 한국경제의 고도압축 성장을 촉발시켰는가? 한국경제 고도성장의 요인에 대해서는 다양한 연구들이 있는데 여기서는 김동헌 외(2011) 연구에서 제시한 부문을 중심으로 요약하고자 한다.[1]

1   한국경제의 고도성장 요인에 대한 연구들로는 강광하 외 (2008), 김광석·박준경 (1979), 김낙년 (1999), 박영구 (1999, 2001), 배진한 (2008), 변형윤 (2012) 등이 있다.

[그림 1] 한국의 연도별 실질 GDP 추이

단위 : 조원

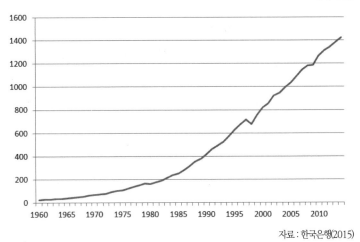

자료 : 한국은행(2015)

[그림 2] 한국의 연도별 GDP 성장률 추이

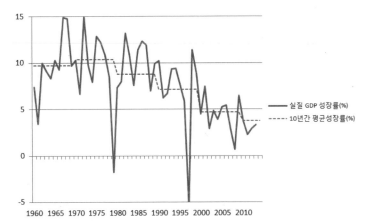

실질 GDP 성장률(%)
10년간 평균성장률(%)

자료 : 한국은행 (2015)

2) 한국경제 성장의 핵심 요인

김동헌 외(2011)는 한국경제 성장모델을 정형화하는 과정에서 한국경제 고도성장의 핵심적 요인을 4가지 관점에서 요약하고 있다: ①제조업의 성장과 대외지향적 무역정책, ②정부의 역할, ③시장경제 체제 및 효율적 자원배분 전략, ④인적자본 축적과 높은 생산성. 물론 이외에도 다양한 요인들이 한국경제 고도성장을 이끌었다는 데는 의심의 여지가 없지만 그 요인들을 종합해 보면 상기 4가지 관점에서 요약해 볼 수 있을 것 같다.

가. 제조업의 성장과 대외지향적 무역정책

한국경제 고도성장의 중심에는 단연코 제조업의 성장과 이와 연계된 수출지향적 산업정책이다. [표 1]은 산업 부문별 연평균 성장률의 추이를 보여주고 있다. 1960년대부터 1990년대까지 한국경제성장률을 견인한 것은 중화학공업을 중심으로 한 제조업의 성장이었다. 한국정부는 경제개발 단계에 따라 필요한 산업구조를 효과적으로 구현하기 위해 제조업을 중심으로 적극적인 산업정책을 펼쳤다. 제조업 연평균 성장률은 경제성장률을 훨씬 상회하면서 국가경제 전체의 성장을 견인해 온 것이다. 경제개발 단계별로 제조업의 성장과정을 간략히 정리하면 다음과 같다.

일제 강점기에 제조업 시설이 주로 한반도 북쪽에 자리하고 있었고 1950년 3년간에 걸쳐 한국전쟁을 겪으면서 한국의 제조업 상황은 매

우 열악하였다. 따라서 1950년대에는 국민들의 생필품 수요에 의해 제
조업이 주로 수입대체산업형태로 생산시설의 토대를 미약하나마 마련
하였고 그 배후에는 미국의 경제원조가 주요한 원천이었다. 한국정부
는 기초 소비재산업을 육성하여 국민경제의 안정을 기한다는 취지로
국가의 특혜적인 지원과 저임금 노동력으로 제조업 부문의 성장 불씨
를 피우려고 노력했다.

[표 1] 산업구조 변화에 따른 산업부문별 연평균 성장률 추이

	1953~60	1961~70	1971~80	1981~90	1991~2000	2001~09
농림어업	2.3	4.4	1.6	3.5	1.9	1.8
광업 및 제조업	12.1	15.7	14.1	11.4	8.2	5.3
광업	-	-	4.7	-0.2	-1.3	-0.3
제조업	12.7	16.8	15.8	12.2	8.4	5.4
경공업	-	-	12.7	7.0	1.1	-0.6
중화학공업	-	-	17.2	14.4	9.8	6.6
전기.가스.수도 사업 및 건설업	9.3	19.2	10.3	10.3	2.7	3.3
전기.가스.수도	-	-	15.8	17.6	10.3	5.8
건설업	-	-	10.1	9.7	1.4	2.6
서비스업	3.8	8.6	6.8	8.4	6.1	3.6
국내총생산	3.8	8.4	9.0	9.7	6.5	3.9

자료 : 김동헌 외(2011)

그러나 정부 보호와 지원에 의한 수입대체공업화정책은 시장원리에
벗어난 원조물자와 외화자금 배정으로 비경쟁적 이권추구행위와 비효
율적 자원배분에 따른 인위적 독점 형성, 달러 공정환율의 저평가에 따

른 수입대체 촉진과 수출 억제, 원조물자와 대충자금의 특혜적이고 편중적 배정에 따른 정경유착, 대외 원조에 의존하는 종속적인 경제체재 등으로 인해 효과적인 제조업 발전을 견인하지 못하였다. 그 당시 제조업의 전체 비중은 10% 내외에 머물렀고 여전히 전통적인 1차산업이 한국경제를 지배하고 있었다.

1960년대에 들어서 한국정부는 수입대체산업의 한계를 인지하고 경공업을 중심으로 수출지향적인 방향으로 정책기조를 변경하는 동시에 경공업의 중간재 수요에 대한 수입억제를 위해 중화학공업의 수입대체 산업화를 추진하였다. 1962년부터 경제개발 5개년 계획을 추진하면서 비교우위 무역이론에 근거하여 노동집약적 경공업 육성에 집중하고 수출증대를 통해 무역시장에서 경쟁력 강화를 도모하였다. 또한 60년대 후반 정부 주도로 대규모 산업시설 및 각종 사회간접자본 확충을 중점적으로 추진하였다. 또한 조세지원, 금융지원, 행정지원으로 구성된 수출진흥종합시책을 기반으로 수출지원정책을 본격화시키고 외환제도개혁을 통해 자원배분의 효율성 제고와 규모의 경제 달성을 통한 경제성장을 추구하였다.

1960년대 한국의 산업은 경공업의 성장을 기반으로 산업구조가 급격히 변화하면서 제조업 비중이 1960년 10.8%에서 1972년 25.25%로 급증한 반면 농림수산업의 비중은 41.3%에서 25.2%로 급감하였다. 이와 같이 경공업을 중심으로한 대외지향적 공업화는 고도경제성장의 발판이 되었고 중화학공업의 수입대체를 벗어나 중화학공업의 수출지향 산업화를 추진하기 위한 시발점이 되었다. 그러나 경공업 중심의 수출지향정책의 한계점은 자본재나 투입재의 수입대체를 유도하지 못해 경상수지 적자의 누증을 초래한 점이다.

1970년대에 들어서 세계경제가 석유파동으로 불황에 접어들고 경공업의 수출경쟁력이 하락하고 중화학공업의 수입대체산업화의 한계가 지적되면서 한국정부는 1973년부터 중화학공업의 수출지향산업화를 위한 집중 지원으로 정책기조를 변경하였다. 한국정부는 철강, 화학, 비철금속, 기계, 조선, 전자의 6개 전략사업을 선정하고 중화학공업 육성을 위한 강력한 지원체제를 구축하였다. 1973년 "국민투자기금법"을 제정하여 재정융자 및 금융지원을 추진하고 전후방 연관효과와 시너지효과를 극대화하기 위해 민간기업의 적극적 참여를 유도하는 금융 및 세제상의 광범위한 우대정책을 펼쳤다. 또한 중화학공업화를 위해 필요한 기술인력 육성을 위한 각종 전문학교 및 직업교육기관을 확대 신설하고 중화학공업 기술 개발을 위한 정부출연 연구소 설립을 적극적으로 추진하였다.

이러한 중화학공업화 정책 추진 결과, 1970년대 중화학공업은 연평균 20.9%의 높은 성장률을 달성하여 1970년대 7%를 상회하는 경제성장률을 달성하는 데 결정적인 기여를 하였다. 또한 수출상품에서 중화학공업 비중이 1970년 12.8%에서 1980년 41.5%로 급격히 증가하였다.

한국경제는 정부의 중화학공업정책 성과에 힘입어 산업구조 고도화의 계기를 마련하고 선진국형 산업구조의 기틀을 마련하였다.

[그림 3] 1980년 전후 제조업 성장률 추이

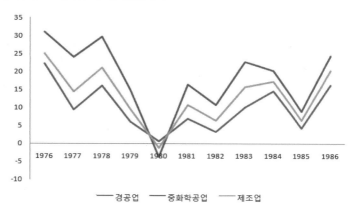

자료 : 김동헌 외(2011)

그러나 중화학공업에 대한 과잉 및 중복투자와 부실화, 대외여건의
악화와 대내 경쟁력 취약으로 조선 및 건설 등의 산업불황이 1980년
대에 발생하고 특정 산업 및 기업 위주의 지원정책으로 인한 경쟁력
집중 및 산업불균형 문제가 심화되면서 정부주도형 중화학공업 육성
정책의 부작용이 지적됨에 따라 정부는 1980년대 제5차 경제사회발
전 5개년 계획을 기초로 중화학공업 투자 조정 및 구조불황산업의 합
리화를 추진하는 이른바 산업합리화와 산업구조조정을 추진하였다.
즉, 산업기술 및 생산성 향상을 위한 산업구조 고도화와 국제경쟁력 향
상을 위해 기술 향상 및 인적자본지원 중심의 기능별 지원정책을 추진
하였다. 산업구조조정 및 부실기업조정을 본격적으로 시행하기 위해
1985년 "조세감면규제법"을 개정하여 산업합리화 지원제도를 추진하
였다. 또한 대기업 경쟁력 집중 현상을 완화하고 선진형 경제제도 구축

을 위해 공정거래제도 및 주력업체, 주력 업종제도를 시행하였다.

정부가 중화학공업을 중심으로 산업합리화 정책을 추진한 결과, 1980년대 초중반 경제성장률 및 투자증가율이 높은 수준을 유지하였고 제조업 내 중화학공업 비중이 70%를 상회하였으며 중화학공업제품의 수출비중도 증가하였다.

또한 지속적인 수입규제정책이 국내산업 경쟁력을 약화시키고 부실화 요인 중의 하나로 부각됨에 따라 정부는 83년 수입자유화 5개년계획을 기점으로 적극적인 수입자유화를 추진하여 1995년 단순평균관세는 7.9%, 수입자유화율은 99%까지 상승하였다.

그러나 1980년대 한국경제는 제도변화 및 대외적 환경변화로 글로벌 경쟁 심화에 직면하였고 급격한 임금의 상승과 생산성 하락으로 세계상품시장에서 경쟁력을 잃어가는 상황에 처했다. 정부는 1990년대에 들어서 경쟁촉진을 통해서 국가경쟁력을 제고시키고 기술혁신과 품질향상만이 경쟁우위를 창출함을 인식하면서 적극적인 연구개발 투자를 추진하였다. 또한 첨단기술산업에 대한 세계적 개발추세와 한국경제의 새로운 성장동력을 창출하기 위해 첨단기술산업에 대한 투자정책을 펼치기 시작했다.

그러한 적극적인 연구개발정책에 힘입어 연구개발 투자는 1981년 3,688억원에서 1997년 12조 1,858억원으로 증가하고 GDP 비중도 0.81%에서 2.69%로 증가하였다. 1981년 이후 연구개발투자 증가율과 경제성장률간 유사한 추세가 관측됨에 따라 연구개발투자가 경제성장에 매우 중요한 요소임을 유추할 수 있다.

[그림 4] 연구개발투자 증가율과 경제성장률

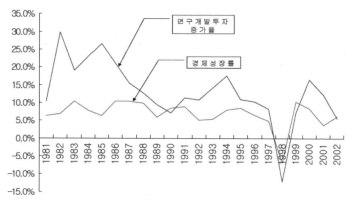

자료: 김동헌 외(2011)

이 시기의 연구개발정책은 1980년대 초반까지 중심이 되었던 과도한 정부주도 개발에서 벗어나 민간이 주도하는 연구개발의 시발점을 형성하였고 기업이 기술혁신을 주도하는 주체로서 정부지원을 활용하여 경제성장의 주체로 등장하기 시작하였다. 이러한 민간주도형 투자지원정책은 첨단기술산업 분야를 중심으로 제조업의 생산성과 경쟁력을 지속적으로 제고시키는 기반이 되었다.

한국경제와 같이 자원이 빈약하고 내수경제가 미약한 국가에서는 경제개방 및 수출을 통한 강력한 대외지향정책이 경제성장에 중요했다고 볼 수 있다. 개방과 경제성장간 관계에 대한 연구에 따르면 개방은 자원배분의 효율성 제고와 기술진보에 따른 생산성 향상을 통해 경제성장을 촉진시킨다. 대외지향정책은 경제개방을 통해 생산특화와 교환이익을 창출하여 경제성장을 가져온다.

[그림 5] 경제개방과 경제성장간 관계

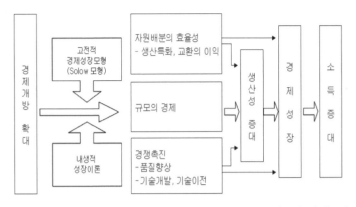

자료: 김동헌 외(2011)

한국경제는 1960년대 경제개발 초기 단계에서 자원배분의 효율성 제고와 규모의 경제 달성을 통한 경제성장을 꾀하기 위해 대외지향정책을 펼치기 시작했다. 수출지향 산업화 정책은 1960년대 경공업을 육성시켰고, 1970년대 및 1980년대에는 중화학공업, 1990년대 및 2000년대는 첨단산업의 성장을 가져옴으로써 경제개발 단계에 따라 제조업 성장을 견인할 수 있는 활로가 되어준 것이다.

개도국의 대외무역 지향성과 생활수준에 대한 OECD 연구에 따르면 강력한 대외지향성을 추구하는 개도국이 그렇지 않은 국가들보다 1인당 국민소득 증가율이 훨씬 높게 나타남을 보여주고 있다(OECD 1998, 1999). 1970-1989년 사이 대외개방을 적극적으로 추진한 15개 개도국, 74개 소극적 개도국, 그리고 OECD 국가 연평균 1인당 GNP 증가율이 각각 4.5%, 0.7%, 2.3%로 나타나 적극적으로 대외개방을 추진한

국가들이 훨씬 높은 생활수준의 향상을 경험하는 것이다(OECD 1999). 프란켈 및 로머(Frankel & Romer 1999)는 GDP 대비 무역액(수입 및 수출) 비중이 1% 증가할 때 1인당 소득이 2% 증가한다는 연구결과를 보여 주고 있다. 또한 중국과 인도도 개방을 적극적으로 추진하기 시작하면 서 1980 2000년 동안 연평균 각각 10% 및 6%의 GDP 성장률을 기록 하였다.

[표 2] 개도국의 대외지향성과 생활수준

	연평균 1인당 GNP 증가율 (%)		
	1963-1973	1974-1985	1986-1992
강력한 대외지향국	6.9%	6.0%	5.8%
중도적 대외지향국	4.9%	2.2%	2.5%
중도적 대내지향국	3.9%	1.8%	-0.1%
강력한 대내지향국	1.6%	-0.3%	-0.1%

자료: OECD(1998), 김동헌 외(2011)

한국은 1962년 1차 경제개발 5개년계획을 추진하면서 수출주도형 성장전략을 채택하여 대외지향적인 경제정책을 적극적으로 펼쳤다. 그리하여 1965년부터 GDP대비 무역비중이 현저히 증가하기 시작하 였다. 이 시기부터 2000년대 한국사회에서 저출산·고령화의 사회경제 적 문제가 제기되기까지 한국의 경제성장률은 GDP대비 무역비중과 양의 상관관계를 보이는 것으로 관측됨에 따라 대외지향성 정책이 한 국경제 성장에 중요한 요인으로 작용한 것으로 평가된다.

[그림 6] 한국의 대외지향성과 경제성장률 추이

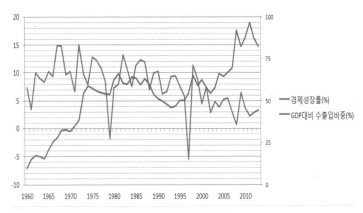

자료 : World Bank (2015)

나. 정부의 역할

한국, 대만, 싱가폴, 홍콩 등 아시아의 작은 호랑이들의 높은 성장률을 가져왔던 산업화의 메커니즘이 무엇인지에 대한 연구에서 발전주의 국가론이 거론된다(World Bank 1993). 발전주의 국가의 개념은 국가정책의 우선순위가 분배가 아닌 성장과 생산성 증대에 있으며, 그 성공의 여부가 국가 관료에 의해 제공된 경제기준에 있고 국가가 사적 자산과 시장에 간여하면서 관료들이 시장을 지도하는 체계이다(김왕배 2013). 발전주의 국가론의 요지는 국가(정부)가 산업화의 프로젝트를 직접 기획하고, 이를 달성하기 위해 민간부분을 육성, 지도, 동원, 지원 및 통제를 해왔다는 것으로 산업화 과정에서 국가의 역할에 주목하는 국가중심적 관점이다(김왕배, 2013).

발전주의 국가론 관점에서 한국의 산업화 전략은 경제기획원을 통한 전반적 산업화정책의 지휘, 수출산업에 대한 조세감면과 관세 및 금리 정책, 노동조합의 억압, 자유무역센터 설립을 통한 외국자본 유치, 한국과학연구소 등을 통한 기술개발, 수출드라이브를 위한 정책지원 등으로 요약된다(김왕배 2013). 한국은 국가 핵심 기구인 정부의 강력한 산업화 드라이브 정책이 산업화를 주도하였고 경제기획원과 상공부 행정관료들이 그 역할을 수행한 것이다. 60년대 경제개발 초기에 대일청구권자금, 월남 파병 및 독일로 광부와 간호사 수출을 통한 달러 송금, 정부신용에 의한 차관 확보 및 외자도입 등을 통해 산업화 자본을 확보하였다. 수출지향적인 산업화를 추진하기 위해 수출부문에 대한 전반적인 유인체계를 수립하였다. 또한 1960년대 후반 정부주도로 대규모 산업시설 및 각종 사회간접자본 확충을 중점적으로 추진하여 산업화의 초석을 마련하였다.

특히 한국정부의 가장 빛나는 역할은 경제개발 단계에 따른 적절한 산업화 정책을 수립하고 이를 적극적으로 추진한 점이다. 즉, 산업화 초기에는 경공업 산업정책, 도약기(가속기)에는 중화학공업 육성정책, 확장기에는 산업합리화 정책, 성숙기에는 국가경쟁력 제고와 연구개발 투자정책 등을 정부 리더십 하에 주도면밀하게 추진한 것이다. 이 과정에서 언제나 수출지향적 산업화정책을 견지하여 제조업 성장을 유도하였고 제품의 가격경쟁력을 위해 노동력에 대한 저임금을 유지하였다.

경제발전 초기단계에서는 보편적 빈곤이 만연하고 자본축적이 열악하며 사회 인프라가 조성되어 있지 못하다. 따라서 민간주도에 의한 시장 메커니즘은 국민에게 경제성장에 대한 강한 의지를 불어넣어주지 못하기 때문에 경제성장을 추진하기 위한 정부의 강력한 의지와 역할이 중요하다. 한국정부는 1970년대 초반 새마을운동을 전개하여 빈곤 탈출과 정신개조, 잘 살 수 있는 가능성을 심어주는 등 국민에게 경제성장 의욕을 고양시켰다. 이를 위해 정부가 나서서 적극적으로 경제성장을 추진하는 정책을 펼쳐 나가야 한다는 필요성을 홍보하였으며 교통 및 통신 등 농촌 하부구조의 조성에 기여하여 사회 전반의 정신적 인프라 구축을 가져왔고 정부의 적극적 정책 추진에 대한 긍정적 인식을 유도하였다. 이는 향후 한국경제의 공업화 과정에서 필요한 인적자원을 양성시키는데 뿌리가 되었다(김동헌 외 2011).

[그림 7] 한국 제조업 성장과 경제개발 약사

경제발전 가속화 단계에서는 초기에 중점을 두었던 경공업에서 국제경쟁력 하락과 성장의 한계를 경험하기 때문에 중화학 공업을 중심으로 전략사업을 선정하고 이들 산업에 정부지원을 집중적으로 투여하는 산업정책과 무역정책이 필요하다. 1970년대 한국은 중화학공업을 전방위적으로 육성하기 위하여 석유화학공업육성법, 철강공업육성법 등

특정 공업 진흥법을 제정하고 중화학공업추진위원회를 발족하여 정부의 강력한 지원체제를 구축하였다. 또한 전후방 연관효과와 시너지 효과를 극대화하기 위해 민간기업의 적극적 참여를 유도하는 조치로 국민투자기금법을 제정하여 다양한 금융 및 세제상의 우대조치 등 정책적 지원을 추진하여 선진국형 산업구조의 기틀을 마련하였다(김동헌 외 2011).

경제발전 성숙단계에서는 산업합리화 추진, 개방과 경쟁의 촉진, 공정거래위원회 설치 및 공정거래법 제정, 민간주도체제로 산업정책의 기조 변경 등을 통하여 시장경제기능을 활성화시킴으로써 생산성 향상을 추구하는 경제체질 개편을 위해 정부의 역할이 중요하다. 1980년대 한국정부는 중화학공업 투자 조정 및 구조불황산업의 합리화를 추진하고 공정거래법 제정, 공정거래 위원회 설치 등을 통해 자율, 경쟁, 개방의 시장경쟁 여건을 조성하였고, 공업발전법의 제정을 통해 민간주도체로 산업정책 기조를 변경하였으며, 기업이 기술혁신을 주도하는 주체로서 제조업의 생산성과 경쟁력 강화를 선도해가는 경제환경 조성을 위해 노력하였다. 또한 1990년대에는 새로운 성장동력으로서 첨단기술산업에 대한 정부의 투자지원 정책을 적극적으로 펼쳐 국가경제의 지속적 성장을 견인하는 역할을 감당하였다.

다. 시장경제 체제 및 효율적 자원배분 전략

한국은 체제경쟁에서 북한을 이겨야 하고 체제를 유지하기 위해서는 군사력을 키워 안보태세(반공)를 투철히 하는 것과 국민생활 수준을 높이기 위해 경제력(근대화)을 키우는 것이 최우선이었다. 발전주의 국가의 산업화를 가능하게 하는 이념적 배경은 국가민족중흥주의였다(김왕배 2013). 1950년 한국전쟁 이후 경제 발전 초기에는 국가안보가 정권의 정당성과 안정성을 부여받는데 중요한 이념적 토대가 되었고 시민운동을 통하여 자생적 민주발전을 추구하는 서구식 자유민주주의와는 뿌리와 상황이 달랐다. 그러나 국가안보와 경제력 확장에는 공통 분모가 있었다. 국가안보를 위해서는 자주국방을 실현시키는 방위산업을 육성해야 하는데 방위산업은 철강, 기계, 전자, 화학 등 중화학 공업 육성에 기초하였다. 따라서 국가안보를 위한 궁극적인 길은 중화학공업화를 통한 국가 경제력 확장과 직결되어 있었다.

비록 한국사회를 중흥하기 위한 부국강병의 민족주의가 서구식 자유민주주의에 기반을 둔 경제발전을 추구하는 상황과 거리가 멀었지만 적어도 경제력 제고를 위한 자유시장경제 체제는 발전주의 국가의 산업화 체제에 중요한 기반이었다. 그래서 각종 경제 인프라, 자본시장, 재산권 관련제도 등 선진경제에서 보편적으로 기반하고 있는 경제제도적 환경의 선진화에 적극적인 행보를 취하였다. 예컨대, 1970년대 공업화 이후 경쟁촉진 효과를 통해 국가경쟁력 제고를 추진하기 위하여 자유무역주의적인 방향으로 전환하면서 한국경제 시장메커니즘은 한층 강화되었다. 또한 1990년대 이후 WTO, OECD 가입 등에 따라 국제경제적 위상을 제고하고 개방화 및 세계화를 추진했으며 1997년 외환위기 이후 국가경제의 광범위한 구조적 개혁을 통해 경제 체질을 획기적으로 개선했던 것은 모두 세계시장경제 질서 하에서 자원배분 효율성을 제고시키는데 기여한 노력들이었다.

왜 시장경제체제가 한국경제 성장에 주요한 요인 중의 하나였는가? 한국과 같이 치열한 체재경쟁을 벌이면서 국가안보가 최우선인 국가에서는 자율적이고 효율적인 민간 중심의 시장경제체제보다 국가권력이 절대적인 우위를 갖고 시장을 지도하는 체제가 당연시된다. 경제발전 초기단계에서는 국가가 경제성장을 추진하기 위해서 강력한 의지와 역할을 내세우면서 사적시장과 시장에 적극적으로 간여하였다. 그러나 한국정부는 경제발전 단계에 따라 시장경제체제의 효과적 작동을 통해 자원배분의 효율성을 제고시키려는 노력을 기울였고 적절한 제도와 정책을 펼쳤다. 이러한 노력은 궁극적으로 국가경제발전에 민간기업의 선도적 역할을 촉발시키고 시장경제의 경쟁효율성과 국제경쟁력 강화를 가져온 것이다. 오늘날 장기적 관점에서 지속적인 경제성장을 추구해온 대부분의 나라들에서 바로 이러한 시장경제체제의 이점을 최대한 누리면서 자원배분의 효율성을 적극적으로 견지했다는 세계 경제사적 증거들을 상기해 볼 때, 한국이 자유시장경제 체제를 적극적으로 수용한 것은 한국 경제성장의 주요한 요인으로 작용했을 것으로 판단됨에는 의심의 여지가 없다.

라. 인적자본 축적과 높은 생산성

바로 및 리(Barro and Lee, 1993, 1996, 2001)는 교육을 통한 인적자본 축적이 경제성장에 지대한 영향을 미친다는 것을 살펴보기 위하여 전 세계 국가들의 교육수준을 측정하였으며 실증적 분석결과, 교육수준이 경제성장에 긍정적인 영향을 미치는 것을 보여주고 있다. 내생적 성장 모형에서 보여주듯이 경제발전 초기단계에서 빈곤퇴치를 위한 강한 열망과 의지는 높은 교육열의로 표출되고 이는 경제내의 주체들 간 상호작용을 통해 높은 인적자본을 축적시키며 개인들의 잠재적 생산성을 향상시켜 경제성장에 기여하게 된다. 즉, 교육수준이 높은 노동력은 높은 생산성을 창출하여 경제성장을 촉진시킨다는 것이다. 또한 교육훈련으로 인해 숙련된 노동력이 많아지고 선진국의 고도기술 습득 능력을 배양시켜 경제성장을 증대시키게 된다.

한국은 1960년대 경제개발 초기단계에서 선진국에 비해 3차교육 평균년수가 낮았고 세계 146개국 평균치와 유사하였지만 풍부한 저숙련 노동력이 경공업산업화를 뒷받침하였으며 1970년대 후 중화학공업의 산업화를 진행하면서 필요한 숙련 노동력의 공급을 고등 교육의 강화로 충족시켰다. 이러한 노동력의 양적·질적 공급은 한국 국민의 높은 교육열의에 의해 뒷받침된 것이다. 한국의 경우, 높은 교육열의가 자조, 자립, 근면의 새마을 운동으로 표출되었고 이는 초기 인적자본 축적 및 노동력의 제공을 통해 경제성장에 기여하였으며 경제성장은 더 많은 교육기회를 제공함으로써 이른바 교육과 경제발전 간 선순환 구조를 형성하였다(김동헌 외 2011).

1960년대 이후 경제발전과 함께 상급학교 진학률이 현저히 높아졌으며 이는 노동의 양적·질적 증가와 인적자본의 축적을 초래하였다. 또한 높은 교육열의는 풍부한 노동력을 제공할 뿐만 아니라 적절한 직업훈련을 통해 노동시장의 유연성을 제고시켜 자원의 효율적 배분을 향상시켰

으며 기업의 연구개발(R&D) 조성과 확장을 통해 학습효과를 늘려 기술
개발을 견인하고 이는 지속적인 경제성장 동력으로 작용한 것이다.

[표 3] 상급학교 진학률 추이

단위: %

연도	중학교 진학률	고교 진학률	대학 진학률
1965	53.4	69.1	32.3
1975	77.2	74.7	25.8
1985	99.2	90.7	36.4
1995	99.9	98.5	51.4
2005	99.9	99.7	82.1

자료 : 교육인적자원부 & 한국교육개발원 (2008)

한국 경제성장에서 두드러진 특징 중의 하나는 급격한 경제성장과
더불어 노동시장에서도 급격한 변화가 일어난 점이다. 즉, 높은 교육열
의가 인적자본의 축적과 노동력의 양적·질적 공급을 뒷받침해줌에 따
라 급속한 산업화 과정에서 노동력 수요 구조의 급격한 변동을 적절하
게 흡수하여 지속적인 경제성장을 가져온 것이다.

1970년대 이후 급속한 산업화가 추진되면서 이에 필요한 숙련 노동
력을 공급하기 위해 고등 및 대학 교육 진학률이 급속하게 증가하여
인적자본의 축적을 가져왔고 이는 산업화를 통한 지속적인 경제성장에

결정적인 기여를 한 것으로 평가할 수 있다. 결국, 한국의 높은 교육열의는 산업화과정에서 적기에 필요한 인적자본 축적을 도모하였고 노동의 양적·질적 공급에 크게 기여한 것이다.

[그림 8] 한국 및 여타 국가의 3차교육 평균년수

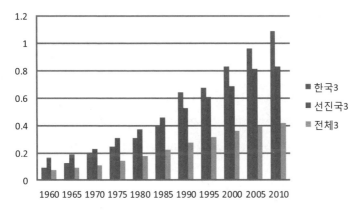

자료 : Barro & Lee (2010)

3. 한국 경제성장과 포스코의 역할

1) 포스코의 위상

포스코는 "철강은 국력이다"라고 철강산업을 공업국가 건설을 위한 기간산업으로 주창한 박정희 대통령의 국가중흥주의 의지를 받들어 "제철보국"만이 빈곤국가를 탈피하고 조국근대화 과업을 이룩할 수 있는 유일한 길이라고 순교자적 사명을 실현했던 박태준 사장이 1968년 4월 1일 포항종합제철주식회사를 설립한 것이 시발점이었다[2]. 이후 대한국제제철차관단(KISA)으로부터의 자금조달 계획이 완전히 무산되면서 포스코 건설이 절명적 위기에 처했으나 박태준 회장의 제철보국에 대한 투철한 사명감으로 일본 철강업계의 지원과 협조를 받아내고 대일청구권자금 전용으로 건설기금을 마련하여 1970년 4월 1일 포항 제1기 공장을 착공하였다.

　1973년 7월 포항 제1기 공장이 완성되어 연산 103만톤 규모의 생산능력을 구비하였으며 세계 철강 역사상 유례없이 가동 원년에 1억달러 이상의 매출액과 약 1200만달러 순이익을 올렸다(서갑경 1997). 이후 지속적으로 철강생산 시설을 확장하여 1976년 2기, 1978년 3기, 1983년 포항 4기를 준공하면서 1983년 연산 910만톤 규모의 철강 생산능력을 갖추었다. 더 나아가 광양지역에 1-4기에 걸쳐 확장 공사를 거듭한 결과 1992년 광양 4기 준공 후 연산 2050만톤의 생산량으로 세계 제3위 철강회사가 되었다. 1998년에는 연산 2654만톤을 생산하면서 조강생산 세계 제1위에 등극하였으며 2013년 현재 포스코는 연산 3840만톤을 생산하면서 아르셀로 미탈, 신일본제철, 헤베이, 보산강철, 유한철강에 이어 명실상부 세계 6위 글로벌 철강회사로 자리매김하고 있다. 또한 한국 총 조강생산량에서 포스코는 약 58.1% 비중의

2　포스코(POSCO)라는 이름은 1968년 설립당시 포항제철주식회사에서 2002년 3월 정관개정을 통해 회사명이 포스코로 바뀌면서 오늘날 널리 통용되는 이름이 되었다.

[그림 9] 포스코의 발자취

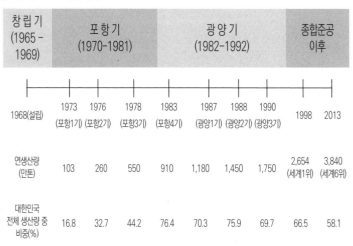

| 창립기
(1965 - 1969) | 포항기
(1970-1981) | | | 광양기
(1982-1992) | | | | 종합준공
이후 | |

	1973 (포항1기)	1976 (포항2기)	1978 (포항3기)	1983 (포항4기)	1987 (광양1기)	1988 (광양2기)	1990 (광양3기)		
1968(설립)								1998	2013
연생산량 (만톤)	103	260	550	910	1,180	1,450	1,750	2,654 (세계1위)	3,840 (세계6위)
대한민국 전체 생산량 중 비중(%)	16.8	32.7	44.2	76.4	70.3	75.9	69.7	66.5	58.1

철강을 생산하고 있는 한국 제일의 철강기업이다.

김병연·최상오(2011)는 포항제철이라는 한 기업의 설립이 전 국가적 사업인 경부고속도로 건설과 같은 영향력을 가진 것으로 평가되는 동시에 경제개발 5개년 계획보다 크게 뒤처지지 않는 파급효과를 가진 것으로 평가되며 이는 포항제철의 성장을 한국 경제발전의 주된 원동력으로 인식하고 있음을 기술하고 있다. 즉, 한국 국민들은 포항제철이 한국경제 전반에 광범위한 영향을 미친 것으로 인식하고 있음을 언급하고 있는 것이다. 그렇다면 포항제철이 어떻게 한국 경제발전에 기여하였는가?

[표 4] 세계 주요 철강 기업 생산량 현황

단위: 백만톤

순위	1991		2001		2010		2013	
	회사	생산량	회사	생산량	회사	생산량	회사	생산량
1	Nippon Steel	28.6	Arcelor	43.1	Arcelor Mittal	98.2	Arcelor Mittal	96.1
2	Usinor	22.8	POSCO	27.8	Bao Steel	37.0	Nippon Steel& Sumitomo	50.1
3	POSCO	19.1	Nippon Steel	26.2	POSCO	35.4	Hebei	45.8
4	British Steel	13.3	Ispat International	19.2	Nippon Steel	35.0	Bao Steel	43.9
5	NKK	12.3	Bao Steel	19.1	JFE	31.1	Wuhan	39.3
6	Kawasaki	10.91	Corus Steel	18.1	Shagang	23.2	POSCO	38.4
7	ILVA	10.9	Thyssen Krupp	16.7	Tata Steel	23.2	Shagang	35.1
8	Sumitomo	10.89	Riva	15.0	US Steel	22.3	Ansteel	33.7
9	Thyssen Krupp	10.3	NKK	14.8	Ansteel	22.1	Shougang	31.5
10	US Steel	9.6	Kawasaki	13.3	Gerdau	18.7	JFE	31.2

자료: World Steel(2014)

2) 한국 경제성장에서 포스코의 역할

전상인(2013)과 김도훈(2007)은 "근대 이후의 역사는 제철의 역사"라
고 할 정도로 제철은 산업화의 초석이며 그래서 철강을 "산업화의 쌀"

58

이라고 표현한다. 근대국가에서 산업화 목표를 꿈꾸던 국가들은 국력의 척도를 철강기술과 생산능력으로 판단하였다. 한마디로 철은 산업사회에 있어서 가장 중요한 기술적 물질이며 국가안보의 핵심이 되는 것이다. 최동용(2007)은 철강산업이 대규모 자본집약적 장치산업으로서 규모의 경제가 큰 산업이며 자동차, 조선, 전자, 기계 등 주요 산업에 필요한 기초 소재를 제공하는 국가기간산업임을 강조하고 있다. 따라서 철강산업은 사업시행에 대한 초기투자 비용이 크지만 타 산업에 대한 파급효과 및 영향력이 크고 투자로 인한 경제적 효과도 막대하여 기업의 성장 발전 및 존속에 지대한 영향을 미치는 것이 일반적 특징이다(임응순 2010).

이런 관점에서 볼 때, 공업화 및 산업화를 통해 지속적인 경제성장을 추진하려면 그 중심에 견고한 철강 산업이 필수불가결함을 알 수 있다. 따라서 1960년대부터 40여년 만에 급속한 공업화 및 산업화를 통해 지속적인 경제성장을 이룩하여 근대국가의 표본이 된 한국경제의 중심에는 포스코라는 글로벌 철강기업이 있었던 것이다. 김병연·최상오 (2011)는 한국 국민들의 인식조사에서 새마을운동, 경제개발 5개년 계획, 경부고속도로·포항제철 건설 등이 산업화에 크게 기여한 주요 요소로 나타났음을 언급하고 있다.

그렇다면 포스코가 급속한 고도경제성장에서 어떠한 핵심적인 역할을 하였는가? 경제학적 관점에서 한 나라의 경제성장을 초래하는 요인들과, 특히 이미 기술한 한국 경제성장의 핵심요인들의 관점에서 포스코가 그 요인들에 기여한 바는 무엇인지를 살펴봄으로써 한국 경제성

장에서 포스코의 핵심적 역할을 규명해 볼 수 있다.[3]

가. 포스코의 산업발전기여를 통한 제조업 성장 견인

철강은 산업화의 쌀이라고 한다. 이에 대한 경제학적 의미는, 철강산업이 규모가 큰 장치산업으로서 타 기업의 많은 제품을 수요하고 다른 산업들에게 철강제품을 주요 중간재로 공급하고 있기 때문에 타 산업과 연관효과가 매우 커서 철강산업의 발전은 경제 산업화를 통한 근대화와 직결된다는 것이다. 경제학에서는 이런 관점에서 한 산업의 타 산업에 대한 기여도를 평가하기 위해 산업연관분석이라는 방법을 이용한다. 산업연관분석은 국민경제를 산업별로 세분하여 산업간 재화와 서비스의 거래로 이루어지는 상호의존관계를 파악함으로써 최종수요 부분이 각 산업의 생산활동에 미치는 파급효과를 계측한다(최동용 2007). 실증분석에서는 각 산업의 투입과 산출관계를 통한 산업간 상호연관관계 등을 수량적으로 분석한다. 따라서 포스코 제품이 주요산업의 중간재로 투입되고 있기 때문에 포스코가 경제성장에 기여한 바를 분석하는 데는 산업연관분석이 중요한 것이다.

많은 기존 연구들에서는 철강산업의 국민경제 기여도를 분석하기 위하여 산업연관분석을 이용하고 있다(한재호 외 1988, 서정헌 1991, 곽상경 외 1992, 김상규 외 1998, 정군오 임응순 2008). 철강기업이 제품을 수요하는 후

---

3   국민경제적 관점에서 포스코가 생산, 고용, 국제수지에 미친 영향과 기간산업으로서 값싼 중간재를 공급한 경제적 효과 분석을 다룬 연구들로는 서울대 사회과학연구소(1987), 산업과학기술연구소(1990), 곽상경 외(1992) 등을 참조하길 바란다.

방연관산업으로는 원자재 산업과 전력, LNG 등 에너지 산업, 건설업, 기계산업, 물류 산업 등이 있으며, 철강기업이 제품을 공급하는 전방연관산업으로는 자동차, 조선, 건설, 기계, 가전, 조립금속 산업 등을 들 수 있다(최동용 2007). 따라서 후방연관효과는 각 산업 간의 상호의존관계 중에서도 타산업의 생산품을 중간재로서 구매하는 정도를 생산유발계수표에서 열의 합계를 통해 추정해낼 수 있다. 전방연관효과는 철강제품을 중간재로 사용하는 산업에 미치는 효과를 의미하는데 생산유발계수표의 행의 합계로 추정할 수 있다.

철강석에서 철강재를 만들기까지 크게 제선, 제강, 압연의 3단계로 구분되고 철강제품은 크게 철강의 성분과 재질, 제강법, 인장강도 등에 따라 봉형강류, 판재류, 강관류, 주단강으로 분류되며, 봉형강류는 주로 건설산업과 일반기계 등에, 판재류는 자동차, 조선, 가전산업 등에, 강관류는 가스관, 송유관, 석유 시추 등에 주로 사용된다. 따라서 철강제품이 쓰이는 산업을 잘 이해하면 철강산업의 전방연관효과를 잘 파악할 수 있고 일관제철소를 확장하거나 철강제품을 생산하기 위해 철강기업이 어떤 중간재를 수요하는지를 잘 이해하면 후방연관효과를 추정하는데 용이하다.

곽상경 외(1992)는 1988년 당시 포스코 철강생산이 국가 전체 총생산고의 70%를 차지하고 있는 철강1차제품 부문의 후방연관효과는 2.59로 추정하였다. 즉, 철강1차제품에 대한 100톤의 최종수요가 있을 때 이로 인한 직 간접 제품의 궁극적 증가가 259톤에 해당된다는 것이다.

당시 21개 산업분류표 기준 기타 산업을 제외하고 철강 1차제품의 후방연관효과가 제일 크게 나왔다. 철강산업의 전방연관효과는 1988년 2.57로 석유화학제품 부문의 3.73, 금융·보험·부동산 부문의 2.76에 이어 상당히 높은 수준을 보였다.

[표 5] 철강 제품 분류 및 용도

주요철강제품			용 도
봉 형 강 류	형	강	공장, 건물, 교량의 기초공사용, 지하철 등 각종 철골 공사용, 선박, 차량 등의 소재로 사용
	봉	강	기계구조용, 무계목강관용, 건설용 볼트·너트·리벳, 마봉강 등의 소재로 사용
	철	근	철근 건축, 토목용 소재
	선	재	선재 각종 철선 및 소형 볼트 너트 소재, 타이어코드
	궤	조	철도용 레일, 크레인 레일, 엘리베이터 레일 등
강관류	무계목강관		고압가스, 화학, 석유시추 등 특수용도로 사용
	용 접 강 관		수도관, 가스관, 송유관, 강관 말뚝, 일반구조용 및 배관용으로 사용
주단강			기계부품 및 공구용품, 각종 롤(roll) 사용

자료 : 『기초철강지식』 한국철강신문(1996)

[표 6] 산업별 전·후방연관효과추이 (1980년-1988년)

번호	산업명	연도별 전방연관효과			연도별 후방연관효과		
		1980년	1985년	1988년	1980년	1985년	1988년
1	농림수산품	2.2188	2.2910	2.2036	2.2188	2.2910	2.2036
2	광산품	1.3659	1.3678	1.3379	1.3956	1.3678	1.3379
3	식·음료품	1.9415	2.1938	2.1409	1.9415	2.1938	2.1409
4	섬유·가죽	1.9936	2.1184	2.0463	1.9936	2.1184	2.0463
5	제재·목제품	1.2870	1.3070	1.2526	1.2870	1.3070	1.2526
6	종이·인쇄·출판	1.9327	2.0533	2.0788	1.9327	2.0533	2.0788
7	석유화학제품	5.4349	4.4164	3.7297	5.4349	4.4164	3.7297
8	비금속광물제품	1.4593	1.5201	1.5338	1.4593	1.5201	1.5338
9	철강1차제품	2.5423	2.6170	2.5652	2.5423	2.6170	2.5652
10	비철금속괴	1.3353	1.3103	1.2808	1.3353	1.3103	1.2808
11	금속제품·기계	1.8862	2.1382	2.4417	1.8862	2.1382	2.4417
12	기타제조업품	1.1306	1.1063	1.1001	1.1306	1.1063	1.1001
13	전력·가스·수도	1.9155	1.9976	1.8247	1.9155	1.9976	1.8247
14	건설	1.2889	1.3229	1.3323	1.2889	1.3229	1.3323
15	도소매	2.2169	2.0338	2.1194	2.2169	2.0338	2.1194
16	음식점·숙박	1.3251	1.3160	1.2523	1.3251	1.3160	1.2523
17	운송·보관·통신	1.7054	1.8140	1.8163	1.7054	1.8140	1.8163
18	금융·보험·부동산	2.4363	2.6764	2.7068	2.4363	2.6764	2.7608
19	공공행정·국방	1.0000	1.0000	1.0000	1.0000	1.0000	1.0000
20	기타서비스	1.1595	1.1846	1.2011	1.1595	1.1846	1.2011
21	기타	1.6303	1.6492	1.5737	1.6303	1.6492	1.5737
	계	39.2345	39.4341	38.5919	39.2345	39.4341	38.5919

자료 : 곽상경 외(1992)

최동용(2007)은 2000년 산업연관표 자료를 통한 분석에서 후방연쇄효과의 정도를 전 산업 평균에 대한 상대적 크기로 나타내는 영향력 계수 추정결과 봉형강류 철강제품 1.315, 자동차 1.306, 판재류 철강제품 1.237, 금속제품 1.135 등 철강제품이 상대적으로 크게 나타났다. 또한 전방연쇄효과가 어느 정도인가를 전 산업 평균에 대한 상대적 크기로 나타내는 감응도계수 추정의 경우, 기타 서비스 3.226, 석유화학제품 2.04, 소재철강제품 1.684, 경공업제품 1.177, 판재류 철강제품 1.1의 순으로 나타나 일반적으로 철강제품이 각 산업부문에 중간재로 널리 사용되는 것을 보여주고 있다.

임응순(2010)은 2007년도 산업연관표 자료를 이용한 분석에서 철강은 전방연쇄효과가 1.795로써 29개 산업부문에서 1위 화학제품 1.923 다음으로 높았고 후방연쇄효과의 경우 철강은 1.250으로써 1위 기타산업 1.449 다음으로 높았다. 임응순(2010)은 철강산업의 경우 전방연쇄효과와 후방연쇄효과가 모두 높아 중간 수요적 제조업형으로 묘사하고 있다.

1980년대부터 2007년까지 철강산업의 전·후방연관효과 분석결과를 종합해보면 철강산업은 전 산업 중에서 전·후방 연관효과가 상당히 높은 산업으로 나타나 철강생산의 60% 이상을 차지한 포스코는 한국 경제성장 과정에서 여타 산업의 중간재 공급에 효과적 기여를 하였을 뿐만 아니라, 여타 산업 제품을 철강생산에 효과적인 중간재로 잘 사용함으로써 타 산업 생산에 상당한 기여를 한 것으로 평가되어, 포스코는 타 산업에 매우 긍정적인 파급효과를 창출하여 한국 경제성장에 기여한 것으로 판단된다.

[표 7] 산업별 전·후방연관효과추이 (2000년)

번호	산업명	전방연관효과		후방연관효과	
		중간수요율	감응도계수	중간투입율	영향력계수
1	농림수산업	0.6947	0.7717	0.3757	0.8592
2	일반광산품	0.9919	0.6554	0.3658	0.8477
3	원료광산품	1.0076	0.6648	0.7989	0.6438
4	경공업제품	0.4765	1.1768	0.7178	1.0863
5	석유화학제품	0.7023	2.0400	0.7226	0.8687
6	비금속광물제품	0.9339	0.9039	0.6604	1.0831
7	소재철강제품	1.0419	1.6837	0.8604	1.1132
8	판재류제품	0.7774	1.0996	0.7533	1.2369
9	봉형강류제품	0.8626	0.7752	0.7859	1.3148
10	비철금속제품	0.8444	0.8355	0.7681	0.8211
11	금속제품	0.7851	0.8703	0.6557	1.1348
12	일반기계	0.4194	0.9540	0.6929	1.1262
13	일반전기전자	0.4652	1.1044	0.7040	0.8739
14	전산가전기기	0.1756	0.5995	0.8239	1.0051
15	자동차	0.4007	0.8774	0.7744	1.3063
16	선박	0.1244	0.5783	0.6795	1.0457
17	기타수송장비	0.5007	0.6104	0.8348	1.0169
18	기타제조업	0.3098	0.5700	0.6597	1.0160
19	전력, 가스, 수도	0.6722	1.0422	0.5440	0.8030
20	건축, 건설	0.1665	0.6198	0.5621	1.0522
21	토목건설	0.0000	0.5301	0.5583	1.0650
22	운수 및 보관	0.3755	0.8112	0.5828	0.8274
23	기타 서비스	0.4151	3.2260	0.3924	0.8527
전체산업평균		0.4859	1.0000	0.5695	1.0000

자료 : 최동용(2007)

[표 8] 산업별 전·후방연관효과추이 (2007)

구분	감응도계수 (전방연쇄효과)	순위	영향력계수 (후방연쇄효과)	순위
1. 농림수산품	0.9614	15	0.9156	19
2. 광산품	0.5869	28	0.8806	20
3. 음식료품	1.0957	9	1.0804	8
4. 섬유 및 가죽제품	0.8103	20	1.0605	10
5. 목재 및 종이제품	1.0537	10	1.0397	15
6. 인쇄 및 복제	0.6669	23	1.0590	12
7. 석유 및 석탄제품	1.3097	5	0.6091	29
8. 화학제품	1.9234	1	1.0595	11
9. 비금속광물제품	0.7400	22	1.0411	14
10. 제1차 금속제품	0.8736	19	0.8445	23
11. 금속제품	0.9704	14	1.2379	4
12. 일반기계	0.9038	18	1.2366	5
13. 전기 및 전자기기	1.0203	12	0.9520	18
14. 정밀기기	0.5931	27	1.0935	7
15. 수송장비	0.9410	16	1.2393	3
16. 기타제조업제품	0.6397	24	1.1353	6
17. 전력, 가스 및 수도	1.1212	8	0.7605	28
18. 건설	0.6077	26	1.0656	9
19. 도소매	1.3190	4	0.8597	22
20. 음식점 및 숙박	1.0263	11	1.0458	13
21. 운수	1.1710	7	0.8146	24
22. 통신 및 방송	0.9104	17	0.9701	17
23. 금융 및 보험	1.2479	6	0.8755	21
24. 부동산 및 사업서비스	1.7951	3	0.7999	27
25. 공공행정 및 국방	0.5293	29	0.8137	25
26. 교육 및 보건	0.6271	25	0.8108	26
27. 사회 및 기타서비스	0.7601	21	1.0015	16
28. 기타	0.9996	13	1.4485	1
29. 철강	1.7954	2	1.2495	2

자료 : 임응순(2010)

전·후방산업연관효과는 각 산업부문에서 생산활동의 중간재 수요에 중점을 두고 산업간 연관관계를 파악하는 반면에 한 산업의 제품에 대한 최종수요의 변화가 생산, 부가가치 및 고용에 미치는 파급효과를 분석할 수 있다. 곽상경 외(1992)는 포스코 생산품에 대한 최종수요 변화가 산업전체의 생산에 미치는 영향을 평가하는 생산유발효과 추정에서 1988년 철강1차제품 부문의 생산유발효과는 2.592로 추정되고 21개 산업 중 가장 높게 나타남을 보여주고 있다. 최동영(2007)은 2000년 산업연관표 분석에서 봉형강류 철강제품의 생산유발계수가 2.481로 가장 높고 다음으로 자동차 2.464, 판재류 철강제품 2.333, 금속제품 2.141의 순임을 보여주고 있다.

곽상경 외(1992)는 포스코의 생산품에 대한 소비 및 투자수요의 변화가 가져오는 부가가치유발효과 추정결과 1988년 0.6290으로 나타나 만약 포스코 제품에 대한 신규수요가 100억원이 발생하면 그로 인하여 유발되는 부가가치가 약 63억원 정도로 추정되었다. 최동영(2007)은 2000년 산업연관표 분석에서 철강산업의 특성상 원자재의 해외의존도가 높기 때문에 철강산업의 부가가치유발계수는 봉형강류 철강제품 0.626, 판재류 철강제품 0.622, 소재 철강제품 0.455 등으로 전체 산업 평균에 못 미치는 것으로 분석되었다.

곽상경 외(1992)는 그 산업에서 최종수요가 10억원 발생할 경우, 직간접적으로 유발되는 노동력의 총인원을 나타내는 노동유발효과 추정에서 1986년 총유발인원 45.7명 중 철강 1차제품 부문이 20명으로 가장 높게 나왔는데 이는 철강 1차제품이 대표적인 노동절약형 산업으로 자본집약적이어서 직접유발효과 (고용계수)는 매우 낮지만 상대적으로 간접유발효과가 높아 타 산업에 미치는 노동유발효과가 상대적으로 높다고 분석하고 있다.

산업연관분석에 대한 기존 연구를 종합해 보면 철강산업의 전·후방 산업연관효과는 매우 높은데 포스코가 한국 철강제품 생산의 70% 이상을 차지하면서 철강산업을 주도해 왔기 때문에 결국 포스코의 산업연관효과는 크고 제조업과 건설업의 발전에 큰 기여를 했다고 볼 수 있다. 이는 한국 경제성장의 관점에서 볼 때, 철강제품을 국제가격보다 낮게 국내에 공급함으로써 관련산업의 생산비를 낮추어 국제 경쟁력을 제고하여 정부의 수출지향적 성장정책 전략에 획기적인 기여를 한 것으로 평가할 수 있다.

곽강수·김대중·강태영(2012)은 1973년 이후 주요 고로사들의 재무실적을 가지고 수익성뿐만 아니라 안정성, 성장성, 생산성, 성장 지배력을 종합적으로 평가한 결과, 한국, 중국, 대만, 일본 등 아시아 지역 기업들의 경영 성과가 우수하였고 특히 포스코의 경영 성과가 경쟁 기업들 중 가장 우수한 성적을 기록하였음을 보여주고 있다. 이들은 포스코가 최고 수준의 원가 경쟁력과 차별화 전략을 통해 경쟁 우위를 확보하였으며, 이를 바탕으로 자동차, 가전, 조선 산업 등에 저렴하고 양질의 소재를 공급함으로써 한국 제조업의 발전과 선순환구조를 만들면서 동반 성장을 가져오는데 기여한 것이라고 평가하고 있다.

[표 9] 산업별 노동유발 내역 (1980~1986)

번호	산업명	연도			
		1980	1983	1985	1986
1	농림수산품	2.7	2.3	1.8	1.6
2	광산품	3.9	3.4	2.1	1.9
3	식·음료품	0.3	0.3	0.3	0.2
4	섬유·가죽	1.3	0.6	0.6	0.6
5	제재·목제품	0.2	0.2	0.2	0.2
6	종이·인쇄·출판	0.7	0.6	0.5	0.4
7	석유화학제품	7.6	5.2	3.9	3.7
8	비금속광물제품	1.6	1.5	1.0	0.9
9	철강1차제품	30.4	25.3	21.5	20.0
10	비철금속괴	0.7	0.7	0.5	0.4
11	금속제품·기계	2.5	2.1	1.6	1.3
12	기타제조업품	0.1	0.1	0.1	0.1
13	전력·가스·수도	1.8	1.2	0.9	0.8
14	건설	1.0	0.7	0.6	0.6
15	도소매	15.8	13.3	8.4	7.0
16	음식점·숙박	1.5	1.7	1.5	1.3
17	운송·보관·통신	3.0	3.3	2.0	1.8
18	금융·보험·부동산	5.3	4.0	2.6	2.4
19	공공행정·국방	0.0	0.0	0.0	0.0
20	기타서비스	1.0	0.9	0.6	0.6
21	기타	0.0	0.0	0.0	0.0
	계	81.5	67.4	50.5	45.7

자료 : 곽상경 외(1992)

[표10] 세계 철강기업 경영 성과 종합 순위 측정 결과(1973~2007년)

기업	Factor1	Factor2	Factor3	종합 점수	순위
POSCO	1.623576	1.068306	0.372612	1.178863	1
BAO Steel	2.150489	0.433292	0.066436	1.147961	2
CSC	1.674895	0.768311	-0.911180	0.835262	3
NSC	-0.445220	1.294712	2.096488	0.660414	4
JFE	-0.639810	1.322276	0.071688	0.156913	5
Arcelor Mittal	0.353510	-1.65363	2.198706	0.075945	6
BHP	0.332522	-0.63951	-0.30706	-0.122150	7
KOBE	-1.026750	1.215360	-0.350930	-0.144980	8
CSN	0.035908	0.104523	-1.282540	-0.216820	9
TKS	-0.555090	-0.353040	0.614907	-0.243970	10
SAAB	0.243342	-0.980990	-0.310060	-0.276660	11
USS	-0.660040	-0.549790	0.829964	-0.312390	12
NISSHIN	-0.525490	0.0045123	-0.693030	-0.372010	13
SUMITOMO	-1.377400	0.815666	-0.247440	-0.416980	14
AKS	-0.456310	-0.634650	-0.089050	-0.43850	15
TISCO	0.177149	-1.842280	-0.810550	-0.696210	16
RAUTARUUKKI	-0.905280	-0.413680	-1.248960	-0.814690	17

자료 : 곽강수·김대중·강태영(2012)

나. 시장지향적 국영기업을 통한 국가주도 산업화 기여

한국경제의 급속한 성장을 견인했던 주요한 요인 중의 하나는 정부
의 강력한 리더십이다. 1960년대 초반 한국은 빈곤이 만연했고 자본축
적이 열악했으며 사회 인프라가 없었기 때문에 민간주도에 의한 성장

전략은 지속적이고 효과적인 경제성장을 견인할 수가 없었다. 이런 상황에서는 국가중심의 발전주의가 경제발전의 이념적 배경이 되어 국가가 산업화 과정에서 중심적이고 주도적인 역할을 담당하여 경제성장을 이끌어야 한다는 것이다. 포스코는 1960년대 국가민족 중흥주의를 주창하던 대한민국 정부의 시대적 사명을 실현하기 위하여 제철보국이라는 경제적 이념으로 결합하여 국가 주도 산업화를 견인함으로써 시장적 국가기업의 역할을 감당하였다.

1960년대 초반 박정희 대통령은 발전주의 국가체제를 통한 민족중흥주의를 이룩하기 위해 부국강병과 국가안보를 실현시켜야 했다. 이를 위해서 산업화를 통해 조국근대화를 추진하고 한국식 민주주의를 완성할 필요가 있었다. 한국식 민주주의는 중화학공업과 방위산업의 육성을 통해 부국강병을 완수하기 위한 경제 과업을 지속적으로 수행하는 것이었다(김왕배 2013). 박정희 정부는 위와 같은 산업화 중심에 종합제철소 건설이 핵심이라고 판단했다. 즉, 국가주도 경제개발을 추진하는 과정에서 제철의 중요성을 확인하고 산업화를 추진하는 과정에서 철강산업의 발전을 위해 적극적으로 노력했던 것이다(전상인 2013).

포스코는 설립 당시 국가주도형 경제발전 및 민족중흥주의라는 시대적 사명을 제철보국 이념으로 실현시켰다. 포스코는 1968년 설립 당시 국가주도형 철강산업을 키우기 위해 세워진 국영기업이었다. 그런데 초대 CEO인 박태준 명예회장의 제철보국에 대한 탁월한 창업정신 및 기업가치 문화는 국가적 소명을 갖는 국민기업을 넘어서 자주관리와 효율적 경영을 표방하는 시장적 원리가 포스코 중심에 자리잡는데 핵심적 역할을 하게 되었고 제철산업 육성을 통한 한국경제의 산업화라는 국가 발전주의 사명을 수행하는데 선봉적 기여를 한 것이다. 따라서 포스코는 공기업과 시장 메커니즘이 결합하여 단순한 국영기업이 아닌 효율성과 생산성을 겸비한 시장적(시장지향적) 공기업의 길을 걸음으로써 한국 경제성장을 이끄는 주요한 원천이 되었던 것이다.

어떻게 포스코의 시장적 공기업 기능이 한국경제의 지속적이고 급속한 성장을 가져오는 데 주요한 역할을 하였는가?

첫째, 포스코는 발전주의 국가 및 국가민족중흥주의 실현을 위한 조국 경제근대화 및 산업화 전략을 가장 잘 보여주는 공기업이었다. 한국전쟁 직후 한국사회는 후진성, 식민지성, 분단, 가난 등의 유산을 안고 있는 초라하기 짝이 없는 후진국이었다. 이런 상황에서 이승만 정권은 정치권력의 부정과 부패로 물들어 있었고 개인의 자유와 권리 등에 기초한 서구식 자유민주주의를 외치던 장면 정권은 민주주의와 자립경제의 확립 및 민족통일의 완수를 제대로 수행하지 못한 무능하고 부패한 상황이었다. 1962년 정권을 잡은 박정희 정부는 한국이 서구식 자유민주주의와 그 뿌리와 상황이 다르다고 인식하고 한국사회를 중흥하기 위해서 가장 시급한 것이 경제 근대화라고 판단하였다. 당시 한국사회는 보편적 빈곤이 만연하고 자본축적이 열악하며 경제 인프라가 조성되어 있지 않았기 때문에 민간주도에 의한 시장 메커니즘은 국민에게 경제성장에 대한 강한 의지를 불어넣어주지 못하고 성장에 대한 씨앗을 키울 수 없었다(김동헌 외 2011). 이런 상황에서 박정희 정부는 국가관료들에 의해 제공된 경제기준을 마련하고 한국식 산업화의 틀을 마련하였다. 한국식 민주주의와 산업화 핵심은 부국강병과 국가안보였다. 국가안보를 위해서는 자주국방을 가능하게 하는 방위산업을 육성해야 하는데, 방위산업은 철강, 기계, 전자, 화학 등 중화학공업의 육성에 기초한다. 따라서 중화학공업과 방위산업의 육성은 한국식 민주주의와 산업화 과업 수행을 위한 박정희 정권의 핵심 목표로 등장한 것이다(김왕배 2013).

  급진적 산업화를 추진한 박정희 정권은 경부고속도로의 건설과 함께 중화학공업을 육성하기 위한 제 2차 경제개발 5개년계획을 세우고 포스코를 필두로 석유화학, 기계, 전자, 전기, 자동차 등의 중화학산업을 육성하였다. 포스코는 국가주도 산업화 선봉장에 서서 국가자금과 국가신용의 차관으로 자본이 마련되어 초기부터 대형 용량의 일관 종합제철소로 건설되었고 공기단축을 통해 비용을 절감하는 등 출발부터 흑자 운영을 달성하면서 국영 기업으로써 큰 성과를 창출한 것이다(김왕배 2013). 철강산업은 대규모 장치산업으로써 규모의 경제가 큰 산업이기 때문에 자본축적이 매우 빈약한 시기에 시장 메커니즘을 통해 민간기업을 설립하여 철강산업을 육성하고 급속하게 국가 산업화를 주도하는 일은 거의 불가능한 상황이었다. 또한 포스코는 국영기업이었기 때문에 기업으로서 이윤추구의 수단만이 되지 않았고 국가경륜의 보다 높은 차원에서 경영되어야 한다는 대의와 가치를 지닌 민족자산의 정수임을 확고히 인식하는 기업경영 자세를 전사적으로 추구하였다(박태준, 1987). 즉, 특정한 개인이 아닌 민족 공동이익을 위한 선량한 봉사자,

관리자로서 국가발전의 기축이 될 철강백년의 진운을 개척하는 자세를 전사적으로 취한 것이었다. 이러한 보국적 자세는 공공기업으로서 포스코의 조직운영원리로 구체화되었고 보통 공기업이 갖게 되는 기업경영의 비효율성을 배제하고 냉엄한 국가 경쟁시대에서 민족과 국가의 생존과 번영을 추구하기 위한 동력으로써 국영기업의 역할을 하는데 주요한 원천이 되었다. 철은 산업의 쌀로써 산업의 쌀을 증진시킴으로써 나라를 부강하게 하여 국민생활을 윤택하게 하며 복지사회 건설에 이바지하는 제철보국 이념은 포스코라는 공기업을 통해 철강산업의 현장에서 실현된 것이었다. 포스코는 제철보국 이념을 국가기간산업인 철강산업에서 실천함으로써 한국경제의 급진적 산업화에 기여하였고 이는 급속하고 지속적인 한국경제 성장을 가져온 주요한 요인 중의 하나가 된 것이다. 류상영(2001)은 포스코의 기업전략과 자율성, 그리고 경제합리성이 박정희 정부의 국가자본주의 산업화 전략과 정치합리성에 부합되어 정부의 강력한 지지와 대통령 직속부서의 성격을 가지면서 한국 경제성장의 동력이었고 당시 시장창조적 국가자본주의를 실현하는 주요 행위자의 하나로 기술하고 있다.

둘째, 포스코는 실용성과 효율적 경영을 실현한 시장지향적 공기업이었다. 대부분의 공기업은 폐쇄적인 관료제에 따라 운영됨으로써 경쟁적인 시장에서 효율적 기업운영을 펼치기가 어렵다. 이명식(2012)은 경쟁이 치열해지는 상황에서 기업이 지속적인 경쟁우위와 월등한 수익성을 누리기 위해서는 시장요구에 경쟁자들보다 더 잘 대응해야 하고 시장 요구의 변화를 예측해야 하는데 이러한 기업의 노력을 시장지향성이라고 언급하고 있다. 공급자의 시장지향성은 거래관계의 불확실성을 감소시키고 경영환경의 변화에 따른 적응력을 제고시키는 역할을 하고 있다. 따라서 시장지향성은 조직 내의 모든 역량을 단일화된 초점으로 결집해 시장의 움직임에 반응케 함으로써 탁월한 성과를 유도하고 성과를 강화시켜 주는 것이다. 시장지향적 기업은 매출액, 총자산이익률, 매출액 성장률, 시장 점유율 등 재무적 성과와 인지된 품질, 고객만족, 직원만족, 신제품 개발과 성공 등 비재무적 성과를 통해 우수한 경영성과를 달성해 가는 것이다.

포스코 박태준 초대 회장은 실용주의적 산업주의 직업관을 견지한 기업인이었다(김왕배 2013). 시장원리에 따라 시장의 흐름에 민감하게 반응하고 국제 철강시장에서 포스코의 생존과 번영을 위해 적시에 시장을 분석하고 흐름을 읽어 대처하는 철저한 시장지향적 경영자였다. 예컨대, 초기부터 포스코의 주요 상대는 선진 외국시장이었기 때문에 박태준 회장은 철을 생산하자마자 바로 외국시장을 겨냥하여 수출을 개시하였다(서갑경 1997). 박태준 회장은 시장의 흐름을 면밀히 읽고 예측하면서 기업조직을 변형시키는 혜안을 발휘했다. 국내 및 국제 철강시장의 수요를 예측하여 생산량을 늘리기 위해 광양만에 제2종합제철소를 건설했다. 박태준 회장은 대부분의 공기업이 폐쇄성과 관료제로 인해 효율적 경영관리를 못해 만성적인 적자기업을 면치 못하는 것을 잘 알고 포스코 경영에 전 국민 주식회사 지주제 전환, 선제적 신기술 도입, 연구개발 및 과학기술분야 확장 등을 적극적으로 펼쳤다(김왕배 2013). 그 결과, 포스코는 공기업으로써 갖는 태생적 한계성을 극복하고 민간기업에 버금가는 효율적 경영관리를 펼친 것이다.

포스코는 이와 같은 시장지향성 추구를 펼치면서 국내 시장에서의 경쟁우위 유지에 목표를 두지 않고 국제시장에서의 경쟁우위 창조를 목표로 공격적인 기업전략을 펼쳤다. 이를 위해 끊임없는 기술혁신과 경영혁신을 추구하였다. 제2제철소의 준공으로 포항제철소는 다품종 소량생산체제로, 광양제철소는 소품종 다량생산체제로 이원화함으로써 기술혁신과 제품차별화에 성공할 수 있었다. 기술연구소와 산업과학기술연구소, 그리고 포항공대 (POSTECH)를 통한 과감한 연구개발 투자와 신기술 축적으로 포스코는 기술경쟁력을 향상시켰다. 또한 인사 및 재무 등 꾸준한 경영혁신을 통하여 경영효율을 제고하고 재무구조를 강화하였다(류상영 2001). 포스코는 공기업으로서 막연한 공공성보다 기업으로서의 상업성을 중시하면서 기업자율성을 강화시켜 나간 것이다. 류상영(2001)은 포스코의 자율성과 시장권력 (market power)이 정부-기업관계를 상호배양적 관계로 전환시키면서 국가와 포스코가 상호 촉매적으로 서로를 지원하고 육성하는 관계로 나아갔고 포스코는 "국가 안의 기업(enterprise within the state)"으로 성장했다고 기술한다.

곽상경 외(1992)는 포스코가 경영 효율성 제고로 제품가격을 낮게 유지하여 국내 경제에 지대한 기여를 했음을 강조하고 있다. 국내산업의 국제경쟁력을 높이기 위해 제품의 가격체계를 조정하여 국제시장에서의 수출가격보다 국내공급가격을 20%나 낮게 유지하고 국내수입가격보다도 10% 정도 낮추었다. 이러한 가격정책은 수출지향적 산업화를 통하여 경제성장을 추진하려는 정부주도 성장전략에 크게 기여한 것으로 평가된다. 결국, 시장지향적 포스코 기업전략은 국내가격제도를 통해 국내연관산업의 수출촉진, 2차 제품산업에 대한 수출경쟁력 제고 지원, 철강제품의 수요확대 및 관련산업의 무역금융지원으로 국내기업의 국제경쟁력 강화에 기여함으로써 급속한 산업화와 경제성장에 지대한 기여를 한 것으로 평가할 수 있다.

다. 기술 개발, 연구개발 투자 및 산학연 협동, 기업복지를 통한
    생산성 제고 및 인적자본 형성에 기여

김병연·최상오(2011)는 포스코의 성장이 국민경제의 성장에 미친 영향을 계량적으로 추정하거나, 포스코가 짧은 기간 동안에 양적으로나 질적으로 세계 일류기업으로 성장할 수 있었던 요인을 분석하는 것에 초점을 맞추는 연구들은 포스코의 국민경제에 대한 기여 및 기업의 성장요인과 정부와 기업 관계의 변화 등을 깊이 이해할 수 있지만 포스코의 한국경제에 대한 기여를 종합적으로 이해하는 데는 한계가 있음을 지적하고 있다. 동 연구는 포스코의 성장이 한국경제 성장에 미친 영향을 직접 효과와 간접 효과로 나누어 대부분의 기존 연구가 직접 효과에 집중된 점에서 벗어나 간접효과 분석에 초점을 맞추고 있다. 예를 들면, 포스코가 어려운 난관을 극복하여 거둔 모든 성공들이 포스코 구성원들, 다른 기업과 근로자들, 더 나아가 국민에게 미친 효과, 포스코의 기업 지배구조나 윤리경영, 인적 자본에 대한 투자 등이 다른 기업들의 정책과 선진 제도의 도입에 미친 영향 등과 같은 간접효과들을 통해서도 한국경제 성장에 긍정적인 영향을 미칠 수 있었던 점을 제시

하고 있다. 류상영(2001)은 포스코 성공 중의 한 요인으로 효율경영체제와 독자적인 연구개발체제를 일찍부터 구축하기 시작하여 자립적인 성장기반을 확립한 것을 강조하고 있다.

임경순(2010)은 포철의 성공요인 중 기술인력 양성 및 기술개선 활동, 현장기술인력의 중요성, 선진기술 습득과정의 심화와 지식의 상호 교류 및 새로운 아이디어 창출, 기초과학에 바탕을 둔 연구개발 전략 및 수요자 중심의 기술개발, 기존 제품의 품질향상 및 공정개선활동을 중시하는 점진적 혁신, 종합적이고 기초과학적 차원에서 종합연구소 추진 등과 같은 과학기술 연구개발 투자가 포스코의 지속적 성장에 크게 기여하였음을 강조하고 있다. 포스코는 해외기술연수와 사내 훈련을 통해 지속적인 기술개선활동을 했으며 특히 작업현장내의 기술개선과 혁신을 강조했다. 기술인력관리는 단순한 기술개발 차원을 넘어 생산성 향상과 초일류 철강기업 건설이라는 전사적 의식개혁운동과 함께 연결되어 추진되었다. 예컨대, 기술인력에 대한 보상체계를 마련하기 위하여 기성제도를 운영하였는데, 이는 탁월한 현장기술을 보유할 뿐만 아니라 인품과 생활태도도 존경 받을 만한 수준에 달하여 회사에서 높은 공헌도와 뛰어난 기술을 함께 인정받는 보국적 기술인을 양성하여 궁극적으로 회사의 경쟁력을 제고시켜 국가 철강산업을 견인하려는 것이었다.

포스코는 설립 당시 일본기술을 도입하여 시작하였지만 건설과 생산을 반복하면서 꾸준하게 성장하였는데 이 과정에서 제철소 규모뿐만 아니라 제철소 기술의 첨단화 전략을 동시에 추구하였다(산업연구원

1997). 철강산업은 장치산업으로서 규모의 경제가 작용하기 때문에 규모를 늘림으로써 생산비를 낮출 수가 있다. 더불어 포스코는 끊임없는 기술개발을 통하여 제철소의 생산성 제고에 결정적인 역할을 하는 연속주조 비율 기술을 획기적으로 개선시켜 나갔다. 이러한 세계 최대 설비를 갖춘 제철소 설비와 최첨단 기술 공법은 포스코의 생산성 제고에 큰 기여를 하였고 포스코를 국제경쟁에서 생존할 수 있는 발판을 마련하게 해주었던 것이다. 포스코는 국제비교우위 확보와 시장의 다변화, 신수요 창출 등이 기술력 수준에 달려 있기 때문에 치열해지는 국제경쟁시장에서 지속적 발전을 꾀하고 선발기업으로서의 위치를 확고히 하기 위해서는 기술개발이 핵심이라고 인지하였다(산업연구원 1997).

포스코는 기술개발을 위해 연구투자에 적극적인 노력을 경주했다. 1977년 부설기술연구소를 건립하고 외부 교육 및 연구기관과 상호 긴밀하게 협력하여 산학연 협력체계를 이루면서 기술개발을 추진하였다. 단순히 선진기술 습득에 만 머무르지 않고 습득한 지식을 상호 교류하는 상호 학습모형을 통해 새로운 아이디어 창출을 꾀하면서 학습효과를 통한 기술혁신을 추구하였다. 수요자 중심의 기술개발을 지향하여 효율적 기술개발과 연구개발의 상용화를 유도하였다. 포스코는 1986년 종합연구소를 설립하여 종합적이고 기초적인 차원에서 연구개발을 체계화하여 단순히 기존제품의 개선과 신제품 개발에만 중점을 두지 않고 장기적 안목에서 기초기술을 개발하고 미래의 유망 첨단제품을 개발하는 연구개발 플랫폼을 추진한다. 이를 계기로 포스코는 기술에 대한 확고한 자주의식을 더욱 고취하고 투철한 기술자립의 기반을 공고히 하였다. 이와 같은 포스코의 기술개발 노력 및 연구투자는 궁극적으로 포스코 기업의 생산성 향상 및 국제 경쟁력 제고를 통해서 결국 한국경제의 생산성 제고에 기여했다고 볼 수 있다.

포스코는 기성제도를 통해 우수한 현장기술인력을 양성하였을 뿐만 아니라 기술연구소 및 종합연구소를 설립하여 철강산업 및 관련 산업 발전에 필요한 연구인력을 양성하였으며 대학, 산업체, 연구소 등을 유기적으로 연결시키기 위해 포항공대(POSTEC)와 포항산업과학연구원(RIST)을 설립하여 산학연 협동체제 구축을 통한 국가 산업 인력을 양성하는데 주요한 기여를 하였다. 국가와 산업의 발전에 교육 및 대학의 역할이 지대하다는 것을 인식한 박태준 초대회장은 당시 이론 중심의 공과대학 교육을 산업현장과 연계시키기 위해 제철연수원에서 여러 가지 자체 보강교육을 개발하여 새로운 교육 방식 구축을 조직적으로 추진하여 제철보국을 구현할 산업인력을 양성하였다.[4] 제철연수원은 설비규모의 확대 및 기업 환경 변화에 대응한 다양한 교육수요가 발생함에 따라 신규 인력의 조기 전력화, 안정 조업 기반의 구축, 직원 의식구조 변화에 따른 창업 정신의 계승 및 발전, 조직의 대규모화에 따른 관리 능력의 확충, 경영의 국제화에 따른 국제화 대응 능력 향상에 중점을 두고 사원교육을 발전시켰다(이상오, 2012).

포스코는 박태준회장의 교육보국 이념을 체계적이고 교육 백년지대계의 관점에서 실현하기 위해 광양제철소 건설 이후 고급두뇌 수요에

---

4   포스코는 1969년 2월 1일 기업의 교육 훈련 전담 기구인 연수원을 설치하여 기술 요원의 국외 위탁 교육과 사내 교육의 목표를 설정하고 이를 중점적으로 추진하였다. (이상오 2012)

대처하기 위한 획기적인 인재확보 방안으로 포항공과대학 설립을 추진하였다. 즉, 포스코는 국가적인 차원에서 미래 산업을 선도해 나갈 유능한 인재를 배출해야 한다는 박태준 회장의 소명의식을 구현하기 위해 연구중심대학인 포항공대를 설립한 것이다(임경순 2010). 포항공대는 설립 이후 저명교수 초빙, 국제적 수준의 교육시설 구비, 산학연 협동체제 구축 및 정예소수인재 선발로 면학과 연구를 위한 제여건을 완비하고 첨단 및 과학기술의 기초응용분야를 교수 연구하며 대학원 중심의 연구위주 대학으로 발돋움함에 따라 한국의 대학들에게 경쟁적인 연구 분위기를 유발시켜 본격적인 연구 체계로 진입하게 하는데 커다란 역할을 하였고 국가 전체의 대학 교육 개혁에도 이바지 했다(Im 1999; 임경순 2010).

위와 같은 포스코의 제철연수원 교육을 통한 산업현장 인력 확보 및 양성, 산학연 협동연구체제를 통한 기술개발 및 연구능력 함양, 그리고 장기적이고 국가적인 관점에서 미래산업을 선도할 고급 두뇌를 양성하기 위한 포항공대라는 연구중심대학의 설립 등은 한국 경제성장에 영향을 미친 주요 핵심요인 중 인적자본 축적에 상당한 기여를 한 것으로 평가된다.

기업은 혁신을 통해 경쟁자들보다 더 빠르고 더 낫고 더 현명하게 성장할 수 있는 메커니즘을 터득하고 궁극적으로 산업발전에 기여하게 된다 (Davila, Epstein & Shelton, 2006). 기업들은 참신한 아이디어를 바탕으로 혁신을 추진하기 때문에 혁신은 경영환경을 뛰어넘어 기업의 성공을 견인하는 경쟁력의 핵심요소이다(Kelley, 2001). 이도화 김창호(2012)는 혁신을 연구개발을 통한 엔지니어 중심의 기술 및 제품 개발을 의미하는 기술혁신과 현장근로자들의 참여에 의한 개선활동이 위주가 되는 고성과 작업장 혁신으로 분리하고 기술혁신과 작업장 혁신이 결합할 때 혁신의 효과는 배가된다고 강조하고 있다. 포스코는 작업장 혁신에 대한 박태준 회장의 신앙적 몰입에 영향을 받아 QC활동인 품질 분임조와 제안제도를 포괄하는 자주관리와 이의 후신인 QSS (Quick Six Sigma) 활동을 통해 전사적인 현장 작업장 혁신을 실행하였다. 이러한 자주관리 활동은 포스코 기업의 노동생산성 및 경영성과를 제고시켜 포스코가 세계적인 경쟁력을 유지하는 원동력으로 평가받고 있다(이도화·김창호 2012).

이도화·김창호(2012) 연구에 따르면, 포스코에 자주관리가 본격적으로 확산된 1979년 이후 포스코의 노동생산성(인당 조강생산량, 톤/인)이 급격히 증가하여 1979-84년 기간의 노동생산성 평균은 530톤/인으로써 1973-78년 기간의 노동생산성 평균 216톤/인에 비해 생산성이 2.5배나 증가한 것으로 추정되었다. 당시 자주관리 주요 활동 테마가 설비효율화와 능률향상으로써 작업효율성 제고에 상당한 기여를 하였고 이는 노동생산성 향상에 긍정적 영향을 주었던 것으로 판단된다. 또한 자주관리에 의해 근로자들의 조업능력이 조기에 향상되고 증설된 신설공기에 숙련 인력 공급을 적기에 가능하게 했다는 점은 자주관리의 간접적 효과로 평가된다.

[그림 10] 포스코 1인당 생산성 추이

단위: 톤/인

자료 : 포스코 35년사(2004)

포스코는 창업 초기부터 근로자가 필요로 하는 다양한 주택, 생활기
반, 문화체육, 장학제도와 교육시설 완비, 우리사주제도에 의한 자산
증식, 선택적 복리후생제도의 의한 근로자 참여형 복지제도라는 기업
복지의 전형을 형성하였다(이용갑 2012). 포스코의 기업복지는 지속적인
흑자경영과 선순환 구조를 이루었다. 즉, 지속적인 흑자경영은 숙련 근
로자의 장기근속을 유도하여 고용안정성의 기반과 기업복지 발전을 위
한 물적 토대를 제공하였고 포스코 근로자들의 안정적 삶의 기반은 끊
임없는 혁신과 생산성 증가를 추구하여 기업의 흑자경영을 가능하게
만든 것이다. 결국, 이러한 선순환 구조는 포스코 생산성 향상을 통해
국가경제의 생산성 향상에 기여한 것으로 평가할 수 있다.

김병연·최상오(2011)는 포스코가 한국사회와 경제에 기여한 내용들을 직접효과와 간접효과로 나누어 포괄적이고 체계적인 분석을 시도하고 있다. 직접효과는 주로 경제적 효과로서 포스코가 질 좋은 철강제품으로 저렴하게 공급함으로써 다른 기업의 경쟁력을 강화시키는 다양한 효과, 예컨대 산업의 전 후방 연관효과, 수입대체효과, 수출효과, 고용효과 등이다. 반면 간접효과는 직접 효과 이외 포스코 성장이 한국 사회와 경제에 미친 영향으로서 한국인의 경제발전 의지, 즉 자신감에 미친 효과와 기업제도의 선진화에 미친 효과 등이다. 동 연구는 당시 언론 보도내용을 이용하여 포스코의 성장과 효과를 분석하는 서지적 방법론과 포스코의 경영성과 자료에 대한 계량적 분석을 이용하여 두 가지 효과를 분석하였다. 분석 결과, 동 연구는 포스코가 한국 경제발전 초기에 중화학공업화를 본격적으로 추진하는 대표적인 선발기업으로 건설과정에서 성공적인 공장 건설 모델을 제공한 점, 대규모 공장 확장 공사를 성공리에 완공하면서 성공에 대한 자신감을 확산시킨 점, 자신감의 확산을 넘어 글로벌 기업으로 우뚝 성장하여 한국경제의 기업성장 모델이 된 점 등은 포스코 설립과 발전이 한국경제에 긍정적인 외부효과를 창출하는데 주요한 요인으로 작용한 것으로 평가하고 있다.

김병연·최상오(2011) 연구는 제도 발전이 미비하고 자원이 빈약하여 동시다발적으로 많은 사업을 진행할 수 없고 경제발전 경험이 일천하여 학습이 필요한 국가들에게 효율적인 경제발전 추진 전략이 무엇인지에 대한 중요한 시사점을 언급하고 있다. 추상적이고 포괄적인 정책보다 포스코와 같은 소수의 중요한 기업에 집중하여 이를 성공 사례로 만들어 내고 이를 학습, 적용, 확산함으로써 한 국가의 성장 동력을 구축하는 것이 개도국의 주요한 경제성장 전략이 될 수 있다는 것이다. 동 연구는 포스코의 성공이 한국경제의 산업화 과정에서 외부효과(Economic externality)를 창출하여 한국경제의 총요소생산성(Total factor productivity)에 긍정적인 영향을 끼쳐 결론적으로 경제 성장에 기여한 것으로 평가하고 있다.

요약하면, 포스코는 제철보국을 실현하면서 국가 미래산업을 선도할 인재육성이라는 박태준 회장의 교육보국 정신을 실천하기 위해 기술개발과 기술혁신, 연구개발 투자, 산학연 협동연구 및 산업 현장인력 양성, 전사적 자주관리를 통한 현장혁신, 기업복지발전과 흑자경영의 선순환 구조, 포스코 성공의 학습 및 확산을 통한 국가 산업화에 외부효과 창출 등을 만들어내면서 국가경제의 생산성 제고 및 인적자본 축적을 도모하여 한국 경제성장에 기여한 것으로 판단된다.

3) 포스코가 한국 경제성장에 미친 영향 : 실증분석

가. 한국 경제성장에 미친 경로

지금까지 한국경제가 지난 40년간 급속한 성장을 경험하게 된 핵심적 요인은 무엇인지 4가지 관점에서 서술하였다. 한국경제 산업화 중심에 있었던 포스코가 급속하고 지속적인 경제성장을 이룩하는데 중요한 역할을 했음에 대하여 기존 연구에서도 다양한 분석방법들이 많이 연구되어왔다. 본 연구에서는 기존연구들이 제시하는 서술적 문헌연구 및 경제적 효과 분석 위주의 접근방식에서 벗어나, 상기 핵심적 요인의 관점에서 실증적 분석을 시도하려고 한다. 먼저 포스코의 성장이 어떻게 한국경제성장에 영향을 미칠 수 있었는지 상기 4가지 핵심적 관점에서 로드맵이 필요하다.

포스코 성장과 한국경제 성장간 로드맵은 국가경제 기반산업인 철강산업의 중심에 서서 글로벌 철강기업으로 부상하는 과정에서 타 산업에 매우 긍정적인 전후방연관효과를 통하여 한국경제 제조업 성장에 핵심적 역할을 감당한 점, 시장지향적 국영기업의 역할을 통하여 국가 산업화 과정에서 정부의 주도적인 역할을 지지하고 수출지향적 대외경제정책을 펼치는데 핵심적 역할을 하였다는 점, 그리고 기술개발 및 혁신, 경영혁신, 자주경영관리, 기업복지, 윤리경영 및 보국이념의 기업철학, 교육보국을 지향하는 교육투자 및 인적 자본 형성 등 포스코의 다양한 직 간접적 역할을 통해 국가경제 생산성 제고 및 인적자본 형성을 통해 한국경제 성장에 기여한 점 등으로 그려 볼 수 있다.

이러한 로드맵에 대한 과학적 분석이나 통계적 분석을 통해 실증적 증거들을 매우 체계적으로 보여주는 것은 그리 쉬운 일은 아니다. 다만 위와 같은 포스코의 선도적 역할을 통해 우수한 기업성과를 예측할 수 있고 이러한 창조적인 기업성과는 제조업 발전을 통해 한국 경제성장에 매우 긍정적인 영향을 미친 것으로 판단해 볼 수 있다. 따라서 본 연구에서는 두 가지 가설적 경로를 설정하고 이에 대한 실증적 분석을 시도하려고 한다.

가설 1: 포스코의 기업성과가 제조업 발전에 긍정적인 영향을 미쳤고 이는 한국경제 성장에 기여했을 것이다.

가설 2: 포스코의 다양한 기술혁신 및 경영혁신, 기업문화 등은 포스코의 생산성을 향상시켰고 이는 제조업발전이나 한국경제의 생산성 제고에 기여함으로써 한국경제 성장에 기여했을 것이다.

가설 1에 대한 실증분석은 두 가지 분석을 통해 시도할 수 있다. 첫째, 제조업 성장률과 포스코 매출증가율간 관계를 분석하는 것이다. 시계열분석에서는 두 변수간 인과관계를 분석하기 위하여 그레인저 인과관계 검증(Granger Causality Test)을 통해 인과관계 존재여부를 판단한다[5]. 둘째, 포스코는 미래 철강수요를 예측하여 제철공장 확장 공사를 선제적으로 펼쳐 나갔다. 따라서 포항 및 광양 제철소 확장 공사가 완공될 때마다 포스코의 생산능력은 증가되고 이는 포스코의 생산성과 제조업 발전에 기여했을 것으로 판단된다. 이에 대한 실증분석은 더미변수(Dummy variable) 접근법을 통하여 간단히 살펴볼 수 있다. 예컨대, 포항의 제 1기, 2기, 3기 및 4기, 광양의 1기, 2기, 3기 및 4기가 준공되는 해에 포스코의 기업성과는 더욱 커지게 되고 이는 제조업 발전을 통해 한국경제 성장에 기여했을 것이다. 이를 실증분석하기 위해 각 확장공

---

5   엄밀히 말하면 그레인저 인과관계 검증은 두 변수간 실제적 인과관계를 분석하는 개념은 아니고 예측의 관점에서 평가하는 개념이다. 즉, 한 변수가 타 변수의 미래값을 예측하는데 도움이 된다면 그레인저 인관관계가 있다고 판단하는 것이다. 하지만 그레인저 인관관계 검정을 통해서 두 변수간 인과관계를 간접적으로 판단하는 것이 보편적으로 활용되고 있다.

사가 준공되는 해를 더미변수로 설정하고 그 해에 특별히 제조업 성장률이 더 높았는지를 검정해 볼 수 있다.

가설 2에 대한 실증분석은 포스코의 생산성(또는 증가율)과 제조업 성장률 및 국가경제 생산성(또는 증가율)간 관계를 분석하는 것이다. 이는 포스코 생산성(또는 증가율)과 제조업 성장률간 회귀분석 또는 포스코 생산성(또는 증가율)과 한국경제 생산성(또는 증가율)간 회귀분석을 통해 포스코 생산성이 제조업발전이나 국가 생산성에 미친 영향을 간단히 평가할 수 있다.

나. 실증분석

포스코는 1973년 7월 예정보다 한 달 빠르게 제1기 공사를 준공하면서 103만톤 규모의 종합제철소를 설립하면서 그해 1억달러 이상의 매출액과 1200만달러에 달하는 순이익 성과를 올려 세계 철강산업 역사상 유례없는 성과를 달성하였다(서갑경 1997). 이후 1976년 5월 포철 제 2기 공장이 준공되면서 포철의 생산능력은 260만톤으로 증대되면서 한국경제의 GDP도 가파르게 증가하기 시작했다.

김명언·이지영(2012)은 리더의 심리적 단어 사용과 조직 맥락 간의 관련성을 살펴보기 위하여 포스코 박태준 회장의 사례를 분석하고 있는데 박태준 회장이 재임했던 기간을 크게 세 단계로 구분하고 있다. 첫 번째는 창업기로 1968년-1973년이고 두 번째는 도약기로 1974년-1985년까지이다. 세 번째는 본격 성장기로 1986년-1992년이다.1973년 제 1기 제철소 공장 완공이후 1974년부터 1985년기간 동안 연평균 매출액 증가율은 43.25%였으며 1986년부터 1992년기간 동안 연평균 매출액 증가율은 17.3%에 달하였다. 박태준 회장 재임기간 중 공장가동 원년 1973년을 제외하고 1973년-1992년 기간 동안 연평균 매출액 증가율은 34%에 달하였다.

[그림 11] 포스코 당기순이익, 매출액 및 명목 GDP 추이

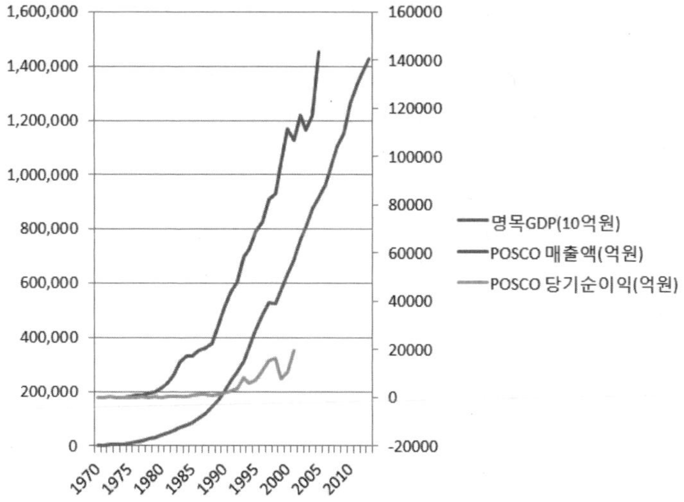

자료 : 한국은행(2015), 포스코 35년사 & 40년사(2004, 2009)

1973년부터 2014년까지 포스코 매출액 증가율과 한국경제 실질 GDP 성장률 간에 상관관계를 파악해보면 두 변수간 양의 상관관계가 나타남을 알 수 있다. 즉, 포스코 매출액 증가율이 높으면 한국 경제성 장률도 높고 매출액 증가율이 낮으면 경제성장률도 낮다는 것이다. 추정된 회귀식에 따르면 포스코 매출액 증가율이 1% 증가하면 한국경제

GDP 성장률이 0.02% 높아진다는 것이다. 이 추정결과는 매출액 증가율이 외생적이라는 가정을 전제하고 있다. 그러나 경제성장률이 높을수록 포스코 매출액 증가율도 높아질 수 있기 때문에 매출액 증가율이 내생적일 수 있으며 따라서 상기 추정결과에 대한 강한 주장을 펴는 데는 무리가 있다. 다만, 포스코 매출액 증가율이 한국 경제성장률에 긍정적인 영향을 미치는 것을 간접적으로 확인할 수 있을 것 같다. 한국경제가 외환위기 여파로 큰 어려움을 겪었던 1999년부터 2001년까지 한국경제 성장률이 마이너스를 기록했던 기간을 제외하면 포스코 매출액 증가율과 경제성장률 간 양(+)의 상관관계는 더 강할 것으로 판단된다.

[그림 12] 포스코 매출액 증가율과 경제성장률간 관계

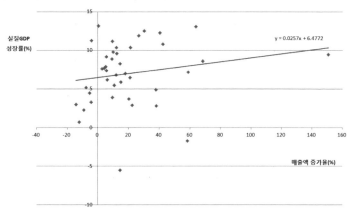

그러나 상관관계 분석은 두 변수 간 인과관계에 대한 방향에 대해서는 아무런 정보를 주지 못하기 때문에 계량경제학에서는 인과관계에 대한 분석을 위해 그렌저 인과관계 검정(Granger Causality Test) 방법을

이용한다. 그렌저 인과관계 검정방법을 간단히 소개한다. 두 개의 변수 x_t와 y_t가 있다고 하자. 우리의 목적이 두 변수 간 인과관계 여부에 대한 검정이라면 다음과 같은 두 개의 모형을 설정할 수 있다:

$$y_t = \alpha_y + \sum_{i=1}^{p} \beta_i y_{t-i} + \sum_{j=1}^{p} \gamma_j x_{t-j} + \epsilon_{yt}, \qquad (1)$$

$$x_t = \alpha_x + \sum_{i=1}^{p} \delta_i x_{t-i} + \sum_{j=1}^{p} \theta_j y_{t-j} + \epsilon_{xt}, \qquad (2)$$

여기에서 $\alpha_i, i = x, y$,는 상수항, $\beta_i, \gamma_i, \delta_i, \theta_i$는 추정계수들, $\epsilon_{xt}, \epsilon_{yt}$는 각 추정식에서 잔차항(error term)을 나타낸다. 모형식 (1)과 (2)의 추정결과에 대하여 두 변수간 그렌저 인과관계가 있는지 검정을 하는 경우 다음과 같이 가설을 설정할 수 있다:

모형식 (1)에서 귀무가설 (H_0) :

x_t는 y_t를 그렌저 인과하지 않는다.

$\Leftrightarrow H_0 : \gamma_1 = \gamma_2 = ... = \gamma_p = 0$ $\qquad$ (3)

모형식 (2)에서 귀무가설 (H_0) :

y_t는 x_t를 그렌저 인과하지 않는다.

$\Leftrightarrow H_0 : \theta_1 = \theta_2 = ... = \theta_p = 0$ $\qquad$ (4)

모형식 (1)과 (2)는 최소자승법(ordinary least squares: OLS)을 통하여 추정할 수 있고 추정결과를 바탕으로 귀무가설 (3)과 (4)에 대하여 각각 왈드검(Wald Test)을 실시할 수 있다. 검정결과 귀무가설 (3)을 기각하게 되면 x_t 는 y_t 미래값을 예측하는데 도움이 되고 이 경우 "x_t 는 y_t 를 그레인저 인과한다(Granger cause)"라고 말한다. 검정결과 귀무가설 (4) 를 기각하게 되면 y_t 는 x_t 미래값을 예측하는데 도움이 되고 이 경우 "y_t 는 x_t 를 그렌저 인과한다(Granger cause)"라고 말한다. 일반적으로 시계열분석에서는 그렌저 인과관계 검정을 통하여 두 변수 간 인과관계를 판단한다.

[표 11] 포스코 매출액 증가율과 제조업부문 성장률간 그렌저 인과관계 검정

구분	1974-2014년 (전체 표본기간)			1974-1994년 (박태준 회장 재임)		
귀무가설	통계량	P-값	검정 결과	통계량	P-값	검정 결과
포스코 매출액 증가율은 제조업 성장률을 그렌저 인과하지 않는다	4.216	0.009	기각	4.844	0.028	기각
제조업 성장률은 포스코 매출액 증가율을 그렌저 인과하지 않는다	4.523	0.006	기각	4.121	0.042	기각

포스코 매출액 증가율과 제조업부문 성장률 간 그렌저 인과관계 검정을 위해 포스코 매출액 증가율을 x_t 라 하고 제조업부문 성장률을 y_t 라고 하자. 표본기간을 1974-2014년과, 주로 박태준 회장 재임기간인 1974년-1994년으로 나누어 그렌저 인과관계 검정을 시도하

였다. 검정 결과, 두 표본 기간의 분석결과는 큰 차이가 없었다. 먼저 포스코 매출액 증가율은 제조업 성장률을 그렌저 인과하지 않는다는 귀무가설이 기각되었다. 이는 포스코의 기업성과가 제조업 성장에 주요한 기여를 했음을 시사하며 기존의 산업연관분석을 통해서 제시된 결과를 뒷받침한다고 볼 수 있다. 즉, 포스코 기업의 성공은 한국 철강산업의 성공이고 이는 전후방산업연관효과를 통해 한국 제조업 부문의 성장을 견인하였다는 것으로 풀이할 수 있다.

또한 반대의 경우로, 제조업 성장이 포스코 기업성과에도 기여하였는지 그렌저 인과관계 검정을 시도할 수 있다. 분석 결과, 제조업 성장률은 포스코 매출액 성장률을 그렌저 인과하지 않는다는 귀무가설이 기각되었다. 이는 제조업부문의 성장이 포스코 기업성장에 기여한 것을 의미하는데 이는 자동차, 전자, 전기 등 분야의 제조업 성장은 철강산업 성장에 긍정적인 영향을 미쳐서 포스코 기업의 성장에 도움을 준 것으로 판단된다. 위와 같은 그렌저 인과관계 검정 결과는 포스코로 대표되는 철강산업과 자동차, 전자, 선박 등의 산업들은 서로 유기적인 관계를 가지고 전후방연관효과를 통해 산업발전의 선순환구조를 형성하여 한국경제 성장을 가져왔다는 것을 시사한다.

포스코의 기업성과가 한국경제 성장에 기여했다는 가설 1에 대한 두 번째 실증분석은 확대기 반영을 통한 더미변수 (dummy variable) 접근법이다. 이미 기술한 바와 같이 포스코 기업성과가 한국 경제성장에 기여했다면 포스코가 제철소 확장 건설을 통하여 조강생산능력을 제고시킬 때마다 포스코의 기업성과는 높아지고 이는 제조업 성장에 기여했

을 것이다. 이에 대한 실증 분석은 다음과 같은 모형식을 통해서 시도할 수 있다:

$$y_t = (\beta_0 + \beta_d D_t) + \sum_{i=1}^{p} \beta_i y_{t-i} + \epsilon_t \qquad (5)$$

D_t는 더미변수로써 포스코의 제철소 확장공사가 준공될 때마다 조강생산능력이 제고되는 연도에는 1의 값을 갖고 그렇지 않은 연도에는 0의 값을 갖는다. 모형식 (5)는 자기회귀모형(Autoregressive(AR) model)으로서 만약 제철소 확장공사가 완료되어 조강생산능력이 제고되어 제조업 성장률이 증가하였다면 추정계수 $\hat{\beta}_d$는 통계적으로 유의한 양(+)의 값을 가질 것이다.

표본기간을 1973년~2014년과 박태준 회장의 재임기간인 1973년-1994년으로 나누고 제조업성장률에 대하여 더미변수 분석을 시도하였다. 포스코가 포항제철소 1기, 2기, 3기, 4기와 광양제철소 1기, 2기, 3기, 4기 준공연도인 1973, 1976, 1978, 1983, 1987, 1988, 1990, 1992년의 경우에 더미변수 D_t값을 1로 주고 나머지는 0으로 설정하여 모형식(5)를 추정하였다.

두 표본기간에 대한 분석결과는 매우 유사하였다. 상수항의 더미변수 D_t의 추정계수 $\hat{\beta}_d$의 값은 모두 양(+)의 값을 갖고 통계적으로 유의하였다. 이러한 추정결과는 포스코가 제철소 확장공사를 준공하여 조강생산 능력이 확장될 때 포스코의 기업성과는 제고되었고 이로 인해 제조업 성장률도 높아지는 것을 의미한다고 볼 수 있다.

[표 12] 포스코 확장 공사가 제조업 성장률에 미친 영향

추정계수	1974-2014년 (전체 표본기간)			1974-2014년 (박태준 회장 재임)		
	계수값	t-통계량	유의성	계수값	t-통계량	유의성
β_0	6.644 (1.680)	3.954	유의함 (1%)	6.929 (2.832)	2.447	유의함 (5%)
β_d	7.408 (2.574)	2.877	유의함 (1%)	6.152 (2.708)	2.271	유의함 (5%)
β_1	0.175 (0.131)	1.335	유의하지 않음 (10%)	0.254 (0.173)	1.468	유의하지 않음 (10%)

주 : 계수값의 ( )는 추정계수의 표준오차(Standard Error)값을 나타내며 유의성의
( )는 귀무가설 검정에 대한 유의수준을 나타낸다.

포항제철소 확장 1-4기 및 광양제철소 확장 1-4기 준공되는 해에 제조업 평균 성장률은 다른 연도보다 약 6-7%가 더 높아지는 것으로 추정된다. 결론적으로 포스코 기업성과는 제조업 성장에 상당한 기여를 하였고 이는 한국경제 성장에 크게 이바지한 것으로 평가할 수 있다.

요약하면, 그레인저 인과관계 분석과 더미변수 접근법을 이용한 실증 분석 결과는 포스코의 기업성과가 제조업 발전에 긍정적인 영향을 미쳤고 이는 한국경제 성장에 기여했을 것이라는 가설 1을 지지하는 것을 보여주고 있다. 즉, 산업의 쌀을 생산하는 포스코 철강기업의 우수한 성과는 제조업 성장을 견인하면서 중화학공업화에 긍정적인 영향을 미쳤고 이는 한국 경제성장에 상당한 기여를 한 것으로 판단할 수 있다.

가설 2는 포스코의 다양한 기술혁신 및 경영혁신, 기업문화 등이 포

스코의 생산성을 향상시켰고 이는 제조업발전이나 한국경제의 생산성 제고에 기여함으로써 한국경제 성장에 기여했을 것을 제안하고 있다. 즉, 미래산업을 선도할 인재육성이라는 박태준 회장의 교육보국 정신을 실천하고 기술개발과 기술혁신, 연구개발 투자, 산학연 협동연구 및 산업 현장인력 양성, 전사적 자주관리를 통한 현장혁신, 기업복지발전과 흑자경영의 선순환 구조, 포스코 성공의 학습 및 확산을 통한 국가 산업화에 외부효과 창출 등을 만들어내면서 국가경제의 생산성 제고 및 인적자본 축적을 도모하여 한국 경제성장에 기여한 측면을 의미한다. 이에 대한 실증분석을 시도하기 위하여 포스코의 생산성 증가율이 한국경제 생산성 증가율에 어떻게 영향을 미쳤는지를 분석하기 위하여 다음과 같은 회귀방정식을 고려하였다:

$$y_t = \beta_0 + \sum_{i=0}^{p} \beta_i x_{t-i} + \epsilon_t \qquad (6)$$

여기에서 y_t 는 한국경제 생산성 증가율을 나타내고 x_{t-i} 는 $t-i$ 년도 포스코 1인당 생산성 증가율을 나타낸다. 포스코의 생산성 증가율의 변화는 단기와 장기에 걸쳐 한국경제 생산성 증가율에 영향을 미칠 수 있음을 고려하여 몇 년의 시차변수를 고려하였다. 자료이용이 가능한 표본기간은 1974년부터 2003년까지 이며 추정결과는 다음과 같다:

$$y_t = \frac{5.835}{(0.953)} - \frac{0.030}{(0.038)}x_t - \frac{0.010}{(0.039)}x_{t-1} + \frac{0.028}{(0.038)}x_{t-2} + \frac{0.057}{(0.027)}x_{t-3} + \epsilon_t \quad (7)$$

$$\overline{R^2} = 0.180$$

추정결과에 따르면 $\beta_0 - \beta_2$는 통계적으로 유의하지 않으나 $\hat{\beta_3}$가 0.057로서 5% 유의수준하에서 통계적으로 유의하게 추정되었다. 즉, 금년도에 포스코 생산성 증가율이 1%p 높아지면 3년 후 국가경제 생산성 증가율은 약 0.06%p가 상승하는 것을 의미한다. 이러한 추정결과는 포스코가 다양한 경영혁신이나 기술혁신, 기업복지, 자주관리, 산학협동 및 교육 등을 추진하여 포스코의 생산성을 증가시키게 되면 약 3년 동안 한국경제에 내재되어 3년 후 한국경제 생산성을 상승시키는 효과를 가져온다는 것을 의미하고 이러한 실증분석 결과는 가설 2의 추론을 뒷받침하는 것으로 풀이할 수 있다.

포스코 성장이 한국 경제성장에 어떻게 기여하였는지를 가설 1과 가설 2를 통해 실증분석을 시도한 결과, 포스코 성과가 높아지면 제조업 성장률이 상승하게 되고 이러한 제조업의 성장은 한국 경제성장에 긍정적인 영향을 끼친 것으로 판단된다. 또한 포스코가 다양한 기술혁신, 경영혁신 및 기업복지를 추진하여 생산성을 제고시키게 되면 이는 수년에 걸쳐 국가경제 생산성을 향상시키는데 기여하고 포스코가 연수 및 교육, 산학협력을 추진하면 국가경제 인적자본 축적에 기여한 것으로 평가된다.

IV. 포스코 성장과 박태준 리더십의 역할

　지금까지 포스코의 성장이 한국경제의 급속하고 지속적인 성장에 상당한 기여를 하였음을 기존 문헌들의 고찰과 포스코 경영성과 및 생산성, 제조업 성장 및 국가경제 생산성 그리고 한국 경제성장률 간 실증분석을 통해 살펴보았다. 포스코는 시장지향적 공기업의 역할, 기술혁신 및 경영혁신, 산학연 협동을 통한 기술 및 연구인력 양성, 복지지향적 기업 문화 등을 통해 탁월한 경영성과와 생산성을 달성하였고 이는 철강산업의 핵심동력 기업으로써 제조업 성장과 한국경제 생산성 제고 및 인적자본 축적에 큰 기여를 함으로써 한국경제 성장에 심도 있는 기여를 한 것으로 평가된다. 한마디로 포스코는 한국경제 성장을 견인한 모범적 기업사례가 된 것이다.

　그렇다면 포스코 성공의 핵심 요인은 무엇인가? 맥컨 및 말란 (McKern & Malan 1992)은 포스코의 성공요인으로 최고경영자의 리더십과 더불어 조직구성원의 사명감과 헌신을 제시하고 있다.

　많은 기존 연구들은 1968년 설립부터 1992년까지 포스코 초대 회장을 맡은 박태준(TJP)의 리더십이 포스코 성장의 핵심적 요인임을 주저 없이 보여주고 있다. 기존 연구들은 박태준 리더십이 포스코 성장에 결정적 기여를 하였다는 것을 다양한 방법을 통해 보여주고 있는데, 대부분 연구들은 포스코 성장에 기여를 한 박태준 리더십의 핵심요소들에 초점을 맞추고 있다. 기존연구들이 제시한 박태준 리더십 경영철학의 핵심적 요소들로는 김왕배(2012)의 보국이념과 국가유기체론, 김민정(2012)의 청렴리더십, 박헌준(2012)의 윤리적 리더십, 백기복(2012)의 용혼경영사상, 송복(2012a, 2012b)의 태준이즘 및 선비사상, 이도화 김창호(2012)의 자주관리경영, 임경순(2010)의 과학기술관, 전상인(2013)의 영웅 리더십, 최진덕 김형효(2012)의 순교자적 사명감, 최진덕(2012)의 결사적 조국애, 최동주(2012)의 제철보국과 신뢰, 이상오(2012)의 교육 리더십, 이용갑(2012)의 복지사상과 기업발전, 허남정(2013)의 극일정신 등을 들 수 있다[6]. 물론, 이외에도 박태준 리더십 경영철학에 대한 다양한 요소들이 제시되었지만 대부분 상기와 같은 핵심적 요인들 안에 포함될 것으로 판단된다.

본 연구에서는 박태준의 선도적 리더십 ⇒ 포스코의 성공 ⇒ 한국경제의 성장 이라는 기본 메카니즘을 전제로 하고 기존연구에서 제시한 다양한 박태준 리더십의 특성들을 종합하여 한국경제 성장에 결정적 기여를 한 박태준 리더십의 핵심은 무엇인지에 초점을 맞춘다. 특히 경제학적 관점에서 리더십의 역할을 집중 조명하는 점에서 기존 연구와 차별적인 입장을 취하고 있다. 즉, 경제학적 관점에서 포스코 경영성과와 한국경제 성장에 핵심적 기여를 한 박태준 리더십의 특성은 무엇인가라는 것이다. 박태준 리더십의 어떤 특성이 한국경제 성장의 핵심적 요인에 중요하게 작용했는지에 중점을 두고 기존 문헌의 재조명과 실

---

6   박태준 리더십 경영철학과 관련한 기존 연구들에 대한 소개는 허남정(2013)에서 잘 요약되어 있다.

증분석을 고려할 것이다.

1. 박태준 회장 재임기간의 경영성과

철강은 국력이라는 철강산업관을 갖고 있었던 박정희 대통령은 1962년부터 일관 종합제철소 건설에 대한 강한 열망이 있었다(류상영 2001). 박정희 대통령은 국가민족중흥주의 기치를 내걸고 중화학공업화와 방위산업 육성을 통해서 국가경제 산업화를 이룩하려는 부국강병을 꿈꾸었다. 철강산업은 국가 기간산업으로써 중화학공업화와 방위산업 육성에 초석이 된다는 것을 인식하고 이를 실현하기 위한 경제개발 계획을 구상하였다. 그런 과정에 박태준 회장은 박정희 대통령의 강력한 민족중흥주의에 영향을 받았고 철은 산업화의 쌀로써 산업의 쌀을 생산하는 철강산업을 국가중흥사업의 대들보라고 생각했다. 즉, 철은 모든 산업의 원료이고 바탕이며 국가를 부흥시키는 산업화의 거름으로서 국가를 부강하게 만든다는 제철보국 정신의 구현은 박태준의 강한 꿈이었던 것이다(김왕배 2013).

포스코는 이러한 박정희 대통령의 국가중흥주의를 실현시키는 철강산업 육성과 박태준 회장의 제철보국 정신의 실현으로 1968년 4월 1일 포항종합제철주식회사라는 이름으로 창립되었다. 박태준 회장은 건설공사의 산실인 포항종합건설본부를 "롬멜하우스(Rommel House)"라고 부르면서 효율적인 건설현장업무를 관할하였고 제철소 건설 프로젝트가 실패하면 직원 전원이 포항 앞바다에 빠져 죽자고 하는 "우향우 정신"을 발휘하는 투철한 사명감으로 1973년 7월 예정보다 한 달 일찍 조강생산 103만톤 규모의 포항제철소 제1기 공장이 준공되었다. 이후 포항제철소 2기, 3기, 4기 확장공사를 준공하면서 1983년 910만톤의 조강생산능력을 갖추었고 조강생산능력 세계 12위국에 올랐다[7]. 박태준 회장은 한국 제 2제철소 프로젝트 유치에 성공하여 1982년 광양제철소 제1기 공장 착공을 이끌어냈고 1992년 광양제철소 제 4기 공장을 완공하여 연간 조강생산능력 2050만톤을 갖춘 세계 제 3위 제철소로 만들었다.

포항제철소가 가동되기 시작한 1973년부터 1992년 기간 동안 박태준은 포스코 회장으로 재임하면서 연평균 매출증가율 34%, 순이익증가율 71.3%, 그리고 1992년 한국경제 GDP 대비 포스코 매출액 비중이 2.3%에 달하는 경이로운 경영성과를 이룩하였다. 1인당 조강생산량으로 측정한 1인당 노동생산성증가율은 연평균 15%에 달하였고 1992년 기준 국내철강생산량 중 포스코 생산량은 71.3% 그리고 생산설비 국산화 비율은 63.1%를 달성하였다. 이러한 눈부신 경영성과로 인해 1992년 세계 유수 기업신용평가기관 스탠다드 앤 푸어스 (Standard & Poors: S&P)는 포스코 기업을 "A+"로 등급을 부과하여 북한과 대치한 상황에서 안보위협에 따른 주요 기업들의 신용등급의 저조

---

7   롬멜하우스는 포항제철소 건설사무소를 지칭하는 말로써, 건설 현장이 흡사 사막전과 같은 이미지 때문에 제2차 세계대전 중 '사막의 여우'라고 알려진 유명한 독일의 야전사령관 에르빈 롬멜(Erwin Rommel)의 이름을 따서 '롬멜하우스'라는 별명이 불리게 되었다(서갑경 1997).

에도 불구하고 신용양호 등급을 부과하여 포스코의 기업우수성을 인정하였다.

[표 13] 박태준 회장 재임(1968년-1992년)중 경영성과

구 분		1973년	1992년	증가율(%)	연평균 증가율(%)
매출액 및 순이익 증대	연간 매출액(억원)	416	61,821	14,861	34.0
	연간 순이익(억원)	46	1,852	40.3	71.3
	GDP대비 매출액 비중(%)	0.8	2.3	287.5	8.0
생산성 향상	연간 조강생산량(천톤)	449	20,012	4457.0	26.2
	직원1인당 조강생산량(톤)	106.6	848.0	8.0	14.9
	국내 철강 생산량 중 비중(%)	15.5	71.3	460	12.9
	생산설비 국산화 비율(%)	12.5	63.1		
기업 신용등급			- S&P:A+ - Moody's :A2		
정부의존도 개선 (주주 중 정부 비중, %)		66.6	20.0		
직원 수(명)		2,581	23,599		
기업복지 수준 향상					
세계 조강생산량 순위		-	3위	-	-

자료: 포스코 35년사(2004) 및 저자 산출

또한 III장 실증분석 [표 10]과 [표 11]에서 보여준 바와 같이 박태준 회장재임기간에 대하여 매출액증가율과 제조업성장률간 그렌저인과관

계분석 결과 포스코 매출액 증가율과 제조업성장률 간 양방향 인과관계가 있음을 확인하였고 더미변수 추정분석결과 박태준 회장재임기간 동안 포항과 광양 제철소가 확장될 때마다 한국경제 제조업 성장은 더 높은 것으로 분석되었다. 특히 박태준 회장은 포스코를 초일류 글로벌 기업으로 육성하기 위해 기술개발, 안전, 품질관리, 현장관리, 자주관리, 기업복지, 산학협력, 연수, 연구개발투자 등 포스코 기술인력 양성과 생산성 향상에 지대한 노력을 기울였다. 이러한 노력에 대한 실증분석은 III장에서 시도한 포스코 생산성 증가율과 한국경제 생산성 증가율간 회귀분석을 통해 확인할 수 있는데 추정결과는 다음과 같다:

$$y_t = \frac{6.924}{(0.992)} - \frac{0.046}{(0.033)}x_t - \frac{0.019}{(0.034)}x_{t-1} + \frac{0.018}{(0.033)}x_{t-2} + \frac{0.054}{(0.023)}x_{t-3} + \epsilon_t \quad (8)$$

$$\overline{R^2} = 0.372$$

추정결과에 따르면 $\beta_1 - \hat{\beta_3}$ 는 통계적으로 유의하지 않으나 $\hat{\beta_4}$ 가 0.054로서 5% 유의수준하에서 통계적으로 유의하였다. 즉, 금년도에 포스코 생산성 증가율이 1%p 높아지면 3년 후 국가경제 생산성 증가율은 약 0.054%p가 상승하는 것을 의미한다. 이러한 추정결과는 박태준 회장재임기간의 실증분석결과와 여타 회장재임기간을 포함한 실증분석결과가 유사하여 포스코 기업의 전반적인 기업성과는 박태준 회장 재임기간 경영성과에 기인하는 것을 추론할 수 있고 이는 김병연 최상오(2011) 연구결과와 부합함을 알 수 있다.

2. 박태준 리더십의 실체 및 역할

박태준 회장은 어떠한 리더십을 발휘하여 포스코를 한국기업 성장 모형의 대표적인 아이콘으로 만들었는가? 경제발전 및 기업성과의 관점에서 박태준 리더십이 어떻게 포스코의 성공을 이끌었고 한국 경제의 급속한 산업화에 기여하여 한국경제성장을 가져왔는지를 살펴보기 위해서는 박태준 리더십의 실체와 역할을 조명해 볼 필요가 있다. 그런데, 기존연구들을 살펴보면 대부분의 연구는 박태준 리더십이 포스코 기업성과에 미치는 영향에 초점을 맞추고 박태준 리더십의 특징과 실체들을 설명하고 있다.

본 연구에서는 한국경제 성장이라는 보다 거시적 관점에서 박태준 리더십의 실체와 역할을 조명하는데 초점을 맞추려고 한다. 즉, 포스코 성장이 한국 경제성장의 핵심요인들에 어떻게 영향을 미쳤는지를 이전 장에서 분석하였는데 여기에서는 박태준 리더십의 특징 중 한국경제성장의 핵심 요인들과 연결될 수 있는 실체들을 분석하고 이러한 실체들이 어떻게 한국경제 성장에 기여하였는지 그 경로들을 살펴보려고 한다.

가. 태준이즘과 제철보국 구현을 통한 제조업 성장 및

　　급속한 산업화에 기여

포스코는 포철 제1기 공장이 준공되면서부터 중화학공업을 중심으로 제조업성장을 이끌어 한국경제 산업화에 기여함으로써 급속한 경제

성장에 공헌하였다. 그렇다면 1973년에 포항제철 제1기 공장을 완공한 지 불과 6-7년 만에 한국 중화학공업화 선봉에 서서 산업화를 이끈 절대적인 추진 동력은 무엇이었는가? 그것은 바로 박태준 회장의 제철보국이념이었다. 박태준 회장의 제철보국이념이란 "제철은 산업화의 기초이고, 산업화는 부국강병의 기초이며, 부국강병의 기초위에서 조국의 민주화도 가능하다. 포항제철의 사명은 국민에게 값싸고 품질 좋은 철강재를 공급하여 국부를 증대하고 합리적인 경영을 통해 사회적 책임을 완수하는 것"이 핵심원리이다.

박태준 회장은 일제 식민지와 남북분단, 그리고 절대 빈곤으로 이어지는 뼈저린 한국 현대사의 비극을 절감하면서 그에 대한 일차적인 책임은 한국인 조상의 무기력이라고 준엄하게 생각했고 일본처럼 강하지 못해 식민지 종주국이 되었음에 깊은 한을 가지고 있었다. 그래서 그는 산업화와 민주화를 통해 부강한 근대국가, 즉 제대로 된 나라를 건설해서 식민종주국의 한을 풀고 나아가 일본보다 더 잘 살아보자는 극일에 대한 강한 의지를 품고 있었다(최진덕 2013). 박태준 회장은 현대사의 비극을 초래한 일본을 이길 수 있는 길은 급속한 경제발전을 가능케 하는 원동력을 세우는 일이고 그 핵심에 글로벌 초일류의 포항제철을 건설하는 것이라고 판단했다. 박태준 회장은 철이 근대 산업문명과 국민국가의 물질적 기반이자 동력이라는 산업화 과정을 잘 이해하고 있었고 산업화와 부국강병을 위해서는 종합제철소 또는 일관제철소 보유가 절대적이라는 제철보국을 외치면서 제철산업에 모든 것을 바치기로 결심했다.

박태준 회장의 제철보국이념은 1962년부터 국가중흥을 향해 발전주의 국가체제를 선두 지휘하던 박정희 대통령의 강력한 철강산업관과 결합하여 국가적 차원에서 지지를 받았다. 박정희 대통령은 국가민족중흥을 위해서 반공과 조국근대화가 급선무이고 이를 위해서 급진적 국가산업화가 최우선과제라고 인식했다. 박정희 대통령은 국가산업화를 위해서 급속한 공업화가 필요하고 그 핵심에는 석유화학, 제철, 조선, 전기전자, 자동차, 선박을 중심으로 한 중화학산업 분야 육성이 필수적이라고 판단했다. 특히 철강공업은 공업국가 건설을 위한 기간산업으로 간주하고 제 2차 경제개발 5개년 계획에 포항제철을 필두로 중화학산업 육성을 추진하였다. 결국, 박태준 회장의 제철보국 이념과 박정희 대통령의 국가민족중흥주의는 포항제철이라는 종합제철소 건설을 통해 경제현장에서 실현이 되었고 이는 급속한 공업화와 제조업 성장 그리고 한국경제 성장을 견인하는 중추적인 동력이 된 것이다.

  그러나 1960년대 당시, 한국경제는 제철소를 건설할 만한 준비된 자본이나 인프라가 전혀 갖추어 있지 않았고 한국 정 재계에서도 제철소 건설이 불가능하다는 심한 반대에 직면해 있었다. 이런 상황에서 설상가상으로 해외자본 조달을 통해 제철소 건설을 추진하기 위해 미국과 유럽 7개 제철회사로 구성된 대한국제제철차관단(KISA: Korea International Steel Associates)으로부터의 자금조달 계획이 완전히 무산되었다(류상영 2001). 박태준 회장은 하와이 구상을 통해 대일청구권 자금 전용 아이디어를 기획하였고 이를 위해 일본 철강업계 및 일본 정부의 지지와 협력을 받아내기 위해 결사적인 조국애로 동분서주하여 결국

1970년 포항제철소 제 1기 공장 착공식을 추진하였다(최진덕 2013).

박태준 회장은 포항제철소 건설과정에서 개척자적 희생정신에서 한 걸음 더 나아가 국가의 발전과 후손의 행복을 위한 "순교자적 희생"을 강조한다(최진덕 2013). 포항제철은 대일청구권 자금이라는 "조상의 혈세"로 지어지기 때문에 포항제철 건설은 반드시 성공되어야 하고 실패하면 조상에게 죄를 짓는 것이니 "우향우 정신"으로 제철소를 성공시켜 나라와 조상의 은혜에 보답하는 자세를 확고한 생활신조로 하였다. 따라서 포항제철은 국민이 내는 세금으로 운영되는 공기업이기 때문에 직원은 공무원으로 공인의 사명을 다해야 하고 나아가 포항제철의 역사적 의미와 역할의 관점에서 볼 때, 단순히 이윤추구의 기업을 넘어 국가경륜의 보다 높은 차원에서 경영되어야 한다는 시대적 대의가 포스코 핵심 경영이념으로 자리 잡았다(김왕배, 2013).

이대환(2004)은 박태준 회장의 결사적 조국애와 순명자적 희생정신을 "짧은 인생을 영원 조국에"와 "절대적 절망은 없다"라는 두 개의 인생 좌우명으로 표현하고 있다. 즉, 첫째는 조국을 영원한 신으로 섬기면서 자신의 덧없는 목숨을 바치겠다는 종교적 차원의 결사적인 조국애를 의미한다. 둘째는 어떤 절망적 상황에 처하더라도 절대로 절망하지 않고 그 상황을 극복할 수 있다는 긍정과 희망, 그리고 확고한 자신감을 말하는 것이다 (최진덕 2013). 송복(2012a)은 한국경제 역사상 포스코라는 공기업을 사기업 이상으로 일으켜 특별한 대성취를 이룩한 박태준 회장의 모든 사건들, 그 모든 요인들을 하나의 맥락으로 만들어 융합하고 종합하는 설명체계를 "태준이즘 (Taejoonism)"으로 서술하고 있다. 송복은 태준이즘을 "절대적 절망은 없다", "절대적 불가능은 없다", "절대적 사익은 없다"라는 세 가지로 요약되는 박태준의 사상이라고 강조하고 있다. 태준이즘은 박태준 회장이 포스코 건설을 통해서 제철보국의 이념을 구현하여 한국경제 급속한 산업화를 이끌었던 종합적 정신 동력이라고 말할 수 있다. 송복 (2012b)은 실천으로서, 현장의 행동으로서, 행위규범으로서 박태준 회장이 선비사상을 가지고 있고 그 핵심은 굳센 의지(지), 소통의 의로움(의), 신뢰의 밧줄(렴), 그리고 감동과 신바람 (애)이라는 점에서 기존 선비사상과 차별화됨을 강조하고 있다.

백기복(2013)은 박태준 회장이 포스코 창업에서부터 성장에 이르는 전 과정에서 보여주고 합리성과 비합리성 모두 포함하는 초합리적 경영가치와 경영방법으로 구현되는 포괄적 사상을 "용혼 경영사상 (Management by great spirit: MBS)"으로 명명하고 있다. 용혼사상이란 국가에 대한 영적 애착심을 갖는 리더가 사명(Mission)을 녹여 불굴의 경영가치를 낳고 경영가치가 제철이나 제련에서처럼 담금질되어 제혼의 경영방식으로 구현되는 것을 의미하고 있다. 박태준 회장은 포스코 창업과 성장의 전 과정을 통하여 결코 흔들리지 않는 일관된 경영가치를 보여줬다는 것이다. 현대 경영학의 기본원리에 따르면 창업을 하고 기업을 경영하기 위해서는 자금, 기술, 인력 그리고 시장이 있어야 하는데 포스코 창업은 자금, 기술, 인력, 시장 자체를 만들어가면서 사업을 일으켜 세워야 하는 힘든 싸움에서 모든 것을 녹여내는 "용혼"의 힘 때문에 가능했다는 것이다. 박태준의 용혼 경영사상은 경계극복의 가치, 공익우선의 가치, 인간존중의 가치, 청렴성장의 가치, 창조혁신의 가치라는 5대 경영가치로 나타났고 사명감이라는 내적 동력을 통해 옳은 방향에 집중하여 끝까지 도전하는 초고강도 활성 에너지라는 제혼동력 실천사상으로 구현된 것이다(백기복 2013). 즉, 국혼에 뿌리를 둔 박태준의 용혼 경영사상은 제철산업 부흥이라는 국가적 사명이 주어졌을 때 모든 한계를 녹여 세계적 철강기업 포스코를 탄생시키는 원동력이 되었다는 것이다(백기복 2013).

박태준 리더십 특성 중 제조업 성장과 한국경제 산업화에 기여한 측면은 다음으로 요약할 수 있다. 박태준 리더십은 박정희 대통령의 국가 민족중심주의와 결합하여 제철보국을 구현하였고 궁극적으로 급속한 한국경제 성장에 기여했다. 박태준 회장은 한국 현대사의 비극을 극복하는 길이 산업화를 통한 부국강병이고 이를 위해서 산업화의 쌀인 철강산업을 육성하는데 자신의 전 생애를 바친 혼신의 리더십을 보여주었다. 박태준 회장은 소신껏, 청렴하게, 사심없이 그리고 온갖 반대와 장애를 뚫는 절대적 절망은 없는 자세를 견지하면서 결사적 조국애와 순교자적 희생정신으로 포스코 건설을 추진하였고 용혼경영사상을 통해 포스코 성장을 주도하였다. 포스코 성장의 대성취를 통해 한국경제 성장에 이바지한 박태준 리더십의 포괄적 종합체계는 태준이즘이고 이는 제철보국의 종합적 정신 동력이다. 결국 박태준 리더십 특성 중 제조업 성장과 산업화에 기여한 측면은 태준이즘 ⇒ 용혼경영사상 ⇒ 제철보국 ⇒ 제조업 성장 ⇒ 급속한 산업화 ⇒ 급속한 한국경제 성장 과정으로 요약할 수 있다.

나. 초일류 기업 추구를 통한 대외지향적 정책에 기여

1960년대 초반 박정희 정권 초기 수입대체형 산업화 전략이 외향적 수출지향형 산업화 전략으로 전환되면서 철강산업도 국가주도 기반산업으로 재설정되었다. 생성기(1968년 1973년)에 포스코는 소유권이 국가에 있었고 급속한 경제성장과 산업화를 추진하고자 하였던 박정희 정부에게는 경제성장의 동력이었다(류상영 2001). 박정희 정부는 포스코를 국가 기반산업으로 육성하여 중화학공업화의 개척자로 내세우고 국가 안보와 수출신장을 전략적으로 수행하는 전략적 산업육성정책의 핵심 주체로 내세웠다. 포스코는 수출위주의 대외지향적 경제정책을 견인하는 선봉기업으로 국가의 전폭적인 지원을 받은 것이다.

박태준은 위와 같은 포스코의 국가적 사명을 깊이 절감하고 제철보국을 구현하기 위해 글로벌 초일류 철강기업 건설을 꿈꾸었다. 포스코가 세계 초일류 철강기업이 되기 위해서는 국제경쟁력이 확보되어야 하고 이러한 국제경쟁력은 저렴한 생산비, 우수한 품질, 효율적 경영, 그리고 지속적 성장을 위한 기술개발에 의해 뒷받침된다는 것을 인식하고 이를 위해 다각적인 노력을 펼쳤다.

박태준은 생산원가는 저렴하지만 품질은 높은 국제경쟁력 있는 국제적 수준의 초일류 기업 건설에 대한 강한 의지를 가지고 창업초기부터 포스코가 국제적 경쟁력을 가지기 위해 초합리적 경영가치를 가지고 이를 실천하였다. 포스코 창립 초기부터 박태준은 국내 철강 수요뿐만 아니라 세계 철강수요를 예측하고 이에 맞는 국제적 수준의 일관종합 제철소 건설을 추진하였다. 철강산업은 규모의 경제가 작용하는 국가

기반산업이기 때문에 종합제철소를 건설해야만 효율적인 철강산업 육성이 가능하다고 판단했다. 국가 산업화 초기 당시 한국에서의 철강제품에 대한 수요는 항상 국내공급을 초과하였고 포스코는 국영기업이었기 때문에 포스코가 생산제품을 모두 국내 기업에 공급하는 것이 당연시 되었으나 박태준은 포스코 생산제품의 20-30%를 지속적으로 수출하면서 포스코가 글로벌 철강업체임을 고집하면서 외국 기업들과의 경쟁에서 국제적인 경쟁력을 갖추는데 열정을 쏟았다(이대환 2004).

박태준은 국제경쟁에서 승리하기 위해서 포스코 성장 단계에 따라 기업 체질을 근본적으로 개선할 필요가 있다고 인식하고 있었다. 공장 건설 초기 단계에서는 성공적으로 공장을 건설하는 것이 중요했고, 공장 건설에 성공한 이후에는 조업 기술의 축적을 통해 비용 이점을 확보하는 것이 중요했지만, 글로벌 기업으로 성장하기 위해서는 조업 기술의 축적만 가지고서는 성공할 수 없다는 것을 인식하고 효율적인 생산관리와 품질관리는 물론, 설비와 공정에서의 기술혁신, 새로운 제품의 개발 등에 근거하여 경쟁할 수 있는 체제를 갖추었다(김병연·최상오 2011). 박태준은 포스코를 초일류 기업으로 육성하기 위해 저가 설비 구매 및 저가 공사를 통한 생산비 절감, 원가와 품질에 대한 투철한 의식, 기술, 안전, 품질, 원가에서 최고수준 지향, 경영혁신 및 기술혁신 노력, 자주 경영관리 노력 등 기업 경영에 있어서 효율 경영철학을 확고하게 실천하였다. 백기복(2013)은 박태준이 혁신경영, 윤리경영, 글로벌 경영, 품질경영, 창조경영, 지속가능 경영 등의 초합리적 가치 경영 추구를 창업초기부터 건설, 확장, 경영 일선에까지 일관적으로 추진하였는데 이는 포스코를 세계 최고 수준의 철강기업으로 만든 핵심적 경영사상(용혼경영사상)임을 강조하고 있다.

박태준은 "무엇이든 세계 최고가 되자"라는 좌우명을 기술과 접목시켜 실천하였다. 그는 회사가 추구하고 있는 국제 비교우위 확보와 시장의 다변화, 신수요 창출 등이 기술력의 수준에 달려 있기 때문에 기술개발은 기업발전의 핵심적인 추진력이라는 점을 강조하면서 R&D 분야에 정성을 기울여 기존의 기술 수준을 계속 향상시켜 나가는 한편, 포스코의 독자적인 연구개발 체제를 확립하고 기술을 개발하여 세계 철강업계에서 지배적인 위치를 지속적으로 점유하려고 노력하였다(임경순 2010; 박철순·남윤성 2012).

박태준이 포스코를 초일류 철강기업으로 육성해야 한다는 의지는 결국 제철보국의 실천적 발로라고 할 수 있다. 박태준은 포스코가 국민의 혈세로 세운 국영기업이기 때문에 효율적 경영과 지속적인 기술개발을 통해 국제수준보다 낮은 가격으로 철강제품을 국내수요자에게 공급함으로써 국내 관련산업의 생산비 절감을 통해 국내 물가의 안정 뿐만 아니라 국내기업의 국제경쟁력을 제고시키는데 기여해야한다는 결사적 사명감을 조직 구성원들과 함께 나누면서 그들의 헌신을 이끌었다. 이러한 박태준의 초일류 철강기업 실현을 위한 선도적인 리더십은 포스코의 선봉적 역할을 통하여 한국 정부가 주도하는 대외지향적 수출위주 성장정책을 펼치는데 주요한 공헌을 한 것이다.

다. 시장지향적 공기업 추구를 통한 정부의 역할 선봉장 포스코는 1968년 설립 당시 총자본금 16억원 중 재무부가 56.2%, 대한중석이 43.8%를 차지하고 있었기 때문에 완전한 국가소유 국영기업이었다. 포스코는 철강공업육성법에 명시된 각종 국가개입과 통제를 받아야 하는 측면이 있는 동시에 국가자본주의 발전을 위한 공격적 국가전략과 전략적 산업육성정책에 의해 국가제도로부터 지원을 많이 받는 국가 안의 국가 내지는 국가기업이었다(류상영 2001). 박태준은 제철보국 실현을 위해 결사적 조국애와 사심을 버리는 순교자적 사명감으로 국가를 우선적으로 발전시키기 위해 산업화의 초석인 철강기업 포스코를 대표적인 공기업으로 육성하고자 하였다. 더불어, 박태준은 포스코가 공기업이면서 국제시장에서 경쟁우위 창조를 위해 끊임없이 공격적이고 상업적인 기업전략을 추구해야 하는 시장지향적 기업임을 매우 중요시했다. 그는 시장지향적 경제관을 가지고 포스코가 국가소유의 공기업으로서 국가 안에 존재하면서도 하나의 자율적인 글로벌 기업으로 성장하려는 기업전략을 지속적으로 추구하였다(류상영 2001). 최진덕(2013)은 포스코가 시장속에 있으면서도 시장을 뛰어넘는 기업, 다시 말해 기업은 기업이되 국가와 민족을 위해 봉사하는 기업이고 박태준은 "국체기용"의 국가관과 기업관을 가지고 포스코의 국가적 사명감을 추진했다고 언급하고 있다.

박태준은 창립 때부터 국가경제에서 포스코가 갖는 중차대한 의미를 강조하고 포스코의 사명을 국민에게 값싸고 품질 좋은 철강재를 공급하여 국부를 증대하고 합리적인 경영을 통해 사회적 책임을 완수하는 것이라고 명시했다. 박태준은 포스코가 공기업이기 때문에 포스코 전

직원은 먼저 국가와 사회에 봉사하고 애국한다는 차원 높은 사명의식을 가지는 것이 마땅하며 공인으로서의 사명감을 끊임없이 전사적으로 요구하였다. 박태준은 발전주의 국가의 산업화 전략추구에서 산업의 쌀인 철을 생산하는 기업은 제조업 및 국가 산업화를 선도하는 국영기업으로써 책무가 있음을 강조했다. 그는 포스코가 국민의 피와 땀으로 만들어진 역사적 민족기업이기 때문에 기업미션, 창업정신, 가치공유를 통해 민족기업의 사명을 추구해야 한다고 보았다. 이러한 순명적 조국애라는 박태준의 리더십은 포스코가 한국경제 산업화 초기부터 국가와 정책적 협의를 긴밀히 펼치면서 시장의 개척자가 되고 시장을 창조하고 육성하면서 한국 경제성장의 동력이 되게 하였고 국가 자본주의를 발전시키는 시장창조적이고 상호배양적인 정부-기업관계를 형성하면서 국가주도의 경제성장을 이끄는데 선봉적인 역할을 이끈 것이다(류상영 2001).

박태준은 포스코가 공기업이기 때문에 권위주의 국가체제 속에서 공기업 조직을 관료제적으로 운영하게 되면 폐쇄적인 관료제의 철칙에 얽매여 경쟁적인 시장의 파고에 휩쓸리는 경향이 높아 결국 경쟁이 치열한 글로벌 시장에서 생존할 수 없다는 것을 잘 알고 있었다. 그는 실용적이고 산업적인 직업관을 가지고 공기업도 시장의 상황에 민감하게 대처하고 다양한 시장의 이윤욕구들을 수용하기 위해 시장의 효율과 성장을 추구해야한다고 보았다. 시장을 지향한 생산자는 상대의 반응을 예측하고 대응하는 명석함이 필요하고 기업의 운영자는 기업자신의 생존과 번영을 위해서 적시에 시장을 분석하고 흐름을 읽어 대처하는 즉결의 예지가 필요하다고 판단했다(김왕배 2013). 이런 관점에서 박태준은 철저한 시장주의자였다. 박태준은 포스코 설립 초기부터 국제 철강시장을 겨냥하여 수출을 개시하였고 장기적인 철강시장의 흐름을 면밀히 읽고 예측하면서 포스코 기업조직을 변형시키는 혜안을 발휘하였다(김왕배 2013). 더불어 박태준은 포스코 제품의 품질 향상과 생산비 절감을 통해 국제 경쟁력을 높이기 위해 한 발 앞선 신기술 도입, 연구개발, 과학기술분야 확장, 산학협력 등을 적극적으로 추진하였다.

위와 같은 박태준의 철저한 시장지향적 공기업 추구는 포스코 기업을 국내적으로 중화학공업화를 추진하는데 핵심적 역할을 도모하여 국가주도 산업화를 선도하고 국외적으로 정부주도 수출위주의 대외지향적 경제정책을 펼쳐 경제발전을 추구하는 전략실천의 선봉장 역할을 감당하게 한 것이다. 만약 박태준이 단순히 공기업을 운영하는 기업인에 머물렀다면 포스코는 글로벌 초일류 기업이 되지 못하였을 것이고 중화학공업화는 효율적이지 못해 정부 주도형 경제발전 전략은 그 빛을 보지 못했을 것이다.

라. 기술혁신, 경영혁신, 교육보국, 선진적 기업문화 추구를 통한
   생산성 향상 및 인적자본 축적

박태준은 포스코 성공을 통해 제철보국을 이룩한 것처럼 장기적으로 산업 및 국가 발전을 위해서 훌륭한 교육을 실천하여 교육보국을 이룩하겠다는 의지가 투철하였다(임경순 2010). 박태준은 기업 경영에 필요한 자금, 물자, 기술, 인력 중에서 가장 중요한 것으로 인력을 꼽았다. 급

속한 경제 성장 과정에서 고도의 기술력과 사명감, 그리고 의욕적인 우수한 인력이야말로 시대를 이끌어가는 견인차라고 인식했다. 1970년 대 당시 한국 공과대학 교육이 산업현장과 유리되어 있어서 공대 교육의 비현실성을 깨닫고 제철연수원을 통해 여러 가지 자체 보강교육을 개발하여 새로운 현장교육 방식 구축을 조직적으로 추진하였다. 박태준은 해외기술연수와 사내 훈련을 통해 지속적인 기술개선활동을 했으며 특히 작업 현장내의 기술개선과 혁신을 강조했으며 작업장의 정리정돈과 청결은 기본의 기본임을 역설하였다. 박태준은 현장기술 개발의 중요성을 고취시키기 위하여 기성제도를 도입하고 기술인력에 대한 보상체계를 마련하였다. 기성제도는 단순히 기술인력의 우수성 뿐만 아니라 인품과 생활태도도 우수한 사람을 인정하고 선발함으로써 모든 직원의 존경을 받아 한 회사에의 높은 공헌도와 뛰어난 기술을 겸비한 사람을 세워 경쟁력있는 현장인력양성을 추구하는 제도였다(박태준 1985).

또한 박태준은 기술에 대한 확고한 자주의식과 투철한 기술자립을 추구하기 위해 각 단위 사업체의 연구개발을 종합적이고 기초과학적 차원에서 지원할 종합연구소 설립을 추진하였고 고급 두뇌에 대한 수요에 대처하고 획기적인 인재확보 방안으로 연구중심대학인 포항공과대학(POSTECH) 설립을 추진하였다. 그는 기업현장에서 혁신을 이끌고 나아가 장기적인 안목에서 고급 기술인력을 양성하기 위해 산학연 협동 체계 구축을 구상하였고 이를 위해 포스코, 산업과학기술연구소, 포항공대간의 유기적인 삼각 연구협동체계를 구축하였다. 이는 우수두뇌

집단을 형성함으로써 기초연구에서부터 연구결과의 상업화에 이르기까지 일관연구를 가능하게 할 뿐만 아니라 연구의 효율성을 극대화하는데 큰 기여를 한 것으로 평가된다(임경순 2010). 박태준은 종합연구소와 연구중심대학을 연계시키는 것이 대규모 과학기술 연구개발 장치를 건설하는 밑거름이라고 하는 국가적 차원의 경영마인드를 피력하였다.

박태준은 기술개발 및 기술혁신, 연구개발 투자를 통해 지속적인 생산성 향상과 국제 경쟁력 제고를 추구하였다. 그는 기술개발이 기업의 지속적 발전의 핵심이고 기술이 기업발전의 추진력이라고 생각했다. 그는 포스코가 추구하고 있는 국제 비교우위 확보와 시장의 다변화, 신수요 창출 등이 기술력의 수준에 달려 있기 때문에 기존의 기술 수준을 계속 향상시켜 나가는 한편 독자적인 기술을 개발하여 국제 철강업계에서 이것을 상품화하려고 했다(박태준 1985). 박태준은 제철소의 생산성을 제고하는데 결정적인 역할을 하는 연속주조의 비율도 계속 증가시키는 노력을 경주했으며 1980년대 초 세계 최첨단 설비를 갖춘 소위 "21세기 형 제철소"를 포항 이외의 지역에 새롭게 건설할 계획을 세워 결국 광양에 세계적인 제철소를 설립한 것이다. 박태준은 자체적인 기술개발 없이는 철강 산업의 국제 경쟁에서 생존할 수 없다는 것을 언제나 절감하고 있었다.

박태준은 작업장 혁신을 통해서도 생산성 향상 노력을 지속적으로 펼쳤다. 작업장 혁신은 현장 근로자들의 참여에 의한 개선 활동이 위주가 되는 고성과 작업장 혁신이다. 현장 근로자들이 그들의 작업장에서 얼마나 새롭고, 효율적으로 개선해 가면서 일하느냐에 따라 그 성과는 중 장기적으로 매우 큰 차이를 가져올 수 있다(배규식 2008). 원래 자주관리는 일본 철강업계에서 현장 제 1선 감독자 및 작업자를 중심으로 한 현장 개선 소그룹 활동을 총칭하는 용어인데 박태준은 자주관리 활동을 도입하여 포스코의 독자적인 작업장 혁신제도를 추진하였다. 박태준은 자주관리를 인간존중 관리라고 개념 짓고 있는데 훌륭한 관리방식은 인간의 본성 및 존엄성을 존중하여 인간의 자아실현을 도우면서 기업의 경영목표를 달성하는 것이라고 보았다(이도화 김창호 2012). 박태준은 직원들에게 스스로 자율 정신과 자주 능력을 개발할 기회를 마련해 주고자 했고, 이것이 자주관리 활동이 되었다. 박태준은 자주관리를 통해 근로자들이 자주적인 문제를 파악, 해결하고 개선책을 실시하는 과정을 경험하며 그들의 역량을 높이고, 동시에 인간을 존중하는 관리를 함으로써 동기부여를 높이려는 목적이었다. 이도화 김창호(2012)는 박태준이 자주관리에 대해 신앙적인 확신을 가지고 강력하게 자주관리 도입과 성장을 주도한 기간에는 자주관리 활동이 왕성하게 이루어지고 그 영향으로 포스코 노동생산성 등 경영성과도 향상되었음을 보여주고 있다.

　박태준은 사심 없는 공인정신과 제철보국과 연계된 기업복지 사상 및 복지사회 건설에 대한 신념을 가지고 선진적 기업문화와 선진 기업복지를 추구하였다. 그는 주인의식이 투철한 회사를 지향하고 회사 직원의 삶과 회사 성장의 불가분의 관계를 확신하고 기업복지 추구를 통하여 복지국가를 지향하였으며 전사적 차원의 복리후생제도를 실천하였다. 박태준은 자가 소유 주택의 제공과 생활 기반시설의 확충, 장학제도와 교육시설의 완비 및 우리사주제도에 의한 자산증식, 선택적 복리후생제도에 의한 근로자 참여형 복지제도라는 기업복지의 전형을 형성하였다(이용갑 2012). 이러한 박태준의 기업복지 추구는 숙련 근로자의 장기근속을 유도하여 기업의 흑자 경영을 가능하게 한 요소로 작용하였으며 이는 포스코 노동생산성 향상에 기여했다고 평가할 수 있다.

요약하면 박태준은 기술개발 및 기술혁신, 연구개발 투자를 통한 국제 경쟁력 제고, 자주관리 노력을 통한 작업장 혁신, 제철보국과 연계된 기업복지의 추구 등을 통해서 포스코의 지속적인 생산성 향상 노력을 추구하였으며 이는 국가경제 생산성 제고에 기여하면서 궁극적으로 한국경제의 급속하고 지속적인 성장에 공헌한 것으로 볼 수 있다.

3. 박태준 리더십과 포스코 성과 : 실증분석

가. 리더십의 특징과 정량화

리더십과 경제발전간 실증분석 연구를 진행하기에 앞서, 먼저 리더십이 어떠한 개념인지에 대한 이해가 필요하다. 리더십에 대한 정의는 명백한 개념이 확립되어 있지 않고, 연구자의 관점에 따라 다양하게 정의되고 있다. 리더십에 관한 연구는 1900년대 초반에 민주와 독재의 효과에 대한 연구에서부터 시작되었으며, 어떤 사람이 결정권을 갖는지에 관한 논의로부터 리더십에 대한 연구로 발전하였다(Bass 1985). 스톡딜 (Stogdill 1974)은 1902년부터 1967년까지 약 65년간의 리더십에 대한 정의를 조사한 결과, 72가지 형태의 정의가 존재 하지만, 일반적으로는 집단의 목표를 위해 사회적 영향력을 미치는 과정으로 정리하고 있다.

리더십은 크게 거래적 리더십(Transactional Leadership)과 변혁적 리더십(Transformational Leadership)으로 나누어진다. 거래적 리더십(Transactional Leadership)은 리더와 구성원들 간의 서로 필요로 하는 요소를 교환거래하여 효과적으로 조직 목표를 달성하는 것이다. 즉, 구성원들은 할당된 업무를 충실히 이행하는 노력을 보이고, 리더는 구성원들에게 그 노력에 대한 적절한 보상을 제시하는 교환거래 방식이다. 따라서 거래적 리더십에서는 구성원들이 업무능력에 대한 보상을 받고, 리더들은 조직 목표의 완성으로 이익을 얻는다. 거래적 리더십은 규칙을 따르는 의무가 있기 때문에 리더들은 변화를 촉진하기보다 조직의 안정유지를 우선시한다. 그러나 구성원들이 그들의 노력에 대한 보상을 받기 위해 규칙에 순응하지만, 조직 목표에 대한 열의는 발생시키지 않는 것이 일반적이다.

종래의 모든 리더십 이론이 거래적 리더십 이론이라는 주장을 비판하면서 발전된 이론이 변혁적 리더십(Transformational Leadership)이다. 브룬스(Bruns 1978)에서 변혁적 리더십이 처음 제시되었고, 이후 바스(Bass 1985)에 의해 구체화되었다. 변혁적 리더십은 리더가 구성원들에게 기대되는 공동 목표를 제시하고 목표 달성을 위해 함께 노력할 것을 호소하여 부하들의 가치관과 태도의 변혁을 통해 목표를 달성하는 지도력에 관한 이론이다. 거래적 리더십이 목표달성과 보상의 교환거래라면 변혁적 리더십 이론은 리더가 구성들에게 장기적 비전을 제시하고 그 비전을 위해 노력하도록 고무시키는 것이다. 구성원들은 그들의 정서 가치관 행동규범 등을 바꾸어 목표달성을 위한 의지와 자신감을 만드는 변혁의 과정을 보인다.

브룬스(Bruns 1978)는 변혁적 리더십을 '리더와 구성원이 모두 더 높은 도덕적 수준을 갖도록 만드는 과정'이라고 정의하고 있다. 따라서 리더는 거래적 리더십의 경우처럼 구성원의 두려움 증오 탐욕 질투 등과 같은 하등수준의 감정을 이용하는 것이 아니라 자유 정의 평등 평화 등과 같은 고차원적인 이상과 도덕적 가치에 호소함으로써 구성원들로 하여금 스스로 의식을 변혁시키고 조직의 목표를 위해 노력한다는 것이다.

바스(Bass 1985)는 거래적 리더십과 브룬스(Bruns 1978)의 변혁적 리더십 이론, 그리고 카리스마적 리더십 이론을 종합하였다. 바스(Bass 1985)에 따르면 구성원들로 하여금 개인적 이해관계를 넘어 기대 이상의 성과를 올리도록 높은 수준의 욕구를 충족시키며, 업무성과 중요성 및 가치를 인식하도록 하여 구성원들을 동기 부여시키는 영향력 행사가 변혁적 리더십이라는 것이다.

바스(Bass 1985)는 리더십이 거래적 리더십과 변혁적 리더십으로 나누어지고, 거래적 리더십은 다시 상황적 보상(Contingent reward)과 예외적 관리(Management-by-exception)로 나뉘며, 변혁적 리더십은 다시 카리스마적 리더십(Charismatic leadership), 지적인 자극(Intellectual stimulation), 개별적 고려(Individualized consideration)로 분류한다. 이러한 분류를 정리하면 [표 14]와 같다.

[표 14] 리더십의 분류

리더십		
거래적 리더십	상황적 보상 (Contingent Reward)	구성원의 노력 리더의 보상
	예외적 관리 (Management-by-exception)	구성원이 조직 목표달성 과정에서 실패한 경우, 리더가 개입
변혁적 리더십	카리스마적 리더십 (Charismatic leadership)	구성원은 리더를 존경 및 신뢰 리더는 구성원에게 사명감 부여
	지적인 자극 (Intellectual Simulation)	구성원들의 창의력을 자극
	개별적 고려 (Individualized Consideration)	리더는 구성원 개별에게 관심을 보임 구성원은 자신의 가치가 인정받고 있음을 인지

자료: Bass (1985)

Allen et al.(2006)는 브룬스 (Bruns 1978)와 바스(Bass 1985)의 변혁적 리더십이 리더의 진취성과 결단력이 개개인의 변혁으로 이어진다고 보는 것과는 다르게, 변혁적 리더십의 개념을 확장하여, 리더십이 권한을 가진 한 개인의 결단이 아닌, 하나의 체계(system)에 속한 많은 사람들이 하나가 되어 공동으로 변혁을 이루어 가는 것임을 강조한다. 이러한 신개념의 리더십은 분권적(Shared), 참여적(participatory), 집단적(collective), 협업적 (collaborative), 협조적(cooperative), 민주적(democratic), 유화적(fluid), 포용적(inclusive), 관계적(relational) 리더십 등 다양한 이름으로 불리고 있다. 집단 리더십은 세계화, 일상생활의 다양성, 변화, 정보 기술의 발전 속도, 복잡함, 다양한 가치에서 오는 긴장, 소득 불평등, 지속적 교육의 요구 등이 증가하며 나타나게 된다. 이러한 리더십의 주요 역할은 번영과 평화로운 삶의 질 성장을 뒷받침 해주는 환경을 창조하는 것, 자연과 조화를 이루어 차기 세대에게 지속가능한 조화를 물려주는 것, 상호관심과 책임공유의 사회를 만드는 것 이라고 할 수 있다.

리더십이 조직의 성과나 발전에 영향을 미치는 실증분석을 시도하기 위해서는 리더십을 정량화하는 과학적 방법이 중요한데 사실상 리더십 개념은 매우 추상적인 속성을 가지고 있기 때문에 리더십을 정량화하는 작업은 매우어려운 과정이다. 리더십을 정량화하는 방법에 관한 연구는 바스(Bass 1985)를 들 수 있다. 바스(Bass 1985)는 리더십의 다섯 가지 요소를 정량화하기 위해, 군인들을 대상으로, 73개의 다양한 요인을 반영하여 리더십 설문(MLQ: Multi-factor Leadership Questionnaire)을 만들었다. 그러나 바스(Bass 1985)의 MLQ는 질문이 중복되거나, 분류하기 모호한 질문들이 있어, 이를 보완한 리더십 정량화에 관한 연구가 Bycio, Hackett and Allen(1995)에 의해 이루어졌다. Bycio, Hackett and Allen(1995)은 MLQ에서 각각의 세부 리더십 항목을 독립변수로 두고 해당하는 문항을 추출해 설문조사를 실시하였다. 응답자는 간호사들(97%가 여성, 평균 37세)이며, 상사가 설문문항과 같은 행동을 자주 보이는 정도에 따라 0점부터 4점까지 5등급으로 답하게 된다. 종속변수로는 부가적인 노력도(extra effort), 리더에 대한 만족도(satisfaction with the leader), 리더의 영향력 등이 있다. 이 연구의 결과로는 변혁적 리더십이 상기 종속변수들에 대해 거래적 리더십 보다 더욱 양(+)의 영향을 미치며, 세부 항목에서 예외적 관리 변수는 모든 종속변수들에 음(-)의 영향을 미치고, 카리스마적 리더십은 모든 종속변수들에 대해 가장 큰 양(+)의 영향을 미치는 것으로 나타났다.

나. 리더십과 경제발전

리더십과 지역 경제발전에 관한 연구로는 Stimson et al.(2005)이 있다. Stimson et al.(2005)는 강한 주도적 리더십(Strong proactive leadership)은 미래 발전 비전을 가져오고 전략과 계획을 통해, 지역의 역량을 향상시켜 조직 및 제도 변화(institutional change)를 일으킨다고 주장한다. 또한 이러한 변화로 형성된 효과적인 기관(Institution)과 인프라 구조가 부존자원(Resource endowment)과 시장 환경을 사용할 수 있는 메커니즘을 작동하게 하여, 지속가능한 발전(Sustainable development)을 이루어 지역 경제발전(RED: Regional Economic Development)이 가능해 진다고 주장한다. 따라서 지역 경제발전(RED)은 다음과 같은 함수의 형태로 나타난다.

$$ED = f(REM\ mediated\,by\ (L, I, E)] \qquad (9)$$

REM은 부존자원 및 시장 환경에 대한 이의 적합도(fit)를 나타내며 (Resource endowments and its fit with market conditions), L(Leadership)은 리더십, E(Entrepreneurship)는 기업가 정신을 나타낸다. I(Institution)는 기관이

나 제도로써 규칙(Rule Structures)을 제공하는 중요할 역할을 하는 사회 조직이라고 할 수 있다. 따라서 지역 경제발전(RED)은 리더십, 기관 그리고 기업가 정신으로 이루어지는 부존자원과 시장 환경 적합도의 함수라고 볼 수 있다.

Stimson et al.(2005)은 사례연구(Case studies)를 통해서 RED 함수의 적절성을 보여주고 있다. 그들은 미국의 두 지역 피츠버그(Pittsburgh)와 휴스톤(Houston), 영국의 두 지역 버밍햄 (Birmingham)과 리버풀(Liverpool), 유럽 프랑스지역의 르네(Rennes), 그리고 아시아의 두 도시국가인 홍콩 (Hong Kong)과 싱가포르(Singapore)에 대한 사례연구를 진행하였다. 피츠버그는 철강 산업의 여파로 1980년대 초반 거대한 실업을 경험했지만, 1980년대 후반에 사적(Private), 공적(Public) 리더가 피츠버그의 교육과 문화, 기술을 발전시키며 지역 경제발전을 이룬 대표적인 사례이다. 휴스턴은 기업윤리의 정신으로 가파른 경제발전을 이루었다. 그러나 리더의 부재로 인해 지역 경제발전의 이익을 누리지 못하였다. 르네는 1980년대 도시 부활의 상징으로 알려져 있다. 르네는 지역사회의 자본 환경에 의해 성공적인 전략(Strategy)을 발전시켰고, 고차원 서비스, 신기술 기업, 삶의 질 향상, 높은 연구 수준, 그리고 취업구조를 중심으로 도시 부활을 이룰 수 있었다. 버밍햄은 의회에서 경제발전을 위한 위원회(Committee)를 만들었고, 지역경제문제에 초점을 맞춘 대표적 예이다. 리처드 놀레스 경(Sir Richard Knowles)의 카리스마적 리더십으로 경제발전 위원회에 힘을 실어 주었다. 비록 이러한 리더십은 다양한 경제적 문제를 낳으며 실패로 종결되었지만, 경제발전에 대한 공공의 관심을 이끌어 냈다. 반면, 리버풀은 버밍햄과 정반대의 경우를 이끌어 냈다. 리버풀의 리더는 리더로서의 자질이 부족했고, 오직 항구(port) 산업에만 의존해야 했던 리버풀은 무역중심이 서유럽에서 북미로 바뀌면서 실업률이 높아졌다. 이러한 상황은 리더의 부재로 20여 년간 지속되었지만, 1987년 시의회가 도시의 경제적 기반을 다양화하는 방안을 모색하면서, 지역 경제 중심으로서 도시부활을 가능하게 하였다. 홍콩은 천연자원의 부족에도 불구하고, 거시경제 환경, 정책 조화, 지역 제도(Institution) 출현 등으로 상업 중심의 발전을 이룰 수 있었다. 싱가포르는 농업 부문, 천연자원, 산업 전통, 기업정신 등의 부재에도 불구하고, 다국적 국가를 표방하는 경쟁적 기반(competitive base for multinationals)을 바탕으로 권위적인 관료주의를 도입하여, 경제발전을 이루었다. 이러한 Stimson et al.(2004)의 사례연구를 통해서 지역 경제 발전(RED)은 리더십, 기관 그리고 기업가 정신으로 이루어지는 부존자원과 시장 환경 적합도에 의해 달성된다는 것을 알 수 있다.

미시적 관점에서 리더십이 경제성장에 영향을 줄 수 있는 경로로는 리더십이 기업의 성과에 어떻게 영향을 줄 수 있는지를 살펴보는 것이다. 조정호, 최수형(1998)은 최고경영자의 리더십 유형이 정보기술의 성과에 어떠한 영향을 주는지 연구하였으며, 수도권과 경남권의 25개 제조업체를 표본으로 하여, 설문 자료를 수집하였다. 설명변수로는 최고경영자의 구조지향적 리더십과 고려지향적 리더십(배려적인 행동)으로 설문을 설정하고, Likert 5점 척도로 측정하였다. 종속변수인 정보기술 성과 측정은 ①경영 의사결정에 정보기술의 사용 척도(전문가 측면)와 ②

정보기술에 관한 사용자 만족도 조사(사용자 측면)를 통해 측정하였다. 실증분석 결과, 구조지향적 리더십과 고려지향적 리더십 모두 정보기술의 성과와 양(+)의 상관관계가 있음을 확인 할 수 있다. 다만, 사용자 측면에서는 구조지향적 리더십이, 전문가 측면에서는 고려주도적 리더십이 정보기술 기업성과에 더욱 강한 영향을 미치는 것으로 나타났다.

[표 15] 조직성과에 기여하는 리더의 행동

리더의 행동		
과업집중형 리더십 (Task-focused leadership) 임무요구, 임무이행 임무정보요구를 이해하는 것	거래적(Transactional)	보상과 조직목표달성을 교환
	솔선수범 (Initiating structure)	리더가 애매모호함이나 갈등을 최소화하여, 목표달성을 강조하는 정도
	경계 범위 (Boundary spanning0	팀에게 이용 가능한 자원을 증가시키는 정치적 소통과 다양한 정보를 확대시키는 통신망과 관련
인력집중형 리더십 (Person-focused leadership) 상호작용, 인식 구조, 태도가 발전되는 것	변혁적 (Transformational)	리더와 구성원이 공동비전를 향해 변혁
	배려 (Consideration)	리더가 친사회적 관계와 그룹 화합을 유지하는 정도
	권한위임 (Empowerment)	구성원들의 자기리더십(self-leadership)과 자기관리의 발전을 강조하는 리더의 행동
	동기부여 (Motivation)	노력한 구성원들을 승진시켜주는 행동

자료: Burke et al. (2006)

그렇다면 리더십의 특징 중 기업의 성과에 크게 기여하는 부문은 무엇인가? Burke et al.(2006)은 리더십의 특징 중 [표 15]와 같은 리더의 행동이 조직성과(Team performance outcomes)에 크게 기여한다고 설명하고 있다. Burke et al.(2006)은 과업집중형 리더십(Task-focused leadership)과 인력집중형 (Person-focused leadership)이 각각 얼마나 조직성과에 기여하는지를 실증 분석해 보았다. 데이터는 종합메타분석(Comprehensive Meta-Analysis)를 이용하였고, 종속변수인 조직성과는 다시 세 가지 부류로 나뉘는데, 각각 팀 효율성(perceived team effectiveness), 팀 생산성/양(team productivity/quantity), 그리고 팀 학습(team learning)이다. 분석결과, 과업집중형 리더십과 인력집중형 리더십 모두 팀 효율성, 팀 생산성, 팀 학습에서 양의 상관관계가 있음을 확인할 수 있었다.

다. 박태준 리더십의 역할 : 실증분석

상기에서 서술한 박태준 리더십의 실체를 정량화하는 방법은 그렇게 흔치 않고 그 정량화 방법이 계량적 모형을 통해 그 영향을 객관적으로 추정할 수 있는 수준에 미치지 못하고 있는 실정이다. 다만 몇 가지 실증적 연구들을 살펴보면, 이명식(2012)은 박태준과 함께 경영진의 일원으로 시장 지향성 경영에 참여한 핵심 담당자들과의 심층면접을 통해 박태준의 변혁적 리더십이 조직의 시장지향성에 미친 영향을 분석하였다. 분석 결과, 박태준의 리더십이 포스코의 시장지향성과 경영성과에 긍정적 영향을 미친 것으로 나타났다. 김명언 이지영(2012)은 박태준 연설에서 나타난 언어적 차원과 심리적 차원의 변인들은 포스코에 영향을 미치는 중요 사건의 수와 유의미한 관계가 있음을 보여주었다. 박태준은 담당 조직에 영향을 줄 수 있는 중요 사건이 수가 많을수록 조직 구성원들과의 주요 의사소통 수단인 연설문에서 긍정 정서와 부정 정서 단어 모두의 사용빈도를 증가시킨 것으로 나타났다.

백기복(2012)은 박태준에 관련된 결정적 사건 31건을 다양한 문헌에서 추출하였고 이 결정적 사건들을 내용 분석하여 박태준 리더십 핵심 변수들을 전략적 예지, 경제성 중시, 과학적 완벽주의, 국가적 사명감, 인간 우선주의, 청렴의 신조, 과감한 전략적 선택, 성취 압박의 행동, 솔선수범하고 희생하는 행위, 종업원들의 성장 지원, 철저한 현장관리, 원칙고수, 설득과 이해, 그리고 전략적 협상력 14개로 추출하였으며 이들을 기반으로 박태준 리더십 종합 모델을 창안하였다. 백기복은 14개 변수들 중 가장 큰 영향력을 발휘하는 변수는 국가적 사명감이라고 강조했다.

최동주(2012)는 허만(Hermann 2003)의 7가지 지도자 특성별로 박태준 어록에 대한 내용분석 결과, 박태준의 주된 리더십 특성은 '인간존중과 신뢰', '문제 해결을 위한 총체적 개념의 복합성', '과업지향성'영역에서 나타나며 포스코가 단기간에 세계적인 철강회사로 발전할 수 있었던 이유는 박태준이 직원들과의 상호 신뢰를 바탕으로 기술 연구와 자주 관리를 중시하는 데 그친 것이 아니라, 국가의 미래를 내다보고 끊임없는 목표의 수립과 달성을 반복한 선순환 구조에 그 답이 있다는 것을 강조하고 있다. 김명언 김예지(2012)는 박태준이 재임기간동안 행한 신년사 18편, 창립 기념사 21편, 송년사 13편을 대상으로 내용분석한 결과, 박태준이 현실적 낙관주의 형태의 의사소통을 조직 구성원들과 많이 할수록 출선량, 조강량, 매출액 이익률, 매출 총이익, 매출액, 제품 판매량, 영업이익 등의 성과 지표에서 유의미한 증가가 나타났음을 보여주고 있다.

본 연구에서는 박태준의 리더십을 정량화하는 방법을 김병연 최상오(2011) 연구에서 사용한 언론기사 아이디어를 이용한다. 김병연 최상오는 특정 신문의 포스코 기사를 활용하여 포스코가 한국 경제에 미친 직 간접적 영향을 분석하고 있다. 즉, 포스코가 한국경제에 미친 직접 효과뿐 아니라 간접 효과가 중요하다면 그 효과를 전달한 주요 채널은 언론이었다는 판단이다. 그들은 "중앙일보"라는 특정 일간지를 선정하고 1966년부터 1992년까지 포스코에 관한 기사 1679건을 추출하고 조정하여 1674건을 대상으로 기사 내용을 분류하여 분석하였다. 본 연구에서는 김병연 최상오(2011) 연구에서 사용한 언론기사 중 박태준 리더십 보도와 관련된 기사내용을 재분류하였다. 주요 기사항목은 자부심, 기술지원, 종업원 복지, 효율경영, 연구개발, 박태준 회장이다. 본 연구는 상기 기사건수를 종합하여 연도별 시계열자료를 산출하고 이러한 리더십 관련 언론기사 건수가 포스코 경영성과 및 생산성에 영향을 미치는지를 추정한다. 다음과 같은 추정방정식을 설정하여 추정한다.

$$y_t = \beta_0 + \sum_{i=1}^{p} \beta_i x_{t-i} + \epsilon_t \qquad (10)$$

[표 16] TJP 리더십 관련 언론보도 내용 및 건수

연도 \ 항목	자부심	기술지원	종업원 복지	효율경영	연구 및 기술개발	박태준	총계
1973	7	1					8
1974	4						4
1975	7	4					11
1976	21				1		22
1977	5		1		1		7
1978	11				2		13
1979	8		2		2		12
1980	5						5
1981	11				1		12
1982	3			1		1	5
1983	3				2	3	8
1984	4				1		5
1985	2			4	4	1	11
1986	4			3	4		11
1987	1			1	1	1	4
1988	6		2	1		1	10
1989	5			1	1	1	8
1990	6		3	1		4	14
1991	1		2	1	4	1	9
1992	9					12	21

자료 : 김병연·최상오(2011)의 자료를 재편집

여기에서 y_t는 포스코 경영성과를 반영하는 매출액 증가율과 생산성 증가율을 나타내고 x_{t-i} 는 $t-i$년도에 TJP 리더십 관련 기사 건수가 된다. 리더십 요인은 단기와 장기에 걸쳐 기업성과와 생산성에 영향을 미칠 수 있다는 것을 고려하여 몇 년의 시차변수를 포함하였다. 최소자승법에 의한 추정결과는 다음과 같다:

⟨y_t : 매출증가율⟩

$$y_t = \frac{-36.92}{(25.03)} + \frac{0.799}{(0.998)}x_t + \frac{2.083}{(1.195)}x_{t-1} + \frac{1.380}{(1.139)}x_{t-2} + \frac{2.556}{(1.148)}x_{t-3} + \epsilon_t \qquad (11)$$

$$\overline{R^2} = 0.208$$

⟨y_t : 1인당 생산성증가율⟩

$$y_t = \frac{-38.93}{(18.99)} + \frac{1.245}{(0.758)}x_t + \frac{0.951}{(0.907)}x_{t-1} - \frac{0.775}{(0.864)}x_{t-2} + \frac{3.795}{(0.871)}x_{t-3} + \epsilon_t \qquad (12)$$

$$\overline{R^2} = 0.573$$

추정 결과, 종속변수가 매출증가율의 경우 TJP 리더십에 대한 언론보도 건수의 추정계수들은 양의 값으로 추정되었으나 통계적으로 유의하지 않았고 다만 3년전 언론보도 건수는 통계적으로 유의하였다. 이러한 결과는 TJP 리더십이 보다 활동적인 경우에는 몇 년의 시차를 두고 포스코 기업 성과에 긍정적인 영향을 끼쳤다는 것을 의미한다.

종속변수가 1인당 생산성증가율의 경우에도 추정계수가 2년 전 언론보도 건수 (x_{t-2})의 경우를 제외하고 모두 양의 값으로 추정되었고 특히 3년 전 TJP 리더십에 대한 언론보도건수의 추정계수는 통계적으로 유의하였다. 따라서 포스코 1인당 생산성의 경우에도, TJP 리더십이 보다 왕성한 경우에는 몇 년의 시차를 두고 포스코 생산성 향상에 기여한 것으로 풀이할 수 있다.

위와 같은 TJP 리더십에 대한 실증분석 결과를 종합하면, 박태준 회장 재임기간 동안 기술개발 및 기술혁신, 경영혁신, 자주관리를 통한 현장혁신, 연수 및 현장교육, 산학연 협력, 기업복지 등 다양한 리더십 활동들은 포스코의 1인당 생산성을 향상시키는데 기여하였고 이는 포스코의 성공적인 경영성과를 불러 일으켰다. 포스코의 뛰어난 생산성 향상과 우수한 경영성과는 한국경제 생산성을 제고시키고 지속적인 경제성장을 가져오는데 상당한 공헌을 한 것으로 평가할 수 있다.

V. 박태준 리더십의 개발도상국 적용방안

1. 박태준 리더십과 포스코 성공 모델

본 연구에서는 한국경제의 급속한 산업화와 경제성장을 가져온 핵심적 요인들을 파악하였고 포스코의 성장이 이러한 핵심적 요소에 어떻게 영향을 미쳤는지 문헌적 고찰과 실증분석을 통해 살펴보았다. 또한 포스코의 성장에 결정적 기여를 한 박태준 초대회장의 핵심적 리더십의 역할은 무엇이었는지 문헌적 연구와 실증적 분석을 통해 확인하였다. 현대 세계경제사회에서 급속한 경제발전을 추구하려는 개도국은 한국경제성장의 경험을 전수받아 자국의 경제발전을 추구하려는 학습의지가 매우 높고 이를 위한 제도적 도입을 적극적으로 고려하고 있다. 한국은 이러한 개도국의 경제발전을 돕기 위해 다양한 지원을 모색하고 있는데 본 연구는 포스코의 성장모델이 개도국의 경제발전 전략에 적용될 수 있는 방안이 무엇인지 제안하려고 한다.

본 연구에서 보여준 박태준 리더십 역할, 포스코 성공, 그리고 한국경제 발전간 핵심적 인과관계 분석결과를 종합하여 포스코 성장 모델을 정형화할 수 있다. 이런 정형화된 포스코 성장모형은 개도국에 잘 전수되어 개도국의 성공적인 경제발전을 추진하는데 기여할 수 있을 것이다. 즉, 포스코와 같이 소수의 중요한 기업에 집중하여 이를 성공사례로 만들어 내고 이를 학습, 적용, 확산함으로써 한 국가의 경제발전의 동력을 얻는 전략은 개발도상국의 경제발전을 촉발시키는 주요한 출발점이 될 수 있다(김병연·최상오 2011).

　본 연구에서 제안하는 포스코형 성장모형은 무엇인가? 그 핵심은 다음 다섯 가지로 요약할 수 있다.

　첫째, 시장지향적 국가기업을 육성하여 정부주도 경제발전을 추진하는 것이다. 경제발전 초기에는 경제 인프라가 미약하기 때문에 민간주도에 의한 경제발전 전략은 그 추진동력이 약하다. 이러한 상황에서는 정부가 국가기업을 육성하여 산업화를 추진할 수 있도록 강력한 정부의 리더십이 필요하고 국가기업을 통했을 때 그 리더십은 더 강력할 수 있다. 그런데 단순히 국가기업을 육성하게 되면 관료제적 기업운영으로 기업 성과가 효율적이지 못하게 되고 이는 기업의 국제경쟁력을 저하시키게 된다. 따라서 시장의 효율적이고 경쟁적인 요소들을 적극적으로 도입하여 국제경쟁력을 갖는 시장지향의 국가기업을 육성하는 것이다.

　둘째, 대외지향적 경제발전 전략을 견인하기 위해 초일류 국가기업을 육성하는 것이다. 세계 경제발전의 역사에서 배우는 교훈은 대외지향적 발전전략을 추구하는 국가들이 그렇지 않은 국가들보다 평균적으로 더 높은 경제성장률을 경험했다는 것이다. 대외지향적 전략은 기업을 국제경쟁시장에서 치열한 가격 및 품질경쟁을 통해 국제경쟁력을 키우게 하고 이는 기업의 효율성과 생산성을 높이는 결과를 가져오게 된다. 이 과정에서 결국 국제시장에서 생존하는 기업은 초일류 기업인 것이다. 이런 관점에서 볼 때, 포스코는 개방과 경쟁을 통해 초일류기업을 추구함으로써 한국 기업의 성공사례가 된 것이다.

셋째, 산업화와 근대화를 위해 기반이 되는 선도적 기업을 육성하는 것이다. 포스코와 같은 철강기업은 산업화의 쌀인 철강제품을 생산하여 국가 산업화의 기반이 되는 전자, 전기, 선박, 조선, 자동차, 중화학공업 등에 지대한 영향을 미치게 된다. 이들 기업들에게 저렴하고 품질 좋은 철강제품을 공급함으로써 궁극적으로 이들 산업의 국제경쟁력 제고에 기여하게 되는 것이다. 따라서 꼭 철강산업이 아니더라도 국가 산업화를 견인할 수 있는 선도적 산업과 기업을 육성하는 것이 중요하다.

넷째, 기술혁신, 경영혁신, R&D, 산학연 협력체 구축 등 생산성 향상과 인적자본 축적에 지속적인 노력을 경주하는 것이다. 기업의 지속적 발전을 견인하는 것은 끊임없는 기술혁신과 기술개발임을 포스코 성공이 절실히 말해주고 있다. 그리고 장기적으로 국가 및 산업 발전을 주도하는 것은 산업인력과 고급 연구두뇌들이다. 포스코는 생산성 향상과 인적자본 축적을 위해 다양하고 적극적인 노력을 기울였다. 특히 한국과 같이 부존자원이 열악한 국가에서는 인적자본 축적을 통한 기술개발과 생산성 향상은 매우 중요하다. 한국과 유사한 위치에 있는 개발도상국들은 이 점을 깊이 있게 고려할 필요가 있다.

다섯째, 결사적 애국심, 시장지향적이고 합리적 태도, 용혼경영사상을 추구하는 CEO를 육성하는 것이다. 포스코 성공 사례는 기업 경영자의 사상과 경제관이 매우 중요하다는 것을 입증하고 있다. TJP 리더십에서 보여준 바와 같이 국가기업을 운영하는 기업경영자는 사익을 버리고 결사적인 조국애를 갖고 기업을 운영하는 자세가 직원들의 공공의식과 자주적 참여의식을 이끌어내는데 매우 중요하다. 산업화의 기반이 되는 국가기업은 단순한 기업 차원을 넘어 또 하나의 국가와 같은 존재라고 할 수 있다. 따라서 국혼을 가지고 부국강병이라는 미션을 달성하기 위해 여러 가지 실천경영을 추진하는 CEO는 포스코와 같은 성공기업을 만드는데 절대적으로 필요하다.

2. 박태준 리더십 활용방안 : 포스코의 역할

포스코형 성장모형을 어떻게 하면 개발도상국이 잘 활용할 수 있을까? 본 연구는 한국경제 성장에서 포스코 및 TJP 리더십이 얼마나 주요한 역할을 하였는지를 보여주고 이를 바탕으로 개발도상국에 활용할 수 있는 방안에 대한 시사점을 제안하고 있다. 개발도상국 활용방안에는 포스코의 역할과 개발도상국 정부의 역할로 나누어 살펴볼 수 있다. 포스코는 개발도상국이 포스코형 성장모델을 학습하고 자국의 경제발전 전략을 수립하고 추진하는데 어떤 역할을 할 수 있을 것인가? 오늘날 포스코는 국영기업에서 벗어나 민영기업으로 탈바꿈하였지만 청암재단 등을 통해 공공 및 사회적 책임 활동이나 창조적 성과공유 활동들을 끊임없이 추구하고 있다. 또한 이것은 초대 창업자인 박태준 회장의 뜻이기도 하다. 따라서 포스코는 TJP 리더십을 개발도상국에 전파하고 이들 국가들이 효과적으로 학습하여 자국의 경제발전전략에 최대한 활용할 수 있도록 그 협력방안을 모색할 필요가 있다. 협력방안은 두 가지 관점에서 전개될 필요가 있다.

첫째, 포스코는 TJP 리더십 센터를 건립하고 개발도상국의 잠재적 리더들을 육성하기 위한 국제적 리더십 프로그램을 운영하고 지원하는 것이다. 리더십센터는 국제적 프로그램 운영을 통하여 잠재적 리더들에게 TJP 리더십의 핵심 요인을 학습시키고 기업성장전략과 경제성장 전략을 체계적으로 교육시키는 것이다. 이러한 교육은 매우 전문적인 차원에서 진행되어 개발도상국 잠재적 리더들에게 실질적이고 전문적인 연수기회를 제공하는 것이다. 특히 개발도상국 경제정책 결정자를 위한 리더십 프로그램을 운영함으로써 개발도상국 경제발전 전략을 구축하는데 기여할 뿐만 아니라 포스코는 개발도상국과 경제적 협력관계를 구축할 수 있는 기회를 갖게 됨으로써 미래 포스코 성장에도 적지 않은 기여를 할 수 있을 것이다. 또한 포스코 설립 초기부터 국제적 기업으로 성장하기까지 TJP 리더십이 어떻게 전개되었는지 정책결정자들에게 학습시키고 포스코 공장과 박물관 등에서 현장 연수를 제공하여 실질적인 교육 프로그램을 제공함으로써 그들에게 경제발전에 대한 욕구를 진작시킬 필요가 있다.

또한 TJP 리더십의 핵심요인을 체계적으로 발굴하고 개발도상국에 적용할 수 있는 방안에 대하여 끊임없는 연구를 지속할 수 있도록 연구를 지원하는 것이다. 개발도상국 경제발전 전략 연구자들에게 장학금과 연구비를 지원하여 TJP 리더십의 핵심요인들을 체계적으로 연구하고 그들 국가들의 경제발전에 적용할 수 있는 다양한 방안들을 연구할 수 있는 기회를 제공함으로써 개발도상국 경제발전 전략 수립에 도움을 줄 뿐만 아니라 박태준 초대회장의 결사적 조국애 계승에도 기여할 것이다.

둘째, 포스코는 국제적 관점에서 사회적 책임을 실천하기 위해 보다 광범위하고 다양한 사회공헌활동을 펼칠 필요가 있다. 오늘날 국경을 넘어 국제적 기업이 보편화되어 가고 있는 현실에서 포스코가 TJP 리더십 센터에서 추진하는 전문적인 리더십 교육에만 머물러서는 국가와 민족을 위한 글로벌 지도자를 육성하는데 한계가 있다. 왜냐하면 TJP 리더십의 가장 핵심적인 결정체는 결사적 조국애이고 오늘날 결사적 조국애는 국경을 넘어 이웃과 공동체를 위해 공헌하는 사회적 책임으로 연결되기 때문이다. 포스코는 박태준 초대 회장의 뜻을 계승하고 그가 보여준 결사적 조국애를 개발도상국 잠재적 지도자들에게 학습시키기 위해서는 리더십센터와 사회적 책임을 연결시켜 보다 광범위한 차원에서 사회공헌활동을 지원하고 다양한 활동들을 펼칠 필요가 있다.

이를 위해 포스코는 사회적 책임과 연결시켜 개발도상국 경제발전을 위해 필요한 사회공헌활동을 지원하고 보다 광범위한 차원에서 박태준 리더십 프로그램 운영에 적극적인 지원을 펼칠 필요가 있다. 예컨대, 한국언론재단에서는 한국전쟁에 참여하였던 국가들의 기자들을 매년 초청하여 한국 경제, 정치, 문화 등 다양한 방면에서 발전과정을 소개하고 학습시키는 프로그램을 매년 성공적으로 추진하고 있다. 포스코는 위와 같은 프로그램을 벤치마킹해서 개발도상국에게 리더십 교육 및 사회적 공헌활동을 고취시켜 그들 국가 경제발전에 실질적 기여를 할 수 있는 다양한 프로그램 개발을 추진할 필요가 있다.

오늘날 포스코는 박태준 초대회장의 기대에 부응하여 세계 초일류 철강기업으로 우뚝 섰다. 그러나 끊임없는 국제적 경쟁 속에 지속적인 성장을 유지하지 못하고 얼마 되지 않아 무너진 대기업들도 속출하고 있는 냉혹한 국제시장에서 포스코가 초일류 기업으로 지속되는 길은 박태준 초대 회장이 보여준 리더십을 되새기고 끊임없이 전사적으로 공유하는 것이다. 그 일환으로 전문적인 리더십 교육과 광범위한 사회 공헌활동은 포스코를 세계적 일류 기업으로 자리매김하는 최소한의 필요조건임을 상기할 필요가 있다.

3. 박태준 리더십 활용방안 : 개도국 정부의 역할

본 연구에서는 한국 정부의 강력한 리더십이 한국경제 발전에 핵심적인 역할을 했다는 것을 강조하고 있다. 이런 맥락에서 경제발전을 시도하는 개발도상국 정부는 포스코형 경제성장 모형에 깊은 관심을 기울이고 자국의 경제발전 전략 수립에 적극적으로 활용할 필요가 있다. 개발도상국 정부는 구체적으로 어떠한 역할과 방안을 추구해야 할 것인가?

첫째, 개발도상국 정부는 포스코와 협력관계 프로그램을 개발하여 한국경제 성장 모형, TJP 리더십, 포스코 경영, 포스코 기업문화를 학습할 수 있는 연수 프로그램을 적극적으로 기획하고 추진할 필요가 있다. 자국의 경제성장에 대한 경험을 맛보지 못한 상황에서 미래 경제 성장의 과실을 꿈꾸고 실천하는 의지를 갖기 위해서는 개발도상국 정부가 이미 경제성장을 이룩한 한국경제의 모범적인 사례를 학습하고 간접적인 체험을 하는 것이다. 이를 위해서 포스코와 긴밀한 협력관계를 추진하여 포스코가 제공하는 다양한 국제적 리더십 연수 프로그램에 적극적으로 참여하는 것이다.

둘째, 개발도상국 정부는 포스코가 지원하는 리더십 프로그램을 유치하고 장학지원 사업 및 연구지원 사업을 적극적으로 활용하여 박태준 초대회장과 같은 지도자를 발굴하고 육성하기 위해 전력을 다하는 것이다. 박태준 초대회장도 한국의 일제 식민지 시절에 일찍이 산업화 길을 걸었던 일본의 경제발전에 대한 깊은 학습을 통해서 실용적인 경제관을 형성했던 경험이 있었다. 이런 관점에서 개발도상국의 잠재적 지도자들이 한국 경험에 대한 학습 및 연수는 자신들의 경제개발 추진 의지 함양에 매우 긍정적인 영향을 미칠 것이다.

셋째, 개발도상국 정부는 한국정부 및 포스코와 긴밀한 협력관계를 구축할 필요가 있다. 포스코가 창립될 초기에 포스코는 독자적인 기술이 전무하여 일본 철강산업으로부터 많은 것을 배우고 나아가 독자적인 기술을 개발하였다. 경제발전 초기 단계에 있는 개발도상국도 유사한 상황이다. 기술 수준이 낮고 산업화를 추진할 수 있는 인적자본이 미약한 상황에서는 국제적 기업 포스코와 한국정부로부터 적극적인 협조를 받아 자국의 기업과 산업을 육성시킬 필요가 있고 이를 위해서 개도국 정부는 포스코 및 한국정부와 긴밀한 협력관계를 구축하기 위해 적극적인 행보를 펼칠 필요가 있다. 예컨대, 기술개발 및 기술인력 양성을 지원하는 연수프로그램을 수립하고 추진하기 위해 개도국 정부는 한국정부 및 포스코와 전략적 협력관계를 구축하는 것이다.

VI. 결 론

한국경제는 지난 60여년 동안 연평균 경제성장률 4.5%를 상회하는 경이적인 기록을 달성하면서 세계 경제의 모범적인 성장사례로 인정받고 있다. 경제발전 초기에 서방 선진국으로부터 경제원조를 받았던 국가가 이제는 개발도상국 경제발전을 지원하는 국가로 탈바꿈한 것이다. 더불어 한국경제의 국제적 위상이 높아짐에 따라 세계경제에 대한 한국경제의 한 차원 격상된 기여가 요구되고 있는 실정이다. 개발도상국의 입장에서 한국경제 성장 경험으로부터 가장 절실히 요구하는 것은 무엇일까? 그 출발점은 경제발전 초기단계에서 중요한 역할을 담당하는 산업기반 조성과 국제 경쟁력을 견인하는 초일류 기업의 육성 전략의 학습이다. 이런 관점에서 한국경제는 어떻게 산업기반을 조성하였고 포스코, 삼성전자, 현대 자동차 등과 같은 초일류 국제적인 기업들을 육성할 수 있었을까?

본 연구는 지난 40년간 한국경제가 성취한 고도성장의 배경과 그 성장동력으로써 핵심에 있었던 포스코의 역할을 심도 있게 연구하여 포스코형 성장 모형의 실질적 프레임워크를 개발하고 베트남 및 인도 등 아시아를 중심으로 한 개발도상국들이 자국들의 경제성장 전략을 추진하는데 중요한 활용 도구로 이용할 수 있는 방안을 연구하였다. 특히 국가기간산업의 근간이 되었던 철강회사 포스코의 한국경제발전 기여와 포스코 초일류기업 육성에 지대한 공헌을 한 TJP 리더십의 핵심적 요소는 무엇이고 이러한 요소들이 어떻게 작용하여 한국경제발전을 선도하였는지를 집중적으로 조명하였다. 나아가 TJP 리더십을 중심으로 한 포스코 성장모델을 정형화하여 경제개발을 기획하고 있는 개발도상국에게 한국경제발전과 같이 효율적인 경제개발을 추진할 수 있는 전략을 전수할 수 있는 방안이 무엇인지를 제시하였다.

한국경제 고도성장의 핵심적 요인은 4가지 관점에서 요약할 수 있다. 첫째, 제조업의 성장과 대외지향적 무역정책이다. 둘째, 경제발전 전략에 정부의 강력한 리더십과 역할이다. 셋째, 경제발전 단계에 따라 효율적 시장경제 체제를 정착시켰고 효율적 자원배분 전략을 지속적으로 추진한 것이다. 넷째, 높은 교육열의와 교육과 경제의 선순환 구조를 형성하여 최적의 인적자본을 축적하였고 기술개발 및 경영혁신 등을 통해 높은 생산성을 달성하여 지속적이면서 고도의 경제성장을 달성하였다. 위의 4가지 핵심요인 중 가장 중요한 두 가지 요소는 정부의 강력한 리더십과 인적자본의 축적으로 요약할 수 있다.

한국경제 성장의 4가지 핵심 요소들의 관점에서 포스코는 다음과 같은 기여를 하였다.

첫째, 포스코는 산업발전 기여를 통해 중화학공업 및 제조업 성장을 견인하는데 중추적인 역할을 담당하였다. 철강은 산업화의 쌀이고 철강산업은 규모가 큰 장치산업으로써 타 기업의 많은 제품을 수요하고 다른 산업들에게 철강제품을 주요 산업의 중간재로 공급한다. 포스코는 매우 높은 전후방연관효과를 보여 한국경제 산업화에 기여했고 이는 제조업 성장에 크게 공헌한 것으로 평가된다.

둘째, 포스코는 시장지향적 국영기업을 통하여 국가주도 산업화에 기여했다. 경제발전 초기 자본축적이 빈약하고 사회 인프라가 미약한 상황에서 민간주도에 의한 성장전략은 효과적인 경제성장을 견인할 수 없다. 이런 상황에서 포스코는 대한민국 정부의 시대적 사명을 실현하기 위하여 제철보국이라는 경제적 이념으로 중화학공업화의 선봉이 되어 국가주도 산업화를 견인했고 세계 초일류 철강기업이 되기 위해 국제경쟁력을 추구하는 시장적 국가기업의 역할을 충실히 감당한 것이다.

셋째, 포스코는 기술개발, 연구개발 투자, 산학연 협동, 및 기업복지를 통해 국가 생산성 향상 및 인적자본 형성에 기여했다. 포스코는 제철보국을 실현하면서 국가 미래산업을 선도할 인재육성이라는 박태준 회장의 교육보국 정신을 실천하기 위해 기술개발과 기술혁신, 연구개발 투자, 산학연 협동연구 및 산업 현장인력 양성, 전사적 자주관리를 통한 현장혁신, 기업복지발전과 흑자경영의 선순환 구조, 포스코 성공의 학습 및 확산을 통한 국가 산업화에 외부효과 창출 등을 만들어내면서 국가경제의 생산성 제고 및 인적자본 축적을 도모하여 한국 경제성장에 기여했다.

포스코의 성공과 한국경제 성장간 실증분석 결과, 포스코 매출액 증가율은 제조업성장률에 긍정적인 영향을 끼쳤다. 특히 포스코가 제철소 확장 준공을 펼친 년도에는 제조업 성장률이 다른 년도에 비해 훨씬 높은 것을 확인하였다. 또한 포스코 생산성 증가율은 국가 생산성 증가율에 3년의 시차를 두고 긍정적인 영향을 끼치는 것으로 분석되었다.

포스코는 한국경제 성장을 견인한 모범적 기업사례가 된 것인데 포스코 성공의 핵심요인은 무엇인가? 본 연구에서는 TJP의 선도적 리더십 ⇒ 포스코의 성공 ⇒ 한국경제의 성장이라는 메카니즘을 전제로 TJP 리더십의 특성들을 종합하여 한국경제 성장에 결정적 기여를 한 TJP 리더십의 핵심을 분석하였다.

첫째, 태준이즘과 제철보국 구현을 통한 제조업 성장 및 급속한 산업화에 기여한 점이다. 박태준 회장은 소신껏, 청렴하게, 사심없이 그리고 온갖 반대와 장애를 뚫는 절대적 절망은 없는 자세를 견지하면서 결사적 조국애와 순교자적 희생정신으로 포스코 건설을 추진하였고 용혼경영사상을 통해 포스코 성장을 주도하였다. 포스코 성장의 대성취를 통해 한국경제 성장에 이바지한 박태준 리더십의 포괄적 종합체계는 태준이즘이고 이는 제철보국의 종합적 정신 동력이다.

둘째, 박태준은 초일류 기업추구를 통한 대외지향적 정책에 기여했다. 박태준은 포스코의 국가적 사명을 깊이 절감하고 제철보국을 구현하기 위해 글로벌 초일류 철강기업 건설을 꿈꾸었다. 포스코가 세계 초일류 철강기업이 되기위해서는 국제경쟁력이 확보되어야 하고 이를 위해 생산비 절감, 우수한 품질, 효율적 경영, 그리고 지속적 성장을 위한 기술개발에 다각적인 노력을 펼쳤다. 초일류 철강기업 실현을 위한 TJP의 선도적인 리더십은 포스코의 선봉적 역할을 통하여 한국 정부가

주도하는 대외지향적 수출위주 성장정책을 펼치는데 주요한 공헌을 한 것이다.

셋째, 박태준은 시장지향적 공기업 추구를 통해 정부주도 경제발전을 이룩하는데 선봉장의 역할을 감당하였다. 박태준은 포스코 창립부터 국가경제에서 포스코가 갖는 중차대한 의미를 전사적으로 공유하고 제조업 및 국가 산업화를 선도하는 국영기업으로써 책무를 다했다. 또한 포스코 제품의 품질 향상과 생산비 절감을 통해 국제 경쟁력을 높이기 위해 한 발 앞선 신기술 도입, 연구개발, 과학기술분야 확장, 산학협력 등 시장지향적 경영활동을 추진하여 포스코 기업을 국내적으로 중화학공업화를 추진하는데 핵심적 역할을 도모하여 국가주도 산업화를 선도하고 국외적으로 정부주도 수출위주의 대외지향적 경제정책을 펼쳐 경제발전을 추구하는 전략실천의 선봉장 역할을 감당하게 한 것이다.

넷째, 박태준은 기술혁신, 경영혁신, 교육보국, 선진적 기업문화 추구를 통해 생산성 향상 및 인적자본 축적에 기여했다. 박태준은 산업 및 국가발전을 위한 교육의 필요성을 인식하고 교육보국 의지가 투철하였다. 현장인력의 양성, 산학연 연구협력체 구축 등을 통해 산업인력 양성과 고급두뇌 인력양성에 전력을 다하였다. 박태준은 기술개발 및 기술혁신, 경영혁신, 자주관리 및 현장혁신, 선진적 기업복지 등을 통해 포스코 생산성을 지속적으로 향상시켜 국가경제 생산성 향상에 기여했다. TJP 리더십이 포스코 경영성과에 미친 실증분석결과, TJP의 적극적인 경영제언 리더십은 포스코 경영성과와 생산성에 긍정적인 영향을 미친 것으로 분석되었다.

　박태준 리더십, 포스코 성공, 그리고 한국경제 발전간 핵심적 인과관계 분석결과 본 연구는 개발도상국에 적용하기 위해 다음을 제안한다.

　첫째, 포스코형 성장모형의 학습이다. 포스코형 성장모형의 핵심은 ①시장지향적 국가기업을 육성하여 정부주도 경제발전을 추진하는 것, ②대외지향적 경제발전 전략을 견인하기 위해 초일류 국가기업을 육성하는 것, ③산업화와 근대화를 위해 기반이 되는 선도적 기업을 육성하는 것, ④기술혁신, 경영혁신, R&D, 산학연 협력체 구축 등 생산성 향상과 인적자본 축적에 지속적인 노력을 경주하는 것, ⑤ 사적 애국심, 시장지향적이고 합리적 태도, 용혼경영사상을 추구하는 CEO를 육성하는 것이다.

　둘째, 포스코는 박태준 리더십 센터 건립을 통해 리더십 학습, 교육, 그리고 연구를 지속적으로 추진하고 개도국의 잠재적 리더들을 발굴하여 리더십 연수를 주최하고 개도국에 장학금과 연구비 지원을 통해 잠재적 지도자 육성에 기여하며 개도국 정책결정자를 위한 리더십 프로그램을 운영할 필요가 있다. 또한 포스코의 사회적 책임을 다할 수 있는 보다 광범위한 사회적 공헌활동 프로그램을 개발하여 개도국 사회공헌활동을 지원하고 박태준 리더십 프로그램 운영에 적극적인 지원을 펼칠 필요가 있다.

　셋째, 개발도상국 정부는 포스코와 협력관계 프로그램을 개발하여 박태준 리더십, 포스코 경영, 포스코 기업문화를 학습할 수 있는 연수 프로그램을 기획하고 포스코가 지원하는 리더십 프로그램을 유치하며 장학금과 연구지원비를 유치하여 잠재적 지도자 육성에 전력하고 한국 정부 및 포스코와 유기적인 협력관계를 구축할 필요가 있다.

본 연구는 TJP 핵심 리더십이 개발도상국에 효과적으로 전수되어 이들 국가 경제발전 전략 수립 및 개도국 경제발전에 이바지하는 것이다. 또한 현재 제 2의 도약을 꿈꾸고 있는 포스코의 신성장 모형을 한국경제의 중장기적 플랜과 새로이 접목시켜 포스코 중장기적 발전과 한국 경제 발전의 연계성을 지속적으로 확보하는데 중요한 연구자료로 활용되길 기대한다.

Acknowledgement :

본 연구는 포스텍 (POSECH)의 지원을 받아 진행되었다. 저자는 본 연구과정에서 심도 있는 코멘트와 토론을 해준 최광웅 소장(박태준미래전략연구소), 정기준 박사, 그리고 이대환 작가에게 고마움을 전한다. 또한 연구과정에서 훌륭하게 연구조교 역할을 해준 문제영 조교(고려대 대학원 석사과정), 박의환 조교(고려대 대학원 박사과정), 그리고 안선영 조교(고려대 대학원 박사과정)에게도 감사를 전한다.

참고문헌

강광하 외 (2008). 『한국 고도성장기의 정책결정체계』, 한국개발연구원.

곽강수·김대중·강태영 (2012), 세계 철강기업 경영성과 분석: 요인 분석을 활용한 종합 점수화 기법, 『박태준의 경영철학 2』, 아시아 출판사.

곽상경 외 (1992), 『포항제철과 국민경제』, 수정당.

권영민 (2002). "인적자원의 증가와 경제성장: 신 성장 이론에 의한 접근", 『경제학연구』, 제50권 제3호.

김광석, 박준경 (1979). 『한국경제의 고도성장요인』, 한국개발연구원.

김낙년 (1999). 『1960년대 한국의 경제성장과 정부의 역할』, 경제사학.

김도훈 (2007), "철과 강의 제조는 어떠한 경로를 거쳐서 오늘에 이르렀는가?: 근세문명을 도약시킨 제철과 제강기술의 역사적 발전 이야기(1)" 『재료마당』, 20(4).

김동헌·이만종·이홍식·한치록, (2011), 『한국경제성장모델의 수립 및 개발도상국 적용방안에 대한 연구』, 국회입법조사처.

김명언·김예지 (2012), "최고경영자가 행한 연설문에 나타난 현실적 낙관주의의 분류체계와 그 효과," 『박태준의 경영철학 1』, 아시아출판사.

김명언 외 (2012), 『박태준의 경영철학 1』, 아시아 출판사.

김명언·이지영 (2012), "최고경영자의 연설문을 통해 살펴본 조직 맥락과 리더의 심리적 발언 간의 관계: K-LIWC 분석을 중심으로," 『박태준의 리더십』, 아시아 출판사.

김민정, (2012), "개인적 요인분석에 의한 청렴 리더십", 『박태준의 리더십』, 아시아 출판사.

김병연·최상오, (2011), 포스코와 한국경제: 서지적, 실증적 분석을 중심으로, 『경영사학』 제 26집 2호, 5-49.

김상규·이재상·이은영·윤영균 (1998), 『산업연관표를 이용한 POSCO의 국민경제에 대한 기여도 분석』 포스코경영연구소.

김시동 (1987). 『80년대 산업합리화의 추진과정과 대책방향』, 산업연구원.

김왕배 (2012), "발전국가와 민족중흥주의: 청암 박태준의 보국이념에 대한 지식사회학적 탐구", 『테준이즘』, 아시아 출판사.

김왕배 (2013), "박태준의 국가관과 사회관", 『박태준 사상 미래를 열다』, 아시아 출판사.

김원규 외 (2000). 『한국산업의 생산성 분석』, 산업개발원.

류상영, (2001), "포항제철 성장의 정치경제학: 정부-기업관계, 연속논쟁, 지대추구," 『한국정치학회보』, 제 35집 2호.

박태준 (1985), 『제철보국의 의지: 박태준회장 경영어록』, 포항종합제철주식회사.

박태준 (1987), 『신종이산가족』, 포항종합제철.

박영구 (1999). "대외의존과 경제구조: 1970년대 중화학공업과 대외의존도에 관한 실증적 연구", 한국국제경제학회.

박영구 (2001). "정부인가 시장인가: 1980년대 중화학공업조정 이후의 효율성과 시사점," 『국제경영연구』, 한국국제경제학회.

박철순·남윤성 (2012), "포스코 신화와 청암: 청지기 경영자와 기업 경쟁력," 『박태준의 경영철학 2』, 아시아 출판사

박헌준, (2012), "긍정조직 윤리에 대한 창업 CEO의 영향력: 가치일치의 매개효과," 『박태준의 경영철학 1』, 아시아 출판사

배규식 (2008), "한국의 작업장 혁신 어떻게 할 것인가: 작업장 혁신과 촉진 정책," 『국제노동브리프』 6권 11호, 한국노동연구원. 1-3.

배종태 외 (2012), 『박태준의 경영철학 2』, 아시아 출판사.

배진한 (2008), "노동시장과 인적자원개발로 본 한국의 경제발전" 『경제경영연구』

백기복 (2012), "청암 박태준의 리더십: 근거이론과 결정적 사건법을 활용한 종합모델 도출", 『박태준의 리더십』, 아시아 출판사

백기복 (2013), "박태준의 용혼 경영사상," 『박태준 사상 미래를 열다』, 아시아 출판사

백기복 외 (2012), 『박태준의 리더십』 아시아 출판사.

변형윤 (2012), 『한국경제발전의 역사』, 지식산업사.

산업과학기술연구소 (1990), 『포항제철의 산업연관모형 개발』, 산업과학기술연구소.

산업연구원 (1997), 『포항제철의 기업발전사 연구』.

서갑경 (1997), 『철강왕 박태준 경영이야기』, 윤동진 옮김, 한언출판사

서울대 사회과학 연구소 (1987), 『포항종합제철의 국민경제 기여 및 기업문화 연구』, 서울대 사회과학연구소.

서울대 사회과학 연구소 (1991), 『포항종합제철의 기업이념과 기업문화에 관한 연구』, 서울대 사회과학연구소.

서정헌 (1991), 『포항제철 산업연관모형(II)의 개발: 공급측면 산업연관모형을 중심으로』, 산업과학기술연구소.

송복 (2012a), "특수성으로서의 태준이즘 연구," 『태준이즘』, 아시아 출판사

송복 (2012b), "선비의 전형 박태준의 선비사상," 『박태준 사상 미래를 열다』, 아시아 출판사

신태영 (2004). 『연구개발투자의 경제성장에 대한 기여도』, 정책자료2004-03, 과학기술정책연구원.

안상훈, 김기호 (2005). "시장구조와 생산성: 한국 제조업 미시자료의 분석을 중심으로," 『금융경제연구』, 제233호, 한국은행 금융경제연구원.

이대환 (2004), 『세계최고의 철강인 박태준』, 현암사.

이도화·김창호 (2012), "CEO 리더십과 작업장 혁신: 포스코 자주관리 QSS 사례," 『박태준의 리더십』, 아시아 출판사

이명식 (2012), "산업재 시장에서 최고경영자의 리더십이 시장 지향성과 경영 성과에 미친 영향: 콘저-케눈고 모델을 중심으로," 『박태준의 리더십』, 아시아 출판사

이상오 (2012), "청암 박태준의 교육 리더십 연구," 『박태준의 리더십』, 아시아 출판사

이용갑 (2012), "최고경영자의 복지사상과 기업복지 발전: 포스코의 기업복지 발전에 대한 연구," 『태준이즘』, 아시아 출판사

임경순 (2010), "박태준과 과학기술", 『과학기술연구』 10권 2호

임응순 (2010), "국내 철강산업의 경제적 파급효과," 『POSRI 경영연구』 제 10권 제 2호

전상인 (2012), "박태준과 지방, 기업, 도시: 포철과 포항의 병존과 융합," 『태준이즘』, 아시아 출판사

전상인 (2013), "박태준 영웅론: 제철입국의 근대 정치사상," 『박태준 사상 미래를 열다』, 아시아 출판사

정군오·임응순 (2008), "한국 철강산업의 국민경제적 파급효과 분석," 『한국산학기술학회 논문지』 제 9집, 제 3호, 831 839.

조정호·최수형 (1998), "최고경영자의 리더쉽유형이 정보기술의 성과에 미치는 영향에 관한 실증연구," 『산업경제연구』 3권, 239 252.

중화학공업추진위원회 기획단 (1973). 중화학공업육성계획.

중화학공업추진위원회 기획단 (1979). 중화학공업추진형황.

최동주 (2012), "어록의 내용 분석을 통한 청암 박태준의 가치 체계 연구: 허만의 리더십 특성 연구 방법을 중심으로," 『태준이즘』, 서울: 아시아 출판사.

최동용 (2007), "철강산업의 산업연관효과 분석," 『POSRI 경영연구』 제 7권 제 1호

최진덕 (2013), "우리 현대사의 비극과 박태준의 결사적인 조국애," 『박태준 사상 미래를 열다』, 아시아 출판사.

최진덕·김형효, (2012), "국가와 기업을 위한 순교자적 사명감: 박태준에 대한 정신사적 반성과 존재론적 성찰," 『박태준의 정신세계』, 서울: 아시아 출판사.

포스코, (2004), 『포스코 35년사』, 포스코.

포스코 (2009), 『포스코 40년사』, 포스코.

한재호·성덕현·김윤호, (1988), 『포스코와 국가산업경제의 연관성 및 기여도 분석』 산업과학기술연구소.

교육인적자원부 한국교육개발원 (2008). 『2007년 간추린 교육통계』.

통계청 (1995). 통계로 본 한국의 발자취.

한국경제60년사 편찬위원회 (2011). 한국경제60년사.

한국무역협회 국제무역연구원 (2010). 주요 무역동향지표.

한국은행 (2015), 경제통계시스템, http://ecos.bok.or.kr/ .

한국철강신문 편찬위원회 (1996), 기초철강지식, 한국철강신문

허남정 (2013), 『박태준 리더십에 대한 재고찰: 일본 문화적 속성의 발현과 그 변용』, 한양대학교 국제대학원 박사학위 논문.

Allen, K.E., Bordas J., Hickman G., Matusak L.R., Sorenson G., and Witmire K. (2006), *Leadership in the Twenty-First Century.*

Barro, R.J., and J.W. Lee (1993), "International comparisons of educational attainment," *Journal of Monetary Economics* 32, 363~394.

Barro, R.J., and J.W. Lee (1996), "International measures of schooling years and schooling quality," *American Economic Review* 86, 218~223.

Barro, R.J., and J.W. Lee (2001), "International data on educational attainment: updates and implications," *Oxford Economic Papers* 53(3).

Barro, R.J., and J.W. Lee (2013). A New Data Set of Educational Attainment in the World, 1950-2010," *Journal of Development Economics* 104, 184~198.

Bass, Bernard M. (1985), "Leadership: Good, Better, Best," *Leadership and Performance Beyond Expectations,* The Free Press.

Borenzenstein E., De Gregorio and J. W. Lee (1998). How Does Foreign Direct Investment Affect Growth?, *Journal of International Economics,* Vol

45, pp 115~35

Bruns, J. M. (1978), Leadership, New York: Harper & Row.

Burket, C.S., K.C. Stagl, C. Klein, G.F. Goodwin, E. Salas, and S.M. Halpin (2006), "What type of leadership behaviors are functional in teams? a meta-analysis," *The Leadership Quarterly* 17, 288 307.

Bycio, P., R.D. Hackett, and J.S. Allen (1995), "Further Assessments of Bass's (1985) Conceptualization of Transactional and Transformational Leadership," *Journal of Applied Psychology* V.80, No. 4, 468 478.

Coe and Helpman, (1995). International R&D Spillovers, *European Economic Review* 39 No.5, 859-887.

Collier, P., and D. Dollar (2001). *Can the world cut poverty in half? How Policy reform and international aid can meet international development goals,* World Development.

Davila, T. Epstein, M. & Shelton, R., 2006, *Making innovation work,* Wharton School Publishing.

Deininger and Squire (1996). "A New Data Set Measuring Income Inequality," *World Bank Economic Review,* Vol. 10. No.3.

Easterly, W. (2005). "National Policies and Economic Growth: A Reappraisal," *Handbook of Economic Growth,* edition 1, volume 1, 1015~1059.

Frankel, J. A., and D. Romer, (1999), "Does Trade Cause Growth?" *American Economic Review* 89(3), 379~399.

Grossman, G. M. and Helpman, E. (1991) Endogenous Product Cycles, *Economic Journal* Vol.101.

Hauseman, R., and D. Rodrik (2002). "Economic development as self-discovery," NBER Working paper No. 8952.

Hermann, M.G. (2003), "Assessing Leadership Style: Trait Analysis in Post", J.M., *The Psychological Assessment of Political Leaders: With Profiles of Saddam Hussein and Bill Clinton,* University of Michigan Press.

Im, G.S. (1999), "The Birth of the Postech: The Building of a Research University in Korea," in Kim, Yung sik and Bray, Francesca eds., *Current Perspectives in the History of Science in East Asia,* 238-242, Seoul: Seoul

National University.

Kelley, T. (2001), *The art of innovation,* Currency Doubleday.

Kim, Chulsu, (2005). "Chapter 73 Korea," The World Trade Organization: Legal, Economic and Political Analysis.

Krugman, Paul (1994). The Myth of Asia's Miracle, Foreign Affairs.

McKern, B., and R. Malan (1992), POSCO's Strategy in the Development of Korea, Stanford Business School Case, 1992

Mukand, S., and D. Rodrik (2005). "In search of the Holy Grail: Policy convergence, experimentation, and economic performance," *American Economic Review* 95, 374-383.

OECD (1999). *Trade, Investment and Development*

Frankel and Romer (1999) "Does Trade Cause Growth?", *The American Economic Review,* 89(3), pp. 379~399.

Rodrik, D. (1996). "Understanding economic policy reform," *Journal of Economic Literature* 34, 9-41.

Rodrik, D. (2003). "Growth Strategies", NBER Working Paper No. 10050

Stern, N. (2001). "A Strategy for development," ABCDE Keynote Address, Washington DC, World Bank

Stimson, R.J., R.R. Stough, and M. Salazar, (2005), "Leadership and institutional factors in endogenous regional economic development," *Investigaciones Regionales* Vol. 7, 23~52.

Stogdill, R.M. (1974), *Handbook of Leadership,* New York: Press.

Williamson, J. (1990), "What Washington means by policy reform, Latin American Adjustment: How much has happened? *Institute for International Economics,* Washington.

World Bank (1993), "The East Asian Miracles: Economic Growth and Public Policy" *A world Bank Policy Research Report,* Oxford University Press.

World Bank (2001), *Global Development Finance.*

World Steel (2014), *Crude Steel Production Statistics*

A Study on the Role of TJP
Leadership in the Korea Economic
Development and Application to the
Developing Economies

Dong Heon Kim

Dong Heon Kim

Education
BA in Economics, Korea University
MA in Economics, Graduate School of Korea University
Ph.D. in Economics, University of California San Diego, U.S.A.

Professional experience
Assistant and Associate Professor, University of Manchester, U.K.
Visiting Professor, University of California San Diego, U.S.A.
Team leader and Member, Evaluation Committee for the Presidents of governmental institutes, Mistery of Strategy and Finance, South Korea
Professor, Department of Economics, Korea University

Main articles
"A Re-examination of the Predictability of Economic Activity Using the Yield Spread" (JMCB, 2002)
"Nonlinearity in the Fed's Monetary Policy Rule" (JAE, 2005)
"The New Keynesian Phillips Curve: from Sticky Inflation to Sticky Prices" (JMCB, 2008)
"Observed Inflation Forecasts and the New Keynesian Phillips Curve" (OBES, 2008)
"What is an oil shock? Panel Data Evidence" (EE, 2012)
"The Evolution of Monetary Policy Regimes in the U.S." (EE, 2012)
「The Analysis of daily Korea call rate」 (2008), 「The role of money in the monetary policy rule」 (2010), 「The Study on the Effect of the Change in USA Financial Conditions on the Korea Financial Markets: FCI Analysis」 (2013), 「Does the Aging Labor Force Reduce Labor Productivity?: In case of Korea Economy」 (2014), 「A Study on the Framework of Macroprudential Policy Instruments and It's Application Method」 (2014)

Contents

Table Contents

Figure Contents

Summary

Korea, once one of the poorest countries in the world, has successfully achieved industrialization and economic liberalization despite lack of special natural resources and industry infra. Nowadays, Korea economy volume ranked 12th and trade volume 9th in the world in 2011 and its economic growth has been evaluated as the unique case of economic development in the world economy history. Since Korea war in 1950, what have been the key factors for such a successful economic growth about annual 4.5% over 60 years? Especially, the Pohang Steel Company (renamed as POSCO in 2002) founded in 1968 under the strong support of the President Jung-Hee Park government, has played an important role in heavy and chemistry industrialization by providing domestic manufacturing sector with cheap but high quality steel products, strengthening the international competitiveness of ship, automobile, machine, electronics and construction industries, and establishing the foothold for these industries growth. Needless to say, the history of POSCO development runs parallel with the history of Korea economic development.

The success of POSCO could be attributable to the effort at the firm level and the support from Korea government, however, more substantial factor of its success lies in the leadership of the founder and the first president Tae-Joon Park (hereafter TJP). From the founding period, TJP had undertaken the first president leadership of the POSCO and completed the 1-4 Pohang steel factories and 1-4 Gwangyang steel factories by 1992. The annual production significantly increased up to 20.5 million ton, which enabled POSCO to become the third greatest steel company in the world in 1992. Moreover, TJP achieved great management performance such as annual average 34% of sale growth, 71.3% of net profit growth, raising the ratio of POSCO production to Korea GDP up to 2.3% over his term. The productivity growth based on per capita crude steel production was 15% of annual average and the ratio of the POSCO steel production to all domestic steel production was 71.3% and the ratio of the domestic production equipments in the POSCO was 63.1% in 1992.

As the status of Korea in world economy has been constantly improved due to the successful economic growth, the current world economy calls for bigger contribution from Korea. In the perspective of developing countries, what are the most necessary needs that could be deduced from the precedent of Korea's successful economic growth? The starting point is the learning of the useful strategies in order to build the industrial infra that plays an important role at the initial stage of economic development and foster a world-class firm. From this point of view, how did Korea economy build the industrial infra and foster several world-class companies such as POSCO, Samsung Electronics, and Hyundai motor company?

The purpose of this research is to develop a POSCO-type growth model by deeply analyzing the background of Korea's high and rapid economic growth and the role of the POSCO as the key growth engine and to seek applicable plans for Asian developing countries, such as Vietnam and India, to use as important strategies for their own economic development. Especially, we try to deeply investigate the contributions of the POSCO in Korea economic development, which have been the foundation for the establishment of Korea key industries, and thoroughly examine what are the key factors of TJP leadership that greatly contributed to world-class POSCO and how these factors worked in order to lead Korea economic development. Furthermore, we try to standardize a POSCO-type growth model with focusing on the TJP leadership and developing an application plan useful in providing efficient economic development strategy for developing countries actively seeking for efficient economic growth model such as the case of Korea economy.

The key factors of Korea economic growth can be summarized as four aspects. First of all, Korea economy has pursued the substantial growth of manufacturing sector and flexible foreign trade policy. Secondly, Korea government has showed strong leadership in establishing and propelling the economic development strategies. Thirdly, Korea economy has smoothly rooted the market economy system and continuously fulfilled the efficient resource allocations. Fourthly, Korea economy constructed a positive relationship between education and economy, based on the strong education spirit, to accumulate optimal human capital and achieve high and sustainable economic growth by enhancing productivity through technology developments and management innovations. Among above four key factors, two most important factors are the government strong leadership and human capital.

How did the POSCO contribute to the development of Korea economy in terms of above key four factors? First of all, the POSCO has played an important role in leading the heavy-chemical industrialization and the growth and manufacturing sectors through the industrial development. The steel is the seed of industrialization and the steel industry is a large equipment industry, and thus the industrial relation effect tends to be very high because the steel industry demands a lot of goods of other industries and provides the steel products serving as intermediate goods for other main industries. As a result of empirical study on the analysis of the front-back industrial effect, the POSCO ranked as the top or the second top and this result implies that the POSCO made a significant contribution to Korea industrialization and the growth of manufacturing sector.

Secondly, the POSCO contributed to the government-leading industrialization through a market-oriented national firm. In the initial stage of the economic development, the capital accumulation tends to be poor and the social infra is weak, which makes it almost impossible for the private sector to lead effective economic growth. In order to realize the mission of Korea government under this situation, the POSCO took the leading role in the government-leading industrialization with the economic philosophy of "Jae-Cheol-Bo-Gook" and the frontier of the heavy-chemical industrialization. It faithfully fulfilled the role of the market-oriented national firm which pursued strong international competitiveness in order to be a world-class steel company.

Thirdly, the POSCO has made a significant commitment to the enhancement of national productivity and the accumulation of human capital through technology development, R&D investment, industry-academic cooperation and firm welfare. According to the TJP's mission of the POSCO, the envision of the "Jae-Cheol-Bo-Gook" and the education patriotism which indicates that the POSCO should develop human resources so as to lead national future industries, the POSCO has tried to achieve national industrialization and create the positive external effect with technology development and innovation, R&D investment, industry-academic cooperation, the training of field workers, the field innovation via company-wide own management, the positive relationship between the development of firm welfare and the surplus management, and the learning and the dissemination of the POSCO's success. Consequently, all such actions have been dedicated to the enhancement of national productivity and the accumulation of human capital and thus the POSCO has contributed to the Korea economic growth.

As a result of the empirical analysis on the relationship between the success of the POSCO and Korea economic growth, we found that the sale growth of the POSCO had a positive impact on the growth of manufacturing sector. Especially, the growth of manufacturing sector was significantly higher in the expansion year of the POSCO's steel factory than other years. In addition, the growth of the POSCO's productivity had a positive impact on the growth of Korea national productivity with 3 years lags.

What are the key factors of the POSCO's success as the

exemplary firm case that reflects the frontier of Korea economic growth? Myriads of existing literature emphasize the TJP leadership as a key factor for the success of the POSCO. Based on the mechanism: initiative TJP leadership ⇒ the success of the POSCO ⇒ Korea economic growth, this study considers all characteristics of TJP leadership and tries to analyze the key factors which have made a critical contribution to Korea economic growth.

First of all, TJP has made a contribution to significant growth of manufacturing sector and rapid Korea industrialization by the Taejoonism and the realization of the "Jae-Cheol-Bo-Gook." TJP thought that the national prosperity and military power is the way to overcome the Korea tragic modern history and can be accomplished by the industrialization and has shown faithful leadership with all his soul might, and his life-time commitment in order to foster the steel industry, the seed of industrialization. TJP has kept his own confidence, integrity, no self-interest, and no limit for absolute impossibility which encouraged POSCO to overcome all interruptions and obstacles, has tried to build the POSCO with undying patriotism and sacrifice of martyr and has led to the development of the POSCO with the "management by great spirit." The comprehensive synthesis system of the TJP leadership which committed to Korea economic growth by placing POSCO at world-class level with great achievement is termed "Taejoonism." It served as overall spiritual engine of the "Jae-Cheol-Bo-Gook."

Secondly, TJP has committed to the flexible foreign trade policy throughout the pursuit of world-class POSCO. TJP has felt that the mission of the POSCO for Korea would be the realization of the "Jae-Cheol-Bo-Gook" and dreamed of POSCO at world-cass level. In order to achieve the mission, TJP has tried to accomplish global competitiveness of the POSCO and for this end, he has put efforts in the reduction of production costs, the improvement of product quality, the efficient management, and technology development for sustainable growth of the POSCO. The initiative TJP leadership for the realization of the world-class POSCO has been important contribution for Korea government to lead the growth policy of foreign trade-oriented exports with POSCO's frontier role in the exports policy.

Thirdly, TJP has played an important role in achieving Korea government-leading economic development through the pursuit of the market-oriented national firm. TJP has shared the important mission of the POSCO for Korea economy with all workers at the beginning of the POSCO and has tried to fulfill the responsibility as the national firm which should lead to the growth of manufacturing sector and national industrialization. In addition, TJP has focused on the reduction of production costs and the improvement of product quality in order to enhance the international competitiveness and has pursued the market-oriented management such as a one-step ahead introduction of new technology, R&D, expansion of science and technology and industry-academic cooperation. All these activities (have made the POSCO play a key firm role in the heavy-chemistry industrialization and in the government-leading industrialization in the domestic context, and a leading role in the realization of Korea development strategy by pursuing the government-leading foreign trade exports policy in the international context.)

Fourthly, TJP has contributed to the enhancement of productivity and the accumulation of human capital through technology innovation, management innovation, educational patriotism and the pursuit of advanced firm culture. TJP has realized the necessity of education for industrialization and national development and has respected the educational patriotism. TJP has tried to do his best on (in) training of industrial workers and the education of high-brain manpower through the training of field workers and the establishment of the industry-academic research cooperation system. TJP has continuously enhanced the POSCO's productivity and thus contributed to the enhancement of national productivity through technology development and innovation, management innovation, self-management and field innovation, and advanced firm welfare. The empirical analysis has shown that TJP's suggestive leadership for management has had a positive impact on the POSCO's performance and productivity.

As a result of main causality analysis between TJP leadership, the success of the POSCO, and Korea economic development, this study suggests following points for the application of developing countries. First of all, it is the learning of the POSCO-type growth model. The key aspects of the POSCO-type growth model are ① to pursue the government-leading economic development based on the establishment of the market-oriented national firm, ② to foster a world-class national firm which can lead the strategy of foreign trade policy for economic development, ③ to promote a leading firm which can be a foundation for national industrialization and modernization, ④ to pursue continuous efforts on the productivity improvement and the accumulation of human capital such as technology innovation, management innovation, R&D, and industry-academic cooperation, and ⑤ to foster a CEO who pursues undying patriotism, market-oriented and rational attitude and management by great spirit.

Secondly, the POSCO should build the center for TJP leadership in order to pursue the learning, education and research for leadership development and to cultivate the potential leaders in the developing countries and to host the training session for them. In addition, the POSCO has to contribute to the fostering potential leaders by providing the scholarship and the research funds for developing countries and has to run a leadership program for the policymakers of developing countries. Furthermore, the POSCO has to develop a program to take social responsibility and support the corporate philanthropic activity for the developing countries and provide active supports for the management of TJP leadership program.

Thirdly, the government of the developing countries has to develop a cooperative program with the POSCO and plan a training program for the learning of TJP leadership, POSCO's management, and POSCO's firm culture. In addition, the government has to host a leadership program supported by the POSCO, scholarship, and the research funds in order to raise their potential prospective leaders and build a systematic cooperative relationship with the Korea government and the POSCO.

The purpose of this study is to contribute to the establishment and the pursuit of the economic development strategy for the developing countries by effectively providing the key factors of TJP leadership for developing countries. In addition, we hope that this study is utilized as the important reference for integrating the growth models of the newly re-leaping POSCO into the long-term plan of Korea economy, and for maintaining the sustainable relationship between the POSCO and the long-term development of Korea economy.

I. Aim of the Research

Korea has tried to achieve industrialization and economic liberalization although Korea did not have special natural resources and sufficient industry infra, and Korea was one of the poorest countries in the world. Nowadays, the Korea economic growth is evaluated as the unique case of economic development in the world economy history. The background for having the successful economic development within 60 years of such a short periods right after the Korean War in 1960s are to choose the strategy of the exports-leading and foreign trade-oriented industrial development based on the world trade environment which was neighbourly to the trade of the developing countries, to build key industries such as steel and ship industries at initial stage of economic development in a proper time, to accumulate the plentiful human capital via the building of educational infra, and to pursue adequate and active economic policy by Korea government according to the stage of economic development.

Especially, the Pohang Steel Company (renamed as the POSCO in 2002) which was founded in 1968 under the strong support of the President Jung-Hee Park government, has played an important role in the Korea economic growth since 1970 by providing cheap but high quality steel products for domestic manufacturing sector, strengthening the international competitiveness of ship, automobile, machine, electronics and construction industries and establishing the foothold of these industries growth. Needless to say, the history of POSCO development can run all the way to the history of Korea economic development (Kim and Choi 2011). In 2012, the world market share of the POSCO's product is 2.6% and the steel production is 39.9 million tons and the POSCO ranks at 5th world steel company. The steel industry is a capital intensive equipment industry and a national key industry with high economies of scale and supplies fundamental materials for main industries (Choi 2007). Since the initial stage of Korea economic development, the successive establishment of the POSCO and the development of world competitive steel industry have been main factors for leading the Korea economic growth (Kwak et al. 1992, Kim et al. 1998).

What are main reasons for making the miracle of the POSCO and consequently for cultivating Korea economic development? In terms of the growth history of the firms and the theory of national development, the effort of the POSCO at the firm level and the role of Korea government have seemed to make a successful case (Rhyu 2001) but more substantial reason for the success of the POSCO is absolutely the role of the founder TJP. TJP has focused on the development of human resources from the initial stage of the steelwork construction, has been eager to realize the "Jae-Cheol-Bo-Gook", constantly cooperating with workers at the construction site and has greatly contributed to construction of Pohang steel mill with the support of Japanese capital and technology. Then, he has played an important role in achieving the legendary development of the POSCO and establishing the POSCO's unique firm culture which shows strong citizenship. Consequently, as the frontier, TJP leadership has resulted in the legendary success of the POSCO and the success has been the corner stone for fostering the world class steel industry, we can infer that the TJP leadership has played an important role in leading Korea economic growth.

Nowadays, as the result of high economic growth, the status of the Korea economy becomes bigger and bigger in the world economy and the world society needs more contributions of Korea economy. According to this need, the Korea government continuously tries to do its best for supporting Korea's key role in the world society and especially, the Korea hosted G20 summit for the first time as a developing country. From this point of view, as the practical way to reinforce the status of Korea economy in the world economy, the establishment of the Korea economic growth model and its application plan to transmit to the developing countries with intensive economic development, are more magnified than before.

In terms of developing countries, what are most necessary needs from the experience of Korea successful economic growth? The starting point for this question is the learning of the strategy which is useful in order to build the industrial infra that plays an important role at the initial stage of economic development and the establishment of the world competitive firm. From this point of view, how Korea economy has built the industrial infra and has fostered several world-class companies such as POSCO, Samsung Electronics, and Hyundai motor company?

The purpose of this research is to develop a POSCO-type growth model by deeply analyzing the background of Korea high and rapid economic growth and the role of the POSCO as the key growth engine and to seek an application plan which Asian developing countries such as Vietnam and India can use as an important strategy in pursuing their own economic development. Especially, we try to deeply investigate the contributions of the POSCO for Korea economic development which have been the foundation for the establishment of Korea key industries and thoroughly examine what are key factors of TJP leadership which have been great contributions for the world-class POSCO and how these factors have worked in order to lead Korea economic development. furthermore, we try to standardize a POSCO-type growth model with focusing on the TJP leadership and develop an application plan which is useful for providing efficient economic development strategy for developing countries who are actively seeking efficient economic growth such as the case of Korea economy.

The expected outcomes of this study could be summarized into two points. First of all, it is to develop a POSCO-type growth model by deeply analyzing the role of the POSCO in the Korea economic development and the TJP leadership which has played a key role in establishing the world class POSCO. Secondly, it is to contribute to the economic development in the developing countries by effectively transmitting the model and supporting the establishment of economic development strategy. Furthermore, it is to set up a base for the sustainable Korea economic growth by encouraging the economic cooperation between Korea and the developing countries. We hope that this study is useful for integrating the growth model of the newly re-leaping POSCO into the long-term plan of Korea economy and for keeping the sustainable relationship between the POSCO and the long-term development of Korea economy.

II. Contents and Scope of this Research

This research is divided into three main parts. First of all, it is to analyze the key growth engine for Korea economic development and examine the role of the POSCO as an icon of the Korea steel industry. (For doing this analysis, we try to re-evaluate whether the success of the POSCO was critical for Korea economic development by addressing a causal relationship between the growth history of the POSCO and Korea economic development in terms of the empirical study.)

Secondly, we examine the reasons of the POSCO's success and the role of TJP leadership. As we infer hypothetically that TJP has shown strong leadership as the first president of the POSCO with all his soul and might from 1968 when the POSCO was founded to 1992 and consequently this leadership has led the success of the POSCO and Korea economic growth, we try to investigate what are the key characteristics of TJP leadership and how this leadership has contributed to the development of the POSCO by using a bibliographical aspect and econometrics method. By means of this research process, we will eventually show directly and indirectly that TJP leadership indeed played an important role in the Korea economic development.

Thirdly, based on research results above, which are supposed to show the important role of TJP leadership in the Korea economic growth via the legendary success of the POSCO, we outline a POSCO-type growth model and find out the role of the POSCO and the government of developing countries in order to apply the growth model to the economic development of developing countries. By means of this process, we will disseminate the core factors of TJP leadership and eventually do deep research on the plan by which the developing country cultivates a TJP-type leader systematically.

1. Korea economic growth and the role of the POSCO

Korea economy has made an economic miracle as a unique case in the world economy over 40 years although Korea did not have sufficient natural resources but has experienced Japanese colony and the Korea war. Despite insufficient natural resource and history of Japanese colony and Korean War, Korea gained its independency from Japan at the end of the Second World War but immediately experienced national division. Then, the Korea faced Korea war with the fight each other among Korean people over 1950-1953. Since the stopfire agreement, Korea was one of the poorest agricultural countries in the world with recovering from the war. However, Korea pushed forward the first historical 5-year plan for the economic development in 1962 and achieved the compact industrialization with pursuing consistently foreign trade policy. That is, As Korea coped with the change in the foreign trade environment quickly and has integrated the exports-leading economic development strategy into the foreign trade policy in order to make a mutual ascent effect, Korea has been a star country which the World bank called as an East Asian Economic Miracle (World Bank 1996). As a result, Korean changed from one of poorest countries in 40 years before to the top 13 in the economy volume and the top 10 at the trade volume in the world economy.

In this chapter, we try to evaluate the policy of Korea economic development and its outcome over 40 years which made the history of miracle in terms of neoclassical and endogenous growth theory and address the key driving forces for Korea economic growth.

In addition, we analyze the role of the POSCO in terms of growth model above driven for Korea economic growth. It is examined how the world class firm led national economic growth in terms of the growth theory and whether in fact, the POSCO made a successful role suggested in the growth theory. In order to investigate the contribution of the POSCO for Korea economic development, we are planning to secure quantitative evidence by using a regression analysis and a counterfactual analysis. We will eventually derive a firm-type growth model for Korea economic growth by deeply shedding light on the role of the POSCO for Korea economic development in terms of academic aspect.

2. The success of the POSCO and TJP leadership

The POSCO established in 1968 has become a national key industry and played a key role in fostering the heavy-chemistry industry in 1970s. The POSCO has stood on tiptoe to the world steel company in late 1990s by the continuous realization of equipment efficiency and the productivity improvement. Nowadays, the POSCO dreams the top world-class company by establishing the technology leadership and the POSCO's own culture. The critical contribution for making the world-class POSCO is the TJP leadership (Baik et al. 2012, Kim et al. 2012, Bae et al. 2012).

In this chapter, we try to investigate how the TJP leadership worked resulting in the growth of the POSCO in terms of bibliographical aspect and find out the quantitative implications by using the regression analysis and the counterfactual analysis more rigorously. For doing this end, we try to produce an index quantifying the TJP leadership and use it in order to analyze the level of contribution to the success of the POSCO.

3. TJP leadership and application plan of the POSCO-type growth model to the development of developing countries

If the TJP leadership had greatly contributed to the success of the POSCO and the success of the POSCO had played an important role in the Korea economic growth, then we can eventually infer that the TJP leadership deeply contributed to

Korea economic growth. In order to materialize this inference, it is necessary to build A POSCO-type growth model. Especially, we examine key elements which are necessary for establishing the economic development strategies of the developing countries with summarizing unique components of the POSCO-type growth model.

The ultimate goal of this research is to find a useful plan in establishing the economic development strategies of the developing countries by utilizing the POSCO-type growth model. For this end, we try to look for the role of the POSCO, Korea government, and the government of the developing countries.

The POSCO has a chance to review their economic cooperative plans with the developing and developed countries and plan their second takeoff with considering the result of this research. Furthermore, the POSCO tries to find new strategies of their growth which can lead the sustainable Korea economic growth.

III. Korea Economic Growth and the Role of the POSCO

Right after the Korea War, the Korea was one of the poorest countries in the world. However, as the Korea started the first 5-year economic development plan in 1962, the Korea pursued the government-leading foreign trade policy and the industrialization strategy through the establishment of heavy-chemistry industries and accumulated human capital based on strong education spirit. As a result, the Korea economy became 13th at the economy volume in the world economy. Korea became one of East Asian Four tigers (Hong Kong, Singapore, Taiwan) and emerged as a star country making the miracle of the world economic growth and was evaluated as the exemplary model for the economic growth of the developing countries.

In this chapter, we try to outline the stylized facts for the countries which experienced high economic growth and, in the similar context, we derive key factors for Korea economic growth. Then, we address the key role of the POSCO in the Korea economic development as we examine how the POSCO contributed to the key factors for Korea economic growth. Especially, we provide quantitative evidence for the role of the POSCO by the econometric empirical analysis.

1. Stylized facts for high economic growth countries

A lot of existing literature about the reasons of economic growth point out the economic policy such as a tax policy as one of main factors to affect the long-term economic growth (Kim et al. 2011). Collier and Dollar (2001) show that the reform of economic policy reduces the national poverty ratio substantially and Easterly (2005) shows theoretically that the change in the economic policy centering in the tax policy has a significant impact on economic growth. Kim et al. (2011) suggest that the change in the government economic policy has a great impact on economic growth by using the neoclassical exogenous growth model. Thus, above literature implies that the proper change in the government policy according to the stage of economic development can be important for the sustainable economic growth.

From this point of view, what are stylized facts that are

observed on the way changing from the low-income economy to the high-income economy according to the stage of economic development? Following Rodrik (2003), Kim et al. (2011) analyze the experiences of the economic growth policy for main countries over the past 40 years and examine the most adequate strategy for the economic growth in terms of the policymakers. According to Rodrik (2003), the economic development policy since 1950 has been developed as follows: the import-substituting industrial policy in 1950s-1960s, the strong foreign trade policy focused on the market-oriented policy in 1970s, the Washington Agreement called by Williamson (1990) for the optimal policy framework in 1980s, and the Washington Agreement and the institutional arrangement which supplements the governance of the government and the firms in 1990s.

However, the economic growth policy of the East Asian countries which have pursued the consistent economic policy and achieved high economic growth is not necessary consistent with the Washington Agreement and the cases of China, India, South American countries, and African countries imply that the reform of institution and policy does necessarily not result in the economic growth. From this point of view, there might not be a unique successive strategy for economic growth which can commonly be applied to all countries. That is, there might not exist a unique optimal way for the developing countries to establish and conduct the economic development policy and various policies are possible depending on the political, economical, and social environment of each country.

Nevertheless, Kim et al. (2011) summarize the stylized facts observed in the countries which experienced high economic growth over past 40 years as four aspects. First of all, a partial reform but not total reform is a starting point for high economic growth. For example, in Korea, the initiation for the 7% of annual average growth rate from 0.6% in pre-1962, was the depreciation of the exchange rate and the increase in the interest rate along with a strong government will for the priority of economic growth policy. This case suggests that the economic development in the developing countries may be initiated by not entire institutional reform but a little scope of reform in institution and policy under the governmental obvious target for economic growth.

Secondly, the reform in policy and institution related with high economic growth is fulfilled with the incorporation of the orthodox factors with the non-orthodox components. It is not possible to have high economic growth without the arrangement of the minimum conditions of economic growth for the orthodox factors such as property right, incentive for market-orientation, management for stable price and fiscal stability. However, the good arrangement for the orthodox factors do not necessarily bring about high economic growth but the non-orthodox components which are deviated from Washington Agreement, such as the financial regulation system, selective export-subsidy policy, and industrial policy, can make a main contribution to high economic growth.

Thirdly, the policy package related to high economic growth is quite different according to each country. For example, the protectionism of Korea and Taiwan is contrast to the free trade of Singapore and even in the inside of the protectionism of Korea and Taiwan, the different policy such as credit supply and tax benefits has been conducted. This implies that the simple and mechanical imitation for the countries which accomplished the successful economic growth can end up with the failure of economic policy.

Fourthly, the sustainable economic growth is far more difficult than just start of economic growth and requires broader institutional reform. Except several East Asian countries such as South Korea, Hong Kong, Singapore, and Taiwan, it was seldom for the countries to experience the sustainable economic growth and then enter to the group of the developed countries. That is, the countries accomplished high economic growth for a time being but most of them lost the driving forces for economic growth soon and experienced the reduction in economic growth. This implies that the temporally short-and medium-term increase in economic growth rate did not always connect to the long-term stable economic growth and ,eventually in order to have sustainable economic growth, the support of active production with reinforcing the institutional aspects of the market system from the initial reform stage and the organization of the institution which can support the flexible response to the external shocks, are very important.

2. The Korea growth model

1) The growth and status of Korea economy

The Korea yearly GDP was 27,000 billion KRW (Korea Won, 2010 base-year price), in 1960, 68,000 billion KRW in 1970, 163,000 billion KRW in 1980, 420,000 billion KRW in 1990, 821,000 billion KRW, 1,265,000 billion KRW in 2010 and since late 1960, the Korea economy experienced the rapid and sustainable economic growth. The annual average of economic growth was 8.72% in 1960s, 9.37% in 1970s, 7.77% in 1980s, 6.14% in 1990s, and 3.67% in 2000s and thus showed the above 6% of annual average growth rate without significant up and down over 40 years except the first oil shock period in 1970s and the Asian financial crisis in 1997-1998 and thus accomplished the incredible economic growth. Korea economy, however, recently faced the significant reduction in economic growth due to the low-birth fertility rate and the aging society.

The annual average growth rate of the per capita GDP in 1960-2000 was above 4.5% for Korea while the growth rates were 2.3% for developing countries and 2.7% for the developed countries. The experience of Korea economic growth amounts to the miracle of economic growth in terms of the history of the world economy. In 2012, the Korea economy volume ranked at the 12th and the trade volume was at the 9th in the world.

[Figure 1] Korea Annual Real GDP trend

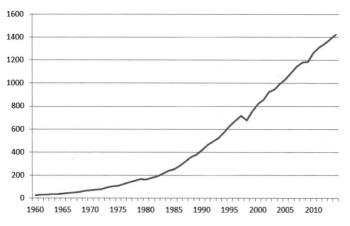

Data : Bank of Korea (2015)

[Figure 2] Korea Annual growth of Real GDP

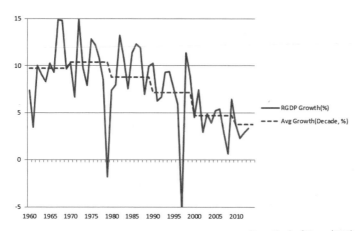

Data : Bank of Korea (2015)

Korea's status upgraded to a higher level as one of G20 member countries and OECD member countries. If so, what are the key factors to initiate high and rapid Korea economic growth over 40 years as the example of the world economy history? There have been various studies on the reasons of Korea economic growth and we summarize key factors focusing on the explanations provided in Kim et al. (2011).[1]

2) Key factors for Korea economic growth

Kim et al. (2011) summarize the key factors for Korea economic growth based on the materialization of Korea economic growth model as four aspects: ① the growth of manufacturing sector and the foreign trade policy, ② the strong government leadership, ③ the market economy system and the efficient resource allocations, and ④ the accumulation of human capital and high productivity. Although there have been other factors for explaining Korea economic growth, we may summarize all factors as above four key factors when considering all together.

---

[1] The studies on key factors for rapid Korea economic growth include Kang et al.(2008), Kim and Park (1979), Kim (1999), Park (1999, 2001), Bae (2008), Byun(2012) etc.

A. The growth of manufacturing sector and

foreign trade policy

In the center of Korea high economic growth there have been definitely the growth of manufacturing sector and related exports-leading industrial policy. [Table 1] shows the annual growth rate of industry sector according to the change in industry structure. The growth of manufacturing sector based on the heavy-chemistry industries led Korea economic growth from 1960s to 1990s. The Korea government has tried to pursue active industrial policy centering the manufacturing sector in order to effectively establish the optimal structure of industry according to the stage of economic development. The annual average growth rate of manufacturing sector was far higher than the growth rate of GDP and thus led overall national economic growth. According to the stage of economic development, we briefly summarize the growth process of manufacturing sector as follows.

The manufacturing sector was very poor in 1950s because main facilities of the manufacturing sector were located in the north of the Korea peninsular and a lot of facilities had been ruined during the 3-years Korea War. Hence, there had been a little weak foundation of the manufacturing sector for production facilities as the type of the imports-substituting industry by the national demand for necessaries and the economic aid of the U.S.A. was the main sources for the background for this industry. The Korea government has tried to ignite the embers of the growth by the beneficiary national supports and the low-age labor forces to the purpose of fostering the fundamental industry for consumption goods and stabilizing national economy.

[Table 1] Annual growth rate of industry sector according to the change in industry structure

	1953-60	1961-70	1971-80	1981-90	1991-2000	2001-09
Agriculture, Fishery	2.3	4.4	1.6	3.5	1.9	1.8
Mining, Manufacturing	12.1	15.7	14.1	11.4	8.2	5.3
Mining	-	-	4.7	-0.2	-1.3	-0.3
Manufacturing	12.7	16.8	15.8	12.2	8.4	5.4
Light Industry	-	-	12.7	7.0	1.1	-0.6
Heavy and Chemical Industry	-	-	17.2	14.4	9.8	6.6
Electricity, Gas, Water and Construction	9.3	19.2	10.3	10.3	2.7	3.3
Electricity, Gas, Water	-	-	45.8	17.6	10.3	5.8
Construction	-	-	10.1	9.7	1.4	2.6
Services	3.8	8.6	6.8	8.4	6.1	3.6
GDP	3.8	8.4	9.0	9.7	6.5	3.9

Sources : OECD (1998), Kim et al. (2011

However, the imports-substituting industry policy by the support and protection of the Korea government was not successful for leading the effective development of manufacturing sector because there were the uncompetitive seeking self-interests, the intentional monopoly with inefficient resource allocations, the accelerations of imports substitution and the restraints of exports by the under-evaluation of the dollar exchange rate, the cozy relations between politics and business by the beneficial and biased allocations of the aid materials and the loan funds, and the subjection of the economic system depending on foreign aids. At that time, the total ratio of the manufacturing sector was about 10% and the traditional first industry has still dominated the Korea economy.

The Korea government realized the limit of the imports-substituting industry in 1960s and pursued the heavy-chemistry imports-substituting industrialization in order to reduce the demand for intermediate goods of the light industry with the change in the policy stance to the exports-oriented policy of the light industry. The Korea government launched the first 5-year economic development plan in 1962, focused on the establishment of the labor intensive light industry based on the comparative advantage theory and pursued the reinforcement of competitiveness in the world trade market through the increase in exports. In addition, the government actualized the export supporting policy based on the synthesis policy for export promotion which was consisted of the tax supporting, finance supporting, and administration supporting and pursued the economic growth through the improvement of resource allocations by the reform in the foreign exchange system and the achievement of the economy of scale.

The Korea industry had a rapid change in the industrial structure based on the significant growth of the light industry in 1960s and the ratio of manufacturing sector in 1960 increased rapidly from 10.8% in 1960 to 25.25% in 1972 whereas the ratio of agricultural and fishery industry significantly reduced from 41.3% in 1960 to 25.2% in 1972. Thus, the foreign trade industrialization has been a foundation for high economic growth and the seed of the exports-oriented industrialization of the heavy-chemistry by the elimination of the imports-substituting policy of the heavy-chemistry industry. However, the weakness of the exports-oriented policy of the light industry is not to substitute the imports of capital goods and input goods and thus to result in the accumulation of the trade deficit.

The Korea government changed the policy stance for strongly supporting the exports-oriented policy of the heavy-chemistry industrialization in 1973 as the world economy experienced the severe recession due to the oil shock, and the export competitiveness reduced and the weakness of the imports-substituting policy of the heavy-chemistry industry was pointed out in 1970s. The Korea government selected the six strategical industries of steel, chemistry, nonferrous metal, machinery, ship, and electronics and established the strong supporting system for fostering the heavy-chemistry industry. The government legislated the "National Investment Funds Act" in 1973 in order to carry forward the fiscal loans and the financial supports and executed the extensively preferential finance and tax policy which could induce the active participation of the private firms with aiming the optimization of the front-back industry effect and the synergy effect. Moreover, the government extended and built various vocational schools and the job training institutes to promote the technicians who were necessary for the heavy-chemistry industrialization and actively pursued the establishment of the government funded research center to support the development of the heavy-chemistry industry.

As the result of the heavy-chemistry industrialization, the annual average growth of the heavy-chemistry industries was 20.9% in 1970s and this achievement greatly contributed to having the above 7% of the economic growth. In addition, the ratio of the heavy-chemistry industries in the exports rapidly increased from 12.8% in 1970 to 41.5% in 1980. As the result of the Korea governmental support for the heavy-chemistry industrialization, the Korea economy established a foothold for the advanced industrialization and made a foundation for the developed industrial structure.

[Figure 3] The growth of manufacturing sector since 1976

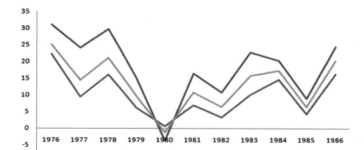

Source: Kim et al. (2011)

In 1980s, however, the industrial recession in the ship and construction industries resulted from the excessive and overlapped investment and the insolvency in the heavy-chemical industry and the deterioration of the foreign economic environment and the weakness of domestic competitiveness. As the side effects of the government-leading heavy-chemistry industrialization were pointed out due to the concentration of the competitiveness caused by the supporting policy for special firms and industries and the problem of the imbalanced industry, the Korea government pursued the industrial rationalization and the structure arrangement of the industry which reformed the investment of the heavy-chemistry industry and rationalized the structurally depressed industries based on the fifth 5-year economic and social development plan. That is, the Korea government pushed forward the technology progress and the functional supporting policy centering on the support of the human capital in order to pursue the advanced industrial structure for the improvement of industrial technology and the increase in productivity and the enhancement in the world competitiveness. In order to enforce the reform in the industrial structure and in the insolvent firms in earnest, the Korea government legislated "Tax Reduction Regulation Act" in 1985 and executed the support system for the industrial rationalization. Furthermore, the government implemented the fair trade system, the major corporation and the core business in order to reduce the competitiveness concentration of the conglomerates and establish the developed economic system.

As a result of the industrial rationalization focusing on the heavy-chemistry industry, the Korea economy kept high economic growth and high investment growth in the early- and mid- 1980s and the ratio of the heavy-chemistry industry in the manufacturing sector was above 70% and the exports ratio of the heavy-chemistry products increased.

Moreover, as the continuous imports regulation policy weakened the competitiveness of the domestic industry and emerged as one of the reasons for insolvency, the Korea government executed the active import liberalization from the initial period of the 5-year plan for the import liberalization in 1983 and the simple average tariff was 7.9% in 1995 and the import liberalization ratio increased to 99%.

However, the Korea economy faced severe global competitiveness due to the institutional change and the foreign environment change and encountered to the decrease in the competitiveness in the world market because of the rapid wage increase and the decrease in the productivity. From early 1990s, the Korea government pursued the active R&D investment with realizing that the national competitiveness could be increased by the promotion of competitiveness and only the technology innovation and the quality improvement can create the competitive advantage. In addition, the government initiated the investment policy on the new high-tech industry in order to accommodate the trend of the world development on the new high-tech industry and to create new growth engine for Korea economy.

[Figure 4] The growth of R&D investment and Economic growth

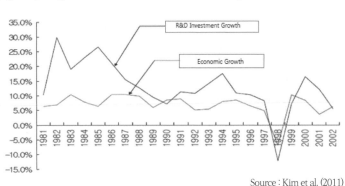

Source : Kim et al. (2011)

As a result of the active policy of the R&D, the R&D investment increased from 368.8 billion KRW in 1981 to 12,185.8 billion KRW in 1997 and the ratio of the R&D to the GDP increased from 0.81% to 2.69% respectively. Since 1981, we can observe the similar trend between the growth of the R&D investment and economic growth and thus may infer that the R&D investment plays an important role in economic growth.

The R&D policy in these periods got rid of the excessive government-leading development which was pivotal by the early 1980s and the R&D led by the private sector has been set up. Moreover, the private firms started to emerge as the main body of economic growth by being the core part initiating the technology innovations and utilizing the government support. This private-sector leading investment support policy has been the foundation for persistently improving the productivity and competitiveness centering around the high-tech industry.

[Figure 5] The relationship between openness and economic growth

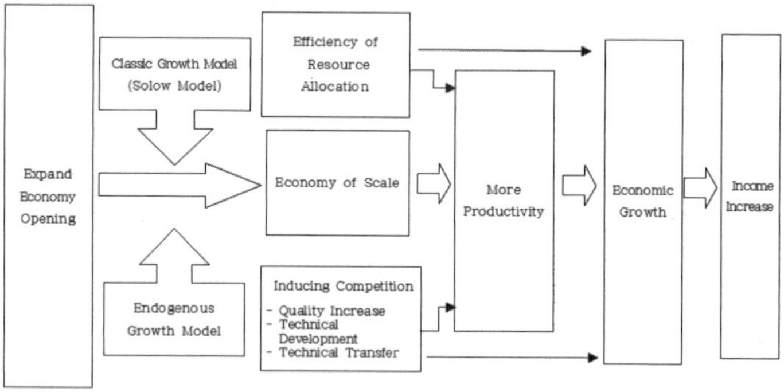

Source: Kim et al. (2011)

In the countries with scarce natural resources and weak domestic economy such as Korea economy, the strong foreign trade-oriented policy has been important for economic growth. According to the study on the relationship between openness and economic growth, the openness promotes economic growth via the improvement of efficient resource allocation and the increase in the productivity by the technology progress. The foreign trade-oriented policy results in economic growth with creating the production specialization and the exchange benefit induced by the openness.

The Korea economy started to pursue the foreign trade-oriented policy at the initial stage of economic development in 1960s in order to achieve economic growth through the improvement of efficient resource allocation and the accomplishment of the economy of scope. As the export-leading industrial policy promoted the light industry in 1960s, the heavy-chemistry industry in 1970s and 1980s, and the growth of the high-tech industry in 1990s and 2000s, the policy has been the good way to lead the growth of the manufacturing sector according to the stage of economic development.

According to the OECD study on the relationship between the foreign trade-oriented tendency and the standard of living in the developing countries, the growth rate of the GDP per capita is much higher in the strong foreign trade-oriented countries than in the other countries (OECD 1998, 1999). As the annual average growth rate of GNP per capita over 1970-1989 was 4.5% in the 15 strong foreign trade-oriented countries, 0.7% in the poor foreign trade-oriented countries, and 2.3% in OECD countries respectively, the countries which actively pursued the foreign trade experienced more improvement in the standard of livings than for other countries (OECD 1999). Frankel and Romer (1999) show that as the ratio of the trade volume (exports + imports) to the GDP increases by 1%, the GDP per capita increases by 2%. In addition, as China and India started to pursue the openness strongly, they achieved the 10% and the 6% of annual average GDP growth over 1980-2000 respectively.

The Korea government strongly pursued the foreign trade-oriented policy by adopting the export-leading growth strategy at the enforcement of the first 5-year economic development plan in 1962. As a result, the ratio of trade volume to the GDP increased significantly from 1965. As the positive correlation between economic growth and the ratio of the trade volume to the GDP in Korea economy was observed from the early 1960s to 2000 in which the lower birth rate and the aging society was raised as a social issue, it is evaluated that the foreign trade-oriented policy played an important role in Korea economic growth.

[Table 2] Foreign trade and standard of living for developing countries

	Average Annual GNP per Capita Growth(%)		
	1963-1973	1974-1985	1986-1992
Strongly Foreign-Oriented	6.9%	6.0%	5.8%
Moderately Foreign-Oriented	4.9%	2.2%	2.5%
Moderately Domestic-Oriented	3.9%	1.8%	-0.1%
Strongly Domestic-Oriented	1.6%	-0.3%	-0.1%

Sources : OECD (1998), Kim et al. (2011)

[Figure 6] Foreign trade and economic growth in Korea

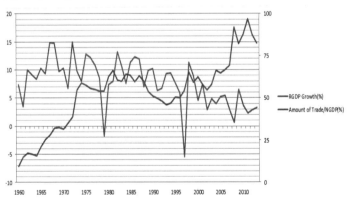

Source : World Bank (2015)

211

B. The role of government

Ones refer to the theory of national development on the study of industrial mechanism that resulted in high economic growth of Asian Tigers such as Hong Kong, South Korea, Singapore, and Taiwan (World Bank 1993). The concept of the national development is the system in which the priority of national policy is not on the division but the increase in growth and productivity, its success depends on the economic criterion provided by the state bureaucracy and the bureaucracy supervises the market engaged in the private property and the market (Kim 2013). The key point of the theory of the national development is the state-centric view paying attention on the role of the state, stating that the government (the state) directly designed the project of the industrialization and for this end, the government fostered, supervised, mobilized, supported, and ruled the private sector (Kim 2013).

In terms of the theory of the state development, the strategy of the Korea industrialization can be summarized as the overall command of the Economic Planning Board for the industrial policy, the policies of the tax reduction, tariff and interest rate for the exporting industries, the suppression of the labor union, the attraction of the foreign capital via the establishment of the free trade center, the technology development via the Korea Science Institute, and the support for promoting exports (Kim 2013). The strong industrial policy by the government in Korea could lead the industrialization and the civil servants in the Economic Planning Board and the Ministry of the Commerce and Industry committed to the role of the government. The government secured the industrial funds at the initial stage of the economic development in the early 1960s via the Korea's property claims against Japan, the Dollar income earned by the dispatches of troops to Vietnam and the miners and nurses to Germany, and the foreign loans and the induction of foreign capitals supported by the government credit. In addition, the government established overall incentive framework for the exports in order to pursue the export-leading industrialization. Furthermore, the foundation of the industrialization has been prepared for the government to pursue the amplifications of the large-scale industrial facilities and various social overhead capitals in priority.

The most prominent role of the Korea government was to establish the proper industrial policy according to the stage of economic development and to actively carry out the policy. That is, the government implemented thoroughly the light industry policy at the initial stage of the industrialization, the heavy-chemistry industrial policy at the leaping (accelerating) period, the industrial rationalization policy at the expansion period, and the policy for the enhancement of national competitiveness and the R&D investment at the matured period under the government leadership. In the process of doing these policies, the government led the growth of manufacturing sector always by supporting the exports-leading industrial policy and kept the lower wage for labor force in order to increase the price competitiveness of the product.

[Figure 7] The growth of Manufacturing sector and the history of economic development in Korea

The strong role and will of the government for economic growth should be important at the early stage of economic

development because the market system based on the private sector leading, does not inspire strong desire for economic growth due to overall popularity of the poverty, weak capital accumulation and poor social infra. The Korea government stimulated the desire for economic growth by inaugurating the "Sae-Ma-Eul"movement in the early 1970s in order to escape the poverty, reform spiritual attitude, and plan the possibility of the rich. For this end, the government advertised the necessity of the government actively pursuing the policy of the economic growth, built the socially overall spiritual infra by contributing to the arrangement of agricultural substructure such as transportation and communication and induced the positive attitude for the active government implementation of the policy. This has been a root for promoting necessary human resources in the process of the industrialization of Korea economy since then (Kim et al. 2011).

It is necessary to have the industrial and trade policies which select the strategic businesses centering on the heavy-chemistry industry at the accelerating period of economic growth because the economy tends to experience the decrease in the world competitiveness in the light industry supported at the early stage and the limit of economic growth. In 1970s, the Korea government legislated special industry promotion acts such as "Petroleum Chemistry Industry Promotion Act" and "Steel Industry Promotion Act" and established the strong support system by launching the Heavy-chemistry Industry Promotion Committee in order to build the heavy-chemistry industry total directionally. In addition, the government built the framework of the advanced industrial structure by legislating the "National Investment Funds Act" as the way of inducing the active participation of the private sector in order to maximize the front-back industry effect and the synergy effect and implementing the support policies such as various preferential treatments in finance and tax (Kim et al. 2011).

In the matured stage of economic development, the role of the government is important for reforming economic constitution pursuing the productivity improvement by vitalizing the market function via the implementation of industrial rationalization, the boost of openness and competition, the establishment of the fair trade committee and the legislation of fair trade act, and the change to the private-sector leading system in the stance of industrial policy. The Korea government in 1980s tried to carry out the adjustment of the heavy-chemistry industry investment and the rationalization of the structurally depressed industry, to set the conditions for autonomy, competition and openness via the legislation of the fair trade act and the establishment of the fair trade committee, to change the stance of the industrial policy to the private-sector leading system via legislating the "Industry Development Act," and to set the economic environment in which the firm is a main body for leading the technology innovation and for guiding the productivity of the manufacturing sector and the reinforcement of competitiveness. Moreover, the government was capable of carrying out the leading role of the sustainable economic growth with actively implementing the government's investment support policy for the high-tech industry as a new growth engine in 1990s.

C. The market economy system and the strategy of efficient resource allocation

In South Korea, both to support national security by having the strong military power and to promote economic power (modernization) to increase the national standard of living were necessary for defeating the North Korea and keeping the South Korea in terms of the system competition. The ideological background to enable the industrialization of the developmental state was the national state revivalism (Kim 2013). In the early stage of economic development in 1950s after the Korea War, the national security was the important ideological foundation for having the justification and stability of the political regime and this political environment was fundamentally different from the Western liberal democracy which pursues the autonomous democratic development via the citizen movement. However, there was a common area in the national security and the economic expansion. While the promotion of the defense industry to enable the self defense is necessary for the national security, the defense industry was based on the establishment of the heavy-chemistry industry such as steel, machinery, electronics and chemistry. Therefore, the ultimate national security was directly connected to the expansion of the national economic power.

Although the democracy for the national prosperity and military power in order to revitalize Korea society was far away from the environment pursuing the economic development based on the Western liberal democracy, the free market system for increasing economic power was the important foundation for the industrialization system of the developmental state.

That is, the Korea government actively tried to implement the advanced modernization of the economic institutional environment which was the foundation of the advanced economy such as various economic infra, capital market, and the institution related to property right. For example, the market mechanism of the Korea economy has been reinforced more with transforming to the free trade policy in order to enhance the national competitiveness via the promotion effect of the competition since the industrialization in 1970s. Moreover, as the Korea joined the WTO and OECD since 1990s, the Korea heightened the international status and implemented the openness and globalization. The substantial improvement of economic constitution right via the extensive structural reform of national economy after the currency crisis in 1997 was due to the effort which contributed to the enhancement of the efficiency of resource allocation under the rule of the world market economy.

Why was the market economy system one of main factors for Korea economic growth? It is to be expected, in Korea that keeps national security as the most priority with having keen system competition, that the system with having national power be at absolute priority and rule the market is considered normal rather than the self-regulating and efficient private-leading market economy system. In the initial stage of economic development, the state actively interrupted in the private sector and the market with advocating strong will and role of the government in order to implement economic growth. However, the Korea government tried to make an effort for increasing the efficiency of the resource allocation via the effective operation of the market economy system according to the stage of the economic development and implemented proper polices and institutions. This effort eventually stimulated the leading role of the private firms for the national economic development and resulted in the improvement of the competition efficiency of the market economy and the reinforcement of the world competition. Nowadays, when ones recall the evidence of the world economy history that most countries having the sustainable economic growth in the long run actively supported the efficiency of the resource allocation with making the best use of the merit of the market economy, there is no doubt that the strong accommodation of the market economy system in Korea must have played an important role in Korea economic growth.

D. The accumulation of human capital and high productivity

Barro and Lee (1993, 1996, 2001) measure the education level of the world countries in order to examine whether the accumulation of human capital via education has a substantial impact on economic growth and as the result of the empirical study, show that the education level has a positive impact on economic growth. As described in the endogenous growth model, the strong desire and will for escaping from the poverty at the initial stage of the economic development are expressed as high education spirit and contribute to economic growth by the accumulation of human capitals via the mutual interaction of the economic agents and the improvement of individual potential productivity. That is, the high educated labor force creates high productivity and thus stimulates economic growth. Moreover, the education and training bring about economic growth by making more skilled workers and increasing the ability of learning the advanced high technology.

The Korea had lower 3rd round average education years than the developed countries in the initial stage of economic development in 1960s and the education years were similar with the average of 146 countries. However, the abundant lower-skilled workers supported the industrialization of the light industry and the supply of the necessary skilled workers has been provided by the reinforcement of higher education as the heavy-chemistry industrialization proceeded in 1970s. This quantitative and qualitative supply of the labor force was supported by high education spirit of Korean people. In Korea, high education spirit was expressed as the "Sae-Ma-Eul movement" of the self-help, self-reliance, and diligence and this contributed to economic growth via the initial accumulation of human capital and the supply of the labor force. Furthermore, as the economic growth provided more opportunities of education, the positive relationship between education and economic growth has been established (Kim et al. 2011).

The admission rate of higher education was increased significantly with economic development since 19960s and this resulted in the quantitative and qualitative increase in the labor force and the accumulation of human capital. Moreover, high education spirit not only provided abundant labor forces but also enhanced the flexibility of the labor market via proper job training and increased the efficient resource allocation. Furthermore, high education spirit led technology development by increasing the learning effect via the establishment and expansion of the R&D and thus this worked as the sustainable growth engine.

[Table 3] Admission rate of higher education

Year	Middle School	High School	College
1965	53.4	69.1	32.3
1975	77.2	74.7	25.8
1985	99.2	90.7	36.4
1995	99.9	98.5	51.4
2005	99.9	99.7	82.1

Sources: Ministry of Education and Human Resources and
Korea Education Development Institute (2008)

One of remarkable characteristics in the Korea economic growth is the rapid change in the labor market with the rapid economic growth. That is, as the high education spirit supported the accumulation of human capital and the quantitative and qualitative supply of labor, the sustainable economic growth has been possible by properly accommodating the rapid change in the demand structure for labor in the process of the fast industrialization.

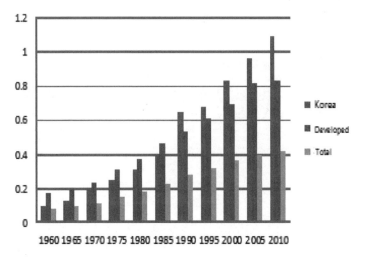

[Figure 8] Average educational year for higher educationin Korea and other countries

Source : Barro and Lee (2013)

It is evaluated that the fast increase in the entrance rate of high school and college to supply the skilled workers required for the rapid industrialization resulted in the accumulation of human capital and this has been important contribution to the sustainable economic growth via the industrialization. Consequently, the educational spirit in Korea were helpful for the accumulation of human capital required for the industrialization in time and greatly contributed to the quantitative and qualitative supply of labor.

3. The role of the POSCO in the Korea economic growth

1) The status of the POSCO

According to the will of the Korea President, Jung-Hee Park, who supported the state revivalism and insisted that the steel industry is the national power and is the foundation of industrialized country, Tae-Joon Park, the first President of the POSCO, started to establish the POSCO on April 1, 1968, in order to respect the President Park's desire and realize the martyr's mission that the realization of the "Jae-Cheol-Bo-Gook" is the only way to escape from the poverty and accomplish the industrialization[2]. Since then, as the financial plan provided by the KISA (Korean International Steel Association) foundered, the establishment of the POSCO was almost at the critical situation. However, TJP was successful for obtaining the support and the cooperation of the Japanese steel association with the thorough mission for the "Jae-Cheol-Bo-Gook" and for preparing the construction funds via the transfer of the Korea's

---

2　The original name of the POSCO(POSCO) was the Pohang Steel National Company in 1968 and the name was renamed as the POSCO in March 2002 via the reform of the articles of association. Since then, the POSCO became popular.

property claims against Japan and the construction of the first Pohang's steel factory was started in April 1, 1970.

[Figure 9] The history of the POSCO

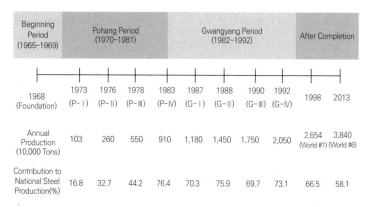

Beginning Period (1965–1969)	Pohang Period (1970–1981)				Gwangyang Period (1982–1992)				After Completion	
1968 (Foundation)	1973 (P-I)	1976 (P-II)	1978 (P-III)	1983 (P-IV)	1987 (G-I)	1988 (G-II)	1990 (G-III)	1992 (G-IV)	1998	2013
Annual Production (10,000 Tons)	103	260	550	910	1,180	1,450	1,750	2,050	2,654 (World #1)	3,840 (World #6)
Contribution to National Steel Production(%)	16.8	32.7	44.2	76.4	70.3	75.9	69.7	73.1	66.5	58.1

Source : POSCO (2004)

The first Pohang steel factory was completed in July 1973 and had the 1.03 million tons of the steel production capacity per year. As the unique case in the world steel history, the POSCO had more than 100 million dollars of sales and 12 million dollars of the net profit in the first operation year (Seo 1997). Since then, the POSCO tried to expand the steel production capacity and completed the second Pohang steel factory in 1976, the third Pohang steel factory in 1978 and the fourth Pohang steel factory in 1983. The production capacity in 1983 was 9.10 million tons per year. As the result of further extensions of the Gwangyang 1-4 steel factories, the production capacity per year of the POSCO was 20.50 million tons and the POSCO ranked as the third steel company in the world in 1992. In 1998, the POSCO produced 26.54 million tons per year and became the world first steel company. In 2013, the production capacity of the POSCO was 38.40 million tons and the POSCO ranked as the sixth steel company in the world with following Arcelor Mittal, Nippon Steel & Sumitomo, Hebei, Bao Steel, and Wuhan respectively. In addition, the ratio of the POSCO's steel production to the Korea total steel production was about 58.1% and the POSCO was the number one steel company in Korea.

Kim and Choi (2011) state that the establishment of the POSCO as a firm may be evaluated not only as the same impact on Korea economy as the construction of the Kyung-bu expressway as a national project but also as the similar ripple effect as the Five years Economic Development Plan and these evaluations can indicate that the growth of the POSCO is the driving force for Korea economic development. That is, the above statement implies that Korean people notice that the POSCO had an extensive impact on overall Korea economy. If so, how did the POSCO contribute to Korea economic development?

[Table 4] Production of Main World Class Steel Companies

unit : million tons

Rank	1991		2001		2010		2013	
	Company	Production	Company	Production	Company	Production	Company	Production
1	Nippon Steel	28.6	Arcelor	43.1	Arcelor Mittal	98.2	Arcelor Mittal	96.1
2	Usinor	22.8	POSCO	27.8	Bao Steel	37.0	Nippon Steel& Sumitomo	50.1
3	POSCO	19.1	Nippon Steel	26.2	POSCO	35.4	Hebei	45.8
4	British Steel	13.3	Ispat International	19.2	Nippon Steel	35.0	Bao Steel	43.9
5	NKK	12.3	Bao Steel	19.1	JFE	31.1	Wuhan	39.3
6	Kawasaki	10.91	Corus Steel	18.1	Shagang	23.2	POSCO	38.4
7	ILVA	10.9	Thyssen Krupp	16.7	Tata Steel	23.2	Shagang	35.1
8	Sumitomo	10.89	Riva	15.0	US Steel	22.3	Ansteel	33.7
9	Thyssen Krupp	10.3	NKK	14.8	Ansteel	22.1	Shougang	31.5
10	US Steel	9.6	Kawasaki	13.3	Gerdau	18.7	JFE	31.2

Source : World Steel(2014)

2) The role of the POSCO in the Korea economic growth

Jun (2013) and Kim (2007) describe that the steel industry is the foundation for industrialization to such an extent as to say that the history after the modern period is the history of the steel and thus the steel is "the rice of industrialization." The countries that dreamed of industrialization among modern countries evaluated the degree of national power based on the steel technology and the production capacity. The steel is the most important technological material in the industrial society and the core for national security in one word. Choi (2007) emphasizes that the steel industry is a large capital-intensive equipment industry with great deal of economy of scale and a national key industry which provides fundamentally needed materials for main industries such as automobile, ship, electronics, and machinery industries. Hence, the general characteristic of the steel industry is that the initial investment cost for the business management is dramatically high but because the ripple effect and industrial influence are high and the investment effect is huge, the steel industry has an influential impact on the growth and the development of other firms (Lim 2010).

From this point of view, the strong steel industry should be essential if one country pursues the sustainable economic growth via industrialization. The POSCO, the world class steel company, has been in the center of Korea economy which accomplished sustainable economic growth only over 40 years since 1960s via rapid industrialization and became an example of modern countries. Kim and Choi (2011) describe that as the result of the national survey, main contributable factors for Korea industrialization were Sae Ma Eul Movement, the Five years Economic Development Plan, the construction of Kyung-Bu Expressway, and the establishment of the POSCO.

If so, what are the key roles of POSCO in Korea's rapid and high economic growth? We investigate the key roles which the POSCO played in the Korea economic growth both in terms of the factors which result in economic growth based on economics and in terms of the key factors which brought about Korea economic growth[3].

3   Please see the Social Science Research Institute at the Seoul National University (1987, 1991), the Korea Institute of Industry, Science and Technology (1990), and Kwak et al. (1992) for existing literature which analyzes what the POSCO had an impact on national production, employment, and the balance of payment in terms of national economic aspect and what were the economic effects of providing cheap intermediate goods as the national key industry.

A. To lead the growth of the manufacturing sector through

POSCO's industry relation effect

The steel is the rice of industrialization. The meaning is that the development of the steel industry is directly connected to the modernization via the economic industrialization because the steel industry as a large scale equipment industry has a lot of demand for the goods of other industries and provide steel products as intermediate goods for other main industries and thus has a great industrial relation effect. In economics, the analysis of the industrial relationship effect is used in order to evaluate the contribution of one industry to other industries. The industrial relation analysis measures the ripple effect which the final demand of one industry has on the production activity of other industries by subdividing the industries and examining the mutual dependent relations made by the transactions of goods and services between industries (Choi 2007). In an empirical analysis, we measure quantitatively mutual dependent relations between industries via the input-output analysis of the industries. Hence, since the products of the POSCO were used as intermediate goods for main industries, the industrial relation analysis is important for examining the contribution which the POSCO made to Korea economic growth.

Lots of existing literature use the input-output analysis in order to analysis the level of contribution of the steel industry (Hahn et al. 1988, Seo 1991, Kwak et al. 1992, Kim et al. 1998, Jung and Lim 2008). The back industries from which the steel industry demands other goods are the industry for raw materials, electricity, energy industry such as LNG, construction, machinery, and the distribution industry. The front industries for which the steel industry provides steel products are automobile, ship, construction, machinery, home appliance, and fabricated metal industry (Choi 2007). The back industry effect can be estimated by measuring the level of the demand for goods of other industries as intermediate goods via the sum of the columns in the input-output table. The front industry effect can be estimated by the sum of the rows in the input-output table, meaning the effect that the steel industry makes on the other industries having the demand for steel products.

The process of the steel production from the raw materials of the steel to the steel products can be sorted as the three processes of the iron making, the steel making, and the rolling. The steel products are divided as the bar shaped steel, the flat-rolled steel, the pipe steel, and the main strong steel. The bar shaped steel is used for construction and general machinery, the flat-rolled steel is used for automobile, ship, and home appliance, and the pipe steel is used for the gas pipe, the oil pipe, and the petroleum drilling. Hence, on the one hand, if ones can understand the industries using the steel products, ones examine the front industry effect very well. On the other hand, if ones can understand what kinds of products as intermediate goods the steel industry demands in order to expand the steel factory or produce the steel products, it is very useful for measuring the back industry effect.

[Table 5] Types and Uses of Steel Products

Types		Uses
Bar Shape Steel	Shape Steel	Foundation Work(Factory, Building, Bridge etc.), Steel Frame Construction(Subway etc.), Vessel, Automobile
	Bar Steel	Machine Structure, Seamless Pipe, Bolt, Nut, Rivet, Cold Finished Carbon Steel Bar
	Steel Reinforcement	Reinforced Concrete Building, Engineering Work
	Wire Rod	Wire Rod, Small Bolt·Nut, Tire Cord
	Rail	Railway, Crane, Elevator etc.
Steel Pipe	Seamless Pipe	High Pressure Gas Pipe, Chemical Pipe, Boring etc.
	Welded Pipe	Water Pipe, Gas Pipe, Oil Pipe, Steel Pipe Pile, General Structure
Cast Forged Steel		Machine Part, Machine Tool, Roll

Source: 「Basic Knowledge on Steel」 Korea Steel and Metal News (1996)

Kwak et al. (1992) show that the back industry effect of the first steel product was estimated as 2.59 in 1988 when the steel production of the POSCO was the 70% in the Korea total steel production. That is, the effect implies that when there was an increase in the demand for the first steel products by 100 tons, the increase in the production of goods and services is 259 tons directly and indirectly. At that time, the estimated back industry effect of the steel industry ranked as the second top among 21 industrial subdivisions. The estimated front industrial effect was 2.57 and ranked as the third top, following the petroleum and chemistry product (3.73) and the finance, insurance and real estate products (2.76).

Choi (2007) shows that as the result of empirical analysis on the input-output table in 2000, the influential coefficients reflecting the back industry effect as the relative size of the industry to the industrial average are 1.315 for the bar shaped steel products, 1.306 for automobile, 1.237 for the flat-rolled steel products, and 1.135 for the metal products and thus the back industry effect is relatively high in the steel products. In addition, in the analysis of the sensitivity figure reflecting the front industry effect as the relative size of the industry to the industrial average, the other services, the coefficients are 3.226 for other services, 2.04 for petroleum-chemistry products, 1.684 for fundamental steel products, 1.177 for the light industry products, and 1.1 for the flat-rolled steel products and thus the steel product is generally used for main industries as intermediate goods.

[Table 6] Front·back industry effect (1980–1988)

No.	Industries	Front Industry Effect			Back Industry Effect		
		1980	1985	1988	1980	1985	1988
1	Agriculture, Fishery	2.2188	2.2910	2.2036	2.2188	2.2910	2.2036
2	Mining	1.3659	1.3678	1.3379	1.3956	1.3678	1.3379
3	Food & Beverage	1.9415	2.1938	2.1409	1.9415	2.1938	2.1409
4	Fabric, Leather	1.9936	2.1184	2.0463	1.9936	2.1184	2.0463
5	Lumber, Wooden Goods	1.2870	1.3070	1.2526	1.2870	1.3070	1.2526
6	Paper, Printing, Publication	1.9327	2.0533	2.0788	1.9327	2.0533	2.0788
7	Petrochemistry	5.4349	4.4164	3.7297	5.4349	4.4164	3.7297
8	Nonmetal Mineral	1.4593	1.5201	1.5338	1.4593	1.5201	1.5338
9	Primary Steel Product	2.5423	2.6170	2.5652	2.5423	2.6170	2.5652

10	Nonferrous Metal	1.3353	1.3103	1.2808	1.3353	1.3103	1.2808
11	Metal Goods, Machinery	1.8862	2.1382	2.4417	1.8862	2.1382	2.4417
12	Etc Manufacturing	1.1306	1.1063	1.1001	1.1306	1.1063	1.1001
13	Electricity, Gas, Water	1.9155	1.9976	1.8247	1.9155	1.9976	1.8247
14	Construction	1.2889	1.3229	1.3323	1.2889	1.3229	1.3323
15	Wholesale and Retail Sales	2.2169	2.0338	2.1194	2.2169	2.0338	2.1194
16	Restaurant, Lodging	1.3251	1.3160	1.2523	1.3251	1.3160	1.2523
17	Shipment, Storage, Telecom	1.7054	1.8140	1.8163	1.7054	1.8140	1.8163
18	Banking, Insurance, Real Estate	2.4363	2.6764	2.7068	2.4363	2.6764	2.7608
19	Public Admin., National Defense	1.0000	1.0000	1.0000	1.0000	1.0000	1.0000
20	Other Services	1.1595	1.1846	1.2011	1.1595	1.1846	1.2011
21	Others	1.6303	1.6492	1.5737	1.6303	1.6492	1.5737
Total		39.2345	39.4341	38.5919	39.2345	39.4341	38.5919

Source: Kwak et al. (1992)

236

[Table 7] Front·back industry effect (2000)

No.	Industries	Front industry effect		Back industry effect	
		RID	ISD	RII	IF
1	Agriculture, Fishery	0.6947	0.7717	0.3757	0.8592
2	General Mining Products	0.9919	0.6554	0.3658	0.8477
3	Raw Material Mining Products	1.0076	0.6648	0.7989	0.6438
4	Light Industry	0.4765	1.1768	0.7178	1.0863
5	Petrochemistry	0.7023	2.0400	0.7226	0.8687
6	Nonmetal Mineral	0.9339	0.9039	0.6604	1.0831
7	Material Steel Products	1.0419	1.6837	0.8604	1.1132
8	Steel Plate	0.7774	1.0996	0.7533	1.2369
9	Bar·Shape Steel	0.8626	0.7752	0.7859	1.3148
10	Nonferrous Metal	0.8444	0.8355	0.7681	0.8211
11	Metal	0.7851	0.8703	0.6557	1.1348
12	General Machine	0.4194	0.9540	0.6929	1.1262
13	General Electronics	0.4652	1.1044	0.7040	0.8739
14	Computer, Home Appliance	0.1756	0.5995	0.8239	1.0051
15	Automobile	0.4007	0.8774	0.7744	1.3063
16	Vessel	0.1244	0.5783	0.6795	1.0457

17	Transport Equipment	0.5007	0.6104	0.8348	1.0169
18	Etc Manufacturing	0.3098	0.5700	0.6597	1.0160
19	Electricity, Gas, Water	0.6722	1.0422	0.5440	0.8030
20	Building	0.1665	0.6198	0.5621	1.0522
21	Engineering Construction	0.0000	0.5301	0.5583	1.0650
22	Transportation, Storage	0.3755	0.8112	0.5828	0.8274
23	기타 서비스	0.4151	3.2260	0.3924	0.8527
Average		0.4859	1.0000	0.5695	1.0000

Source : Choi (2007)

Note : RID denotes the rate of intermediate demand, ISD is the sensitivity figure, RII is the rate of intermediate input and IF is the impact factor.

Lim (2010) shows that in the analysis of 2007 input-output table, the front industry effect for the steel products is 1.795 and ranks as the second top following the 1.923 of the chemistry products and the back industry effect for the steel products is 1.250 and ranks as the second top following the 1.449 of other industries. Lim (2010) describes the steel industry as the intermediate-demand manufacture because the steel industry has both the high front industry and the high back industry effect.

[Table 8] Front·back industry effect (2007)

Industries	ISD (Front industry effect)	Rank	IF (Back industry effect)	Rank
1. Agriculture, Fishery	0.9614	15	0.9156	19
2. Mining Products	0.5869	28	0.8806	20
3. Food and Beverage	1.0957	9	1.0804	8
4. Fabric, Leather	0.8103	20	1.0605	10
5. Lumber, Paper	1.0537	10	1.0397	15
6. Printing, Copy	0.6669	23	1.0590	12
7. Petrochemistry	1.3097	5	0.6091	29
8. Chemistry	1.9234	1	1.0595	11
9. Nonmetal Mineral	0.7400	22	1.0411	14
10. Primary Metal Product	0.8736	19	0.8445	23
11. Metal Product	0.9704	14	1.2379	4
12. General Machinery	0.9038	18	1.2366	5
13. Electronic Equipment	1.0203	12	0.9520	18
14. Precision Instrument	0.5931	27	1.0935	7
15. Transport Equipment	0.9410	16	1.2393	3

16. Etc Manufacturing	0.6397	24	1.1353	6
17. Electricity, Gas, Water	1.1212	8	0.7605	28
18. Construction	0.6077	26	1.0656	9
19. Wholesale and Retail Sales	1.3190	4	0.8597	22
20. Restaurant, Lodging	1.0263	11	1.0458	13
21. Transportation	1.1710	7	0.8146	24
22. Telecom, Broadcasting	0.9104	17	0.9701	17
23. Banking, Insurance	1.2479	6	0.8755	21
24. Real Estate, Business Service	1.7951	3	0.7999	27
25. Public Administration, National Defense	0.5293	29	0.8137	25
26. Education and Health	0.6271	25	0.8108	26
27. Social, Other Services	0.7601	21	1.0015	16
28. Others	0.9996	13	1.4485	1
29. Steel Industry	1.7954	2	1.2495	2

Source : Lim (2010)

The summary of the analysis of the input-output table over 1980-2007 indicates that the steel industry has very high front back industry effect over all industries and the POSCO producing Korea steel more than 60% has not only contributed to the supply of intermediate goods for other main industries but also is dedicated to the production of other industries by using the products of other industries as intermediate goods for the steel production. In sum, it is evaluated that the POSCO has contributed to the Korea economic growth by creating very positive ripple effects for other industries.

Ones can analyze the ripple effect of the change in the final demand for one goods on the production, the value addition and the employment, while the front-back industry effect examines the industrial relations with focusing on the demand for intermediate goods for production activity in each industry. Kwak et al. (1992) show that in the estimation of the production induction effect which measures the effect of the change in the final demand for the products of the POSCO on the productions of all industries, the production induction effect of the first steel products was estimated as 2.592 and highest over 21 industries in 1988. Choi (2007) shows that in the analysis of the 2000 input-output table, the production induction effect of the bar shaped steel products was 2.481 and highest and that of the automobile industry was 2.464, that of the flat-rolled steel products was 2.333 and that of the metal products was 2.141.

Kwak et al. (1992) shows that as the result of the estimation for the value-added induction effect which results from the change in the consumption and investment demand for the products of the POSCO, the estimated effect was 0.6290 in 1988. The estimation result indicates that if new demand for the products of the POSCO increases by 10 billion KRW, the value-addition resulting from new demand is 6.3 billion KRW. Choi (2007) shows in the analysis of the 2000 input-output table that the value-added induction effects of the steel products are 0.626 for the bar shaped steel products, 0.622 for the flat-rolled steel products and 0.455 for material steel products and thus are lower than the industrial average.

In the estimation of the employment inducement effect measuring the direct and indirect effect of the employment resulting from the increase in the final demand by 1 billion KRW, Kwak et al. (1992) show that the total number of the employment inducement effect is 45.7 and the number of the first steel products is 20 and highest in the all industries in 1986. They explain that since the first steel product industry is a typical labor-saving and capital-intensive industry and thus the direct inducement effect (employment coefficient) is low but the indirect inducement effect is significantly high, the employment inducement effect of the steel industry is relatively high to other industries.

In terms of the summary of the existing literature on the input-output analysis, since the front-back industry effect of the steel industry have been very high and the POSCO has led the Korea steel production more than 70%, ones can evaluate that the front-back industrial effect of the POSCO was high and thus contributed to the development of the construction industry and the manufacturing sector. From the point of Korea economic growth, ones can assess that the POSCO greatly committed to the exports-leading growth policy of the Korea government through the reduction of the production costs of the relating industries and the enhancement of the international competitiveness which resulted from the lower price of the domestic steel products than the international price.

[Table 9] labor-inducement effect (1980-1986)

No.	Industries	Year			
		1980	1983	1985	1986
1	Agriculture, Fishery	2.7	2.3	1.8	1.6
2	Mining	3.9	3.4	2.1	1.9
3	Food & Beverage	0.3	0.3	0.3	0.2
4	Fabric, Leather	1.3	0.6	0.6	0.6
5	Lumber, Wooden Goods	0.2	0.2	0.2	0.2
6	Paper, Printing, Publication	0.7	0.6	0.5	0.4
7	Petrochemistry	7.6	5.2	3.9	3.7
8	Nonmetal Mineral	1.6	1.5	1.0	0.9
9	Primary Steel Product	30.4	25.3	21.5	20.0
10	Nonferrous Metal	0.7	0.7	0.5	0.4
11	Metal Goods, Machinery	2.5	2.1	1.6	1.3
12	Etc Manufacturing	0.1	0.1	0.1	0.1
13	Electricity, Gas, Water	1.8	1.2	0.9	0.8
14	Construction	1.0	0.7	0.6	0.6
15	Wholesale and Retail Sales	15.8	13.3	8.4	7.0
16	Restaurant, Lodging	1.5	1.7	1.5	1.3
17	Shipment, Storage, Telecom	3.0	3.3	2.0	1.8
18	Banking, Insurance, Real Estate	5.3	4.0	2.6	2.4
19	Public Admin., National Defense	0.0	0.0	0.0	0.0
20	Other Services	1.0	0.9	0.6	0.6
21	Others	0.0	0.0	0.0	0.0
Total		81.5	67.4	50.5	45.7

Source : Kwak et al. (1992)

Table 10] The ranking of management performance for
world class steel companies (1973–2007)

Company	Factor1	Factor2	Factor3	Score	Ranking
POSCO	1.623576	1.068306	0.372612	1.178863	1
BAO Steel	2.150489	0.433292	0.066436	1.147961	2
CSC	1.674895	0.768311	-0.911180	0.835262	3
NSC	-0.445220	1.294712	2.096488	0.660414	4
JFE	-0.639810	1.322276	0.071688	0.156913	5
Arcelor Mittal	0.353510	-1.65363	2.198706	0.075945	6
BHP	0.332522	-0.63951	-0.30706	-0.122150	7
KOBE	-1.026750	1.215360	-0.350930	-0.144980	8
CSN	0.035908	0.104523	-1.282540	-0.216820	9
TKS	-0.555090	-0.353040	0.614907	-0.243970	10
SAAB	0.243342	-0.980990	-0.310060	-0.276660	11
USS	-0.660040	-0.549790	0.829964	-0.312390	12
NISSHIN	-0.525490	0.0045123	-0.693030	-0.372010	13
SUMITOMO	-1.377400	0.815666	-0.247440	-0.416980	14
AKS	-0.456310	-0.634650	-0.089050	-0.43850	15
TISCO	0.177149	-1.842280	-0.810550	-0.696210	16
RAUTARUUKKI	-0.905280	-0.413680	-1.248960	-0.814690	17

Source : Kwak, Kim and Kang (2012)

245

Kwak, Kim and Kang (2012) show that as the result of the financial evaluation of main shaft furnace companies in terms of profitability, stability, growth, productivity, and market power, the management performance of Asian steel firms such as South Korea, China, Taiwan and Japan is good and especially, the management performance of the POSCO is the best in terms of overall evaluations. They explain that as the POSCO accomplished the competitive advantage through the best cost competitiveness and the distinguished strategy and supplied the cheap but high quality steel products for automobile, home appliance, and ship industries based on the competitive advantage, the POSCO could contribute to the development of Korea manufacturing sector with making a positive relations between the POSCO and the manufacturing sector.

B. The commitment to the government-leading industrialization through a market-oriented national firm

One of the main factors for the Korea rapid economic growth is the strong government leadership. Since South Korea was suffering from poverty and did not have sufficient capital accumulation and social infra in the early 1960s, the growth strategy by the private sector could not lead the effective and sustainable economic growth. In this situation, the effective ideological background was the state-centering development, so the state should lead economic growth by playing the key role in industrialization. The POSCO has played the key role of the market-oriented national firm by incorporating the "Je-Cheol-Bo-Gook" of the economic ideology and by supporting the government-leading industrialization in order to realize the era mission of the Korea government advocating the state revivalism in 1960s.

President Jung-Hee Park in 1960s had to realize the national prosperity and defense and national security in order to achieve the national revivalism via the system of the developmental state. For this end, it was needed that he had to pursue national modernization and to complete Korea democracy via industrialization. The Korean democracy was continuously to fulfill the economic tasks to complete the national prosperity and defense via the heavy-chemistry industrialization and the promotion of the defense industry (Kim 2013). President Jung-Hee Park's government judged that the establishment of the synthetic steel mill was the core in the center of the industrialization. That is, the Korea government tried to make strong effort for the development of the steel industry in the middle of the industrialization because the government assured the importance of the steel industry in pursuing the government-leading economic development (Jun 2013).

The POSCO realized the era mission of the government-leading economic development and the national revivalism with the "Jae-Cheol-Bo-Gook" ideology from the establishment of the POSCO. The POSCO was the national firm to foster the government-leading steel industry when it was founded in 1968. The prominent foundation spirit and the culture of the firm value of the first CEO Tae-Joon Park for the realization of the "Jae-Cheol-Bo-Gook" not only played the key role in settling the self management beyond the national firm and the market principle of the efficient management in the POSCO but also become the spearhead for achieving the mission of the state development which was the Korea industrialization via the promotion of the steel industry. Therefore, the POSCO has become an important source leading Korea economic growth by incorporating the national firm with the market mechanism and by following the way of the market-oriented national firm with efficiency and productivity.

How did the market-oriented national firm of the POSCO play an important role in resulting in the sustainable and rapid Korea economic growth? First al all, the POSCO was the national firm which had the best strategy for national economic modernization and industrialization in order to realize the developmental state and the national revivalism. Right after the Korea War, the Korea society was the very poor developing country with poor bequests such as backwardness, colonization, national division, and poverty. In this situation, President Seung-Man Lee government was corrupted with the political power groups and Prime Minister Myun-Jang government which supported the Western-style liberal democracy based on the individual liberty and right, was incompetent and corrupt not carrying out Korea democracy, the establishment of the self-supporting economy and the accomplishment of Korea reunification. The President Jung-Hee Park taking over the political regime in 1962 noticed that the Korea society was different from the root of the Western-style liberal democracy and thought that the most urgent task for the revival of Korea society was the economic industrialization. Since the poverty was severe, the capital accumulation was weak, and the economic infra was not established in the Korea society at that time, the market mechanism based on the private sector leadership could not inspire strong will for economic growth and raise the seed of economic growth (Kim et al. 2011). In this situation, the President Jung-Hee Park prepared economic criterion provided by civil servants and the frame of the Korea industrialization. The core of Korea democracy and industrialization was the national prosperity and defense and national security. The promotion of the defense industry enabling the self-defense is necessary for national security and the defense industry is based on the promotion of the heavy-chemistry industry such as the steel, machinery, electronics, and chemistry. Therefore, the promotion of the heavy-chemistry industry and the defense appeared as the core target of President Jung-Hee Park government in order to pursue Korea democracy and industrialization (Kim 2013).

The President Jung-Hee Park government tried to pursue rapid industrialization and established the second 5-year economic development plan for the promotion of the heavy-chemistry industry with the construction of the Kyung-bu Expressway. Then, they fostered the heavy-chemistry industry such as petroleum-chemistry, machinery, electronics, electricity and automobile with the frontier of the POSCO. The POSCO was the frontier of the government-leading industrialization and was constructed as a coherent synthetic steel mill at the initial stage with the finance of national funds and the foreign loans. In the first year, the POSCO could make a surplus and create great performance as the national firm through the reduction of the production costs resulting from the shortening of the construction periods (Kim 2013). It was hardly possible to foster the steel industry and make a rapid national industrialization based on the leading of the private sectors by the market mechanism at the period of poor capital accumulation because the steel industry was a large equipment industry with the huge economies of scale. In addition, The POSCO tried to pursue the attitude of the firm management at the corporate level with clearly realizing the key national asset reflecting the cause and the value that the POSCO should not be the only means of the profit-making as a firm but should be managed as a national firm at the state management level (Park 1987). That is, at the corporate level, the POSCO took the responsibility as a frontier in the 100 years of the steel industry which should be the key component for the national development as the good volunteer and manager not for special individual but for national common interests. Such a patriotic attitude has been materialized as the principle of the firm management as a national firm and been an important source for the POSCO to play the role of the national firm in being a driving force ruling out inefficiency of national firm's management and pursuing national existence and prosperity in the severe international competitiveness era. The POSCO realized at the factor site of the steel industry, the patriotism of the steel industry that since the steel is the rice of the industrialization, the improvement of the steel industry contributes to strong nation, to the rich life of the nation, and to the construction of welfare society. As the POSCO realized the patriotism at the steel industry as the key national industry, they contributed to the rapid industrialization of the Korea economy and this contribution could become one of key factors to bring about the Korea economic growth. Rue (2001) describes that the POSCO's corporate strategy, autonomy, and the economic rationality have been the growth engine for Korea economic growth with according to the industrialization strategy of President Jung-Hee Park government's national capitalism and to the political rationality and with having the strong support of the government and the characteristic of the Presidential department and have been one of main behaviors to realize the market-creative national capitalism.

Secondly, the POSCO was a market-oriented national firm to realize practicality and efficient management. Most national firms have a difficulty to operate the efficient management in the competitive market because they tend to be operated according to exclusive bureaucratism. Lee (2012) states that in order for the firm to have sustainable competitive advantage and superior profits, the firm's effort to respond to the market demand better than other competitors and predict the change in the market demand very well is called the market-orientation. The market-orientation of the suppliers decreases the uncertainty of the transaction relations and enhances the applicability resulting from the change in the management environment. Hence, the market-orientation can lead and reinforce excellent performance with concentrating all their capacities into the unified power and with responding to the market movement. The market-oriented firm can achieve good management performance via both financial performances such as sale, total asset-profit ratio, the sale growth, and the market share and non-financial performances such as cognized quality, customer satisfaction, employee satisfaction, and the development and the success of new product.

Tae-Joon Park, the first president of the POSCO, was a businessman to support the occupational view of the practical industrialization (Kim 2013). He was a distinguished market-oriented manager with responding sensitively to the market flow according to the market principle and analyzing the market on time and coping with the market flow in order for the POSCO to survive and prosper in the international steel market. For example, the President Tae-Joon Park started to export the steel with targeting the foreign markets as soon as the POSCO produced the steel. The reason was that the main competitors to the POSCO were the foreign steel firms in the international steel markets (Seo 1998). Tae-Joon Park was very wise with reading and predicting the market flow and adjusting the firm organization. He tried to construct the second coherent synthetic steel mill at the Gwangyang Bay in order to increase the steel production with prediction that the demand in the domestic and international steel market. Tae-Joon Park actively carried out the transition of the stock-sharing plan of the nation, the preemptive introduction of new technology, R&D and the expansion of science and technology in the POSCO's management (with realizing very well that most national firms do not have efficient management due to exclusive bureaucratism and thus do not avoid the chronic deficits (Kim 2013)). As a result, the POSCO could overcome the innate limit as a national firm and make an efficient management almost compatible to the private firm.

The POSCO tried to carry out very aggressive firm strategy with not targeting the competitive advantage in the domestic market but creating the competitive advantage in the world market based on the market-oriented attitude. For this end, the POSCO continuously pursued the technology and management innovation. As the POSCO built the second Gwangyang steel mill and could divide the production system into the dual production systems of the small production of various steel types in the Pohang steel mill and the large production of a few steel types in the Gwangyang steel mill, the POSCO could be successful in the technology innovation and the product differentiation. The POSCO tried to improve the technology competitiveness with the drastic R&D and the accumulation of new technology via the Technology Research Institute, the Industry Science and Technology Institute, and the POSTECH. In addition, they enhanced the management efficiency through the steady management innovation on human resources and finance management and reinforced the financial structure (Rheu 2001). The POSCO tried to reinforce the firm autonomy with focusing not on the public character as a national firm but on the marketability as a firm. Rheu (2001) describes that as the autonomy and the market power of the POSCO could transform the government-firm relation into the mutual cultivation relation and generate the relation of the state and the POSCO supports and promotions each other with mutually autocatalytic behavior, the POSCO grew to "the enterprise within the state." Kwak et al. (1992) emphasize that the POSCO contributed greatly to the Korea economy by keeping the lower steel price resulting from on the enhancement of the management efficiency. In order to increase the international competitiveness of the domestic industries, the POSCO adjusted the price system and set the price of the domestic supply lower by 20% than the exporting price in the international market and lower by 10% than the importing price of the domestic market. It is evaluated that this pricing policy contributed significantly to the government-leading growth policy to pursue the economic growth through the export-leading industrialization. In sum, ones can appraise that as the market-oriented POSCO's strategy based on the local pricing system made a contribution to the export promotion of the domestically related industries, the support of the export competitiveness, the expansion of the demand for the steel product, and the support of the trade finance of the related industries, the POSCO contributed greatly to the rapid industrialization and to economic growth via the reinforcement of the international competitiveness of the domestic firms.

C. The commitment to the productivity improvement and the accumulation of human capital through technology development, R&D investment, industry-academic cooperation, and firm welfare

Kim and Choi (2011) point out that the existing literature which has focused on the econometric estimation of the effect of the POSCO growth on the Korea economy or on the explanation of how the POSCO has been the world class firm quantitatively and qualitatively within such a short period, are useful for understanding the contribution of the POSCO to the Korea economy and the relation between the cause of the firm growth and the change in the government-firm relation but have a limit for comprehensively understanding the contribution of the POSCO to the Korea economy. They divide the effect of the POSCO on the Korea economy into the direct effect and the indirect effect and focus on analyzing both effects while the existing literature has focused on only the direct effect. For example, they present the indirect effects such that all successes of the POSCO to overcome any difficulties have an impact on the POSCO's workers, the other firms and other workers, and the nation and that the corporate governance structure and the compliance management, the investment on human capital of the POSCO have an impact on the policy of other firms and the introduction of the advanced system and state that the POSCO had a positive impact on the Korea economic growth via such indirect effects. Rheu (2001) emphasizes that the POSCO built the efficient management system and independent R&D system at the early period and then established the independent growth foundation.

Lim (2010) considers the reasons of the POSCO's success and emphasizes that the sustainable growth of the POSCO has resulted from the investment on the technology and science and R&D such as the training of technical professionals and the activity of technology improvement, the importance of the field workers, the reinforcement of learning advanced technology, the mutual exchange of knowledge and the creation of new idea, the R&D strategy based on the basic science and the technology development centering on the user, the quality improvement of the existing products, the gradual innovation considering the quality improvement of the existing product and the improvement activity of the production process, and the establishment of the general research institute based on the basic and comprehensive science. The POSCO tried to have the sustainable technology improvement via the foreign technology training and the job training and especially, emphasized the technology innovation and improvement in the field site. The management of technological human resources has been pushed ahead at the firm level with relating the mental reform campaign of the productivity enhancement and the building of the world-class steel company beyond the simple technology development. For example, the master technician program to compensate the good technicians has been operated in order to raise the patriotic technician who has not only excellent field skills but also good personality and thus get the recognition of outstanding skills and high contribution at the company and thus eventually to enhance the company's competitiveness.

The POSCO started with the introduction of Japanese technology at the foundation of the POSCO but grew with the repetition of construction and production. In this process, the POSCO realized not only the expansion of the steel mill but also the new technology of the steel mill (KIET 1997). Since the steel industry has the economies of the scale as an equipment industry, it can reduce the production costs by increasing the size. At the same time, the POSCO tried substantially to improve the strand casting technology to play a key role in increasing the productivity in the steel mill via continuous technology development. The world-class facility of the steel mill and the world-class technology greatly contributed to the productivity improvement of the POSCO and could be the foundation for the POSCO to survive in the world competitiveness. The POSCO recognized that since the securement of the world comparative advantage, the diversification of the markets, and the creation of new demand depend on the technology, the technology development should be the key in order to have continuous development in the world competitive market and to consolidate the frontier position.

The POSCO tried to make a strong effort in the technology

development and the R&D investment. They established the affiliated technology institute in 1977 and pursued the technology development with mutually closely coworking with the outside education and research institute and with making the industry-academic cooperation system. They were not satisfied with simple learning of the advanced technology but pursued the technology innovation with creating new idea via the mutual learning model mutually to exchange the acquired knowledge. The POSCO induced the efficient technology development and the commercialization of the R&D by aiming the technology development centering on the customer. As they built the comprehensive research institute in 1986 and systemized the R&D at the fundamental and total aspects, the POSCO pursued the R&D platform not simply to focus on the improvement of the existing products and the invention of new product but to develop the fundamental technology in terms of the long run and the promising advanced product. Based on this opportunity, the POSCO recognized strong technology independence and reinforced the foundation of the thorough technology independence. Consequently, the effort of the technology development and the R&D in the POSCO could contribute to the improvement of the productivity of the

Korea economy through the productivity enhancement and the increase in the international competitiveness of the POSCO.

The POSCO not only educated the good field workers through the master technician program but also raised the researchers requested for the development of the steel industry and the related industries via the establishment of the technology research institute and the research complex. They founded the Pohang Industry and Science Institute and the POSTEC in order to organically connect the university, the industry and the research institute and thus contributed greatly to the education of the national industrial workers via the establishment of the industry-academic cooperation system. President Tae-Joon Park who recognized that the role of the education and the university is important for the development of the state and the industry, raised the industrial workers to realize the "Jae-Cheol-Bo-Gook" with developing various independent supplementary program at the POSCO's training institute in order to connect the theory-oriented education of the engineering college with the industrial workplace[4].

4   The POSCO established the training institute taking full charge of the training and the education in February 1 in 1969 and pursued the foreign commissioned education of the technicians and the company training in priority (Lee 2012).

As the various educational needs were asked in response to the expansion of equipment facilities and the change in the company environment, The POSCO's training institute developed the education program for the workers with focusing on the early arrangement of new workers, the establishment of stable working base, the inherit and the development of the founding spirit according to the change in the workers' mental structure, the amplification of the management ability due to the organization's large scale, and the improvement of the international reaction capability due to the internationalization of the management (Lee 2012).

The POSCO founded POSTECH in order to realize the ideology of the educational patriotism of the Tae-Joon Park in terms of the systematic and planned education of the 100 years and pushed ahead the innovate plan to secure human resources in response to the increased demand for high brains after the building of the Gwangyang steel mill. That is, the POSCO established the research-oriented POSTECH in order to realize the mission of Tae-Joon Park that the POSCO has to produce the capable human resources to lead the future industry at the state level (Lim 2010). Since the foundation, as the POSTECH prepared all conditions for the study and the research such as the recruitment of the world-class scholars, the fulfillment of the world-class education facility, the establishment of the industry-academic cooperation and the selection of the most elite students and stood as the research-oriented graduate school to teach and research the high-tech and the basic application field of the science and technology, the POSCO played a great role in entering into the system of the full-fledged research and contributed to the college education reform of the state (Im 2010).

In sum, it is evaluated that the securement and the promotion of the field workers based the education of the POSCO's training institute, the technology development and the improvement of research facility via the industry-academic cooperation, and the establishment of the research-oriented POSTECH in order to raise the high brains to lead the future industry in long-term perspective and the state were main factors that had an impact on the Korea economic growth via the accumulation of human capital.

A firm learns the mechanism to grow faster, better, and

wiser through innovation than competitors and eventually contributes to the industry development (Davila, Epstein & Shelton 2006). Since a firm carries out innovation based on a fresh idea, an innovation should be a key factor of the competitiveness to lead the firm's success with surpassing the management environment (Kelley 2001). Lee and Kim (2012) emphasize that the effect of the innovation doubles when both the technology innovation meaning the engineer-oriented technology and the product development through R&D and the high-performance workplace innovation meaning the reform activity via the participation of the field workers are divided and two innovations are combined. As the result of the effect of the President Tae-Joon Park's religious immersion into the filed innovation, the POSCO conducted the filed innovation at the firm level through the activity of the quality working teams such as a quality control activity, the self management encompassing the suggestion program and the successive QSS (quick six sigma) activity. It is evaluated that such a self management activity has been a driving force for keeping the world competitiveness by promoting the labor productivity and the management performance of the POSCO (Lee and Kim 2012).

[Figure 10] POSCO's productivity per person

unit : ton/person

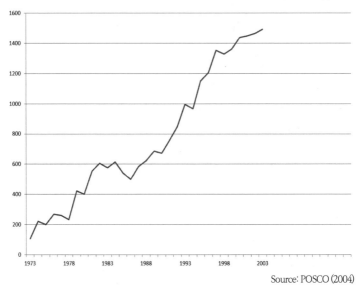

Source: POSCO (2004)

According to Lee and Kim (2012), the labor productivity (per capita steel production, ton/person) of the POSCO increased dramatically right after the full-fledged expansion of the self management in 1979 and the average labor productivity over 1979-1984 was 530 ton/person while the average labor productivity was 216 ton/person over 1973-1978, indicating that the productivity increased by 2.5 times. At that time, the main activity themes of the self management were the improvement in the facility efficiency and the work efficiency and it is evaluated that such a self management contributed greatly to the improvement of work efficiency and thus had a positive impact on the increase in the labor productivity. Moreover, it is evaluated that the proper improvement of the work capacity due to the self management and the proper supply of the skilled workers for newly built factory were the indirect effects of the self management.

The POSCO from the early period of the foundation, made an example framework for the firm welfare which included the support of various housing and lifestyle-base, culture and sports, the scholarship and the education facility, the asset accumulation by a stock-sharing plan for the employees, and the worker-participating welfare by the selective welfare system (Lee 2012). The welfare system of the POSCO achieved the positive relation with the sustainable management surplus. That is, the sustainable surplus management provided the foundation for employment stability and the material base for the development of the firm welfare by inducing the long-term years of labor and the stable life-base of the workers in the POSCO made the POSCO achieve the surplus management by pursuing continuous innovation and the productivity improvement. Therefore, it is evaluated that the positive relation contributed to the productivity improvement of the Korea economy via the increase in the POSCO's productivity.

Kim and Choi (2011) divide the POSCO's contribution to the Korea society and economy into direct and indirect effects and provide the comprehensive analysis. On the one hand, the direct effect is mainly economic effect which includes various effects to reinforce the firm's competitiveness by supplying the cheap but high-quality steel products. For example, there are the front-back industry effects, the import-substituting effect, the export effect and the employment effect. On the other hand, the indirect effect is about the effect of the growth of the POSCO on the Korea society and economy and is the effect on the Korean will for the economic development. That is, it is the effect of the POSCO on the Korean confidence for economic development, and the effect of the POSCO on the advancement of the firm system. They analyze both effects based on the biographical approach to use the newspaper's reports and on the econometric approach to examine the management performance. As the result of the analysis, they evaluate that the foundation and the development of the POSCO functioned as the main factor in creating the positive economic externality for the Korea economy. The examples are that the POSCO provided a successful model for the factory construction as the example leading firm to carry out the heavy-chemistry industrialization in earnest at the beginning of the Korea economic development, the POSCO spread the self confidence for the success with successfully completing the expansion of the large steel factory, and the POSCO was an example model for the firm growth in the Korea economy with standing on the world market as one of global companies.

Kim and Choi (2011) provide an important implication for the effective strategy of the economic development in the countries which have weak institution, poor natural resources, few experiences for economic development, and which cannot carry out a lot of projects at the same time and thus need the learning for economic growth. They suggest that the main strategy for the economic development in the developing countries is that they try to establish a growth engine by focusing on a few important firms rather than the abstract and comprehensive policy, making a successful case and pursuing the learning, the application and the dissemination of this case. Kim and Choi (2011) evaluate that the success of the POSCO created the economic externality in the process of the Korea industrialization and eventually the POSCO contributed to the Korea economic growth by having a positive impact on the total factor productivity (TFP) of the Korea economy.

In sum, the POSCO tried to realize the "Jae-Cheol-Bo-Gook" and materialized the education patriotism of the Tae-Joon Park which could raise the talented human resources to lead the future industry of the state. For this end, as the POSCO carried out the technology development, the technology innovation, R&D investment, the industry-academic cooperation, the education of the field workers, the workplace innovation via the firm-level self management, the positive relation between the development of the firm welfare and the surplus management, and the creation of the economic externality for Korea industrialization via the learning and the dissemination of the story of the POSCO's success, the POSCO supported the improvement of Korea economy's productivity and the accumulation of the human capital and consequently contributed to the growth of the Korea economy.

3) The effect of the POSCO on the Korea economy :
An empirical analysis

A. The channel through which the POSCO affected the Korea economic growth

So far, we explained how the Korea economy experienced the rapid economic growth over previous 40 years in terms of four key factors. Of course, the existing literature has shown using various analyses that the POSCO played an important role in the rapid and sustainable growth of the Korea economy. In this study, we keep away the approach which the existing literature used in terms of descriptive study and the analysis of the economic effect and rather focus on the empirical analysis based on above suggested key factors. At first, we need to build the road map on how the growth of the POSCO affected the Korea economic growth in terms of above four key factors.

We design the road map between the growth of the POSCO and the Korea economic growth in terms of the following aspects. First of all, the POSCO played a key role in the growth of the manufacturing sector via the very positive front-back industry effect for other industries as the POSCO emerged as one of the global steel companies with being the center of the national key steel industry. Secondly, the POSCO supported the government-leading role in the process of the Korea industrialization via the role of the market-oriented national firm and played a key role in the export-leading foreign policy. Thirdly, the POSCO supported the enhancement of the state productivity and the accumulation of the human capital via the various direct and indirect role of the POSCO such as the technology development and innovation, the management innovation, the independent management, the firm welfare, the compliance management, the firm ideology of the patriotism, and the education investment and the accumulation of human capital to aim the education patriotism.

It is not easy to show systematically the scientific or the statistical empirical analysis for these road maps. We, however, merely infer the good management performance via the POSCO's leading role and draw conclusion that the excellent firm performance played a very positive role in the Korea economic growth via the growth of the manufacturing sector. Hence, we try to investigate the empirical analysis based on the two hypotheses as follows:

Hypothesis 1 : The POSCO's management performance had a positive impact on the growth of the Korea manufacturing sector and thus the POSCO contributed to the Korea economic growth.

Hypothesis 2 : The various technology innovation, the management innovation and the company culture of the POSCO resulted in the improvement of the POSCO's productivity and this contributed to the Korea economic growth via the development of the manufacturing sector or the increase in the Korea economy productivity.

The Hypothesis 1 can be carried out by two analyses. First of all, it is to examine the relationship between the growth of the manufacturing sector and the sale growth of the POSCO. In the time-series analysis, the Granger causality test can be used to investigate the causal relationship between two variables[5]. Secondly, the POSCO tried to carry out the preemptive expansion construction of the steel mill based on the forecasting of the future demand for steel products. Hence, we conjecture

5   Strictly speaking, the Granger causality test is not a concept to analyze the real causal relationship between two variables but a concept in terms of forecasting. That is, if the variable x is helpful for the future forecasting of the other variable y, ones state that x Granger causes y. Nevertheless, it is general to use the Granger causality test in order indirectly to evaluate the causal relationship between two variables.

that it is evaluated for the POSCO to increase their production capacity whenever the expansion construction of the Pohang and Gwangyang steel mills was completed and this contributed to the improvement of the POSCO's productivity and the development of the manufacturing sector. For this analysis, we use the dummy variable approach. For example, in the year of the completion of the Pohang's first, second, third and fourth steel factors and the Gwangyang's first, second, third and fourth steel factors, the POSCO's performance would have been increased and this would have contributed to the Korea economic growth via the development of the manufacturing sector. For this analysis, we set the completion year as the dummy variable and examine whether the growth of the manufacturing sector had been increased especially in the same year.

To test the Hypothesis 2, we conduct an empirical analysis to examine the relationship between the POSCO's productivity and the growth of the manufacturing sector and the productivity of the Korea economy. We consider the regression analysis on the POSCO's productivity and the growth of the manufacturing sector or the regression analysis on the POSCO's productivity and the productivity of the Korea economy.

B. Empirical analysis

As the POSCO completed the first Pohang steel factor one month ahead on July 1973 and built the 1.03 million tons of the steel production capacity as a synthesized steel mill, the POSCO had 0.1 billion dollars of the sales and 1.2 million dollars of the net profit at the first year. This performance has been recorded as a unique performance in terms of the history of the world steel industry (Seo 1997). Since then, as the second Pohang steel mill was completed on May 1976, the production capacity of the POSCO increased to 2.6 million tons per year and the GDP of the Korea started to grow rapidly.

Kim and Lee (2012) analyze the case of the first President Tae-Joon Park in order to examine the relation between the use of the psychological words and the group performance and divide the term of Tae-Joon Park into three different periods. The first period is the foundation period of the 1968-1973, the second period is the leaping period of the 1974-1985 and the third period is the full-fledged period of the 1986-1992. Since the completion of the first Pohang steel factory in 1973, the annual average growth rate of the sales were 43.25% over 1974-1985 and 17.3% over 1986-1992 respectively. The annual average growth rate of the sales over the term of the President Tae-Joon

Park over 1973-1992 except the first 1973, was 34%.

[Figure 11] Net profit and sales of POSCO and nominal GDP

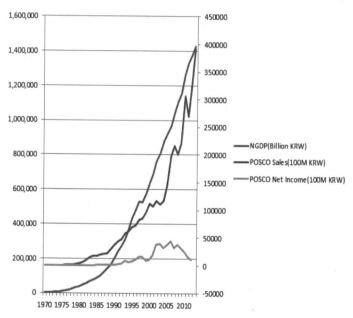

Source : BOK (2015), POSCO (2004, 2009)

There appears to be a positive correlation between the sale growth of the POSCO and the real GDP growth of the Korea economy over 1973-2014. That is, it may indicate that the growth of the Korea economy is high when the sale growth of the POSCO is high and vice versa. According to the estimated regression equation, as the sale growth of the POSCO increases by 1%, the GDP growth of the Korea economy increases by 0.026%. This estimation result is based on the assumption that the sale growth of the POSCO is exogenous. However, as the economic growth is high, the sale growth of the POSCO can rise, and thus, we cannot exclude the possibility of the endogenous sale growth of the POSCO and if so, we may not strongly insist the result of our estimation. Even so, it seems to be certain indirectly that the sale growth of the POSCO had a positive impact on the Korea economic growth. When we exclude the Korea currency crisis period of the 1999-2001 in which the GDP growth was minus, it is evaluated that the positive correlation between the sale growth of the POSCO and the economic growth was much stronger than the non-excluding periods.

Since, however, the correlation analysis does not provide any information on the causal direction between two variables, ones use the Granger causality test in order to examine the causal relation in the econometrics. We briefly introduce the Granger causality test as follows. Let x_t and y_t be two variables. If our interest is to test the causal relation between two variables, we set following two models:

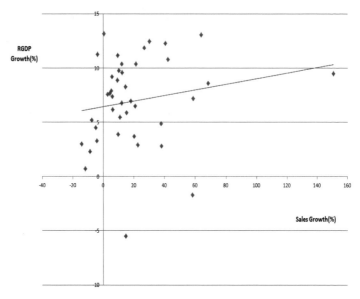

[Figure 12] The relationship between POSCO's sale growth and Korea economic growth

$$y_t = \alpha_y + \sum_{i=1}^{p} \beta_i y_{t-i} + \sum_{j=1}^{p} \gamma_j x_{t-j} + \epsilon_{yt}, \tag{1}$$

$$x_t = \alpha_x + \sum_{i=1}^{p} \delta_i x_{t-i} + \sum_{j=1}^{p} \theta_j y_{t-j} + \epsilon_{xt}, \tag{2}$$

where $\alpha_i, i = x,y$ is a constant term, $\beta_i, \gamma_i, \delta_i, \theta_i$ are the coefficients to be estimated, and epsilon $\epsilon_{xt}, \epsilon_{yt}$ are the error terms of the two equations. In order to test the Granger causal relation between two variables based on the estimation of the two equations, we set the following hypothesis:

H_0 in the model (1): x_t does not Granger cause y_t.

$$H_0 : \gamma_1 = \gamma_2 = ... = \gamma_p = 0 \qquad (3)$$

H_0 in the model (2): y_t does not Granger cause x_t.

$$\Rightarrow H_0 : \theta_1 = \theta_2 = ... = \theta_p = 0 \qquad (4)$$

The Equations (1) and (2) can be estimated by the OLS (ordinary least squares) and we can test the hypotheses (3) and (4) by using the Wald Test based on the estimation result. As the result of the hypothesis test, if we reject the hypothesis (3), it is said that x_t does Granger cause y_t and x_t is helpful for the forecasting of the future y_t.

Let x_t and y_t be the sale growth of the POSCO and the growth of the manufacturing production respectively for the Granger causality test. We conduct the Granger causality test for two different samples: the 1974-2014 of the whole sample period and the 1974-1994 of the term of the President Tae-Joon Park[6]. As the result of the test, we did not find the significant difference over two samples. First of all, the null hypothesis (3) that the sale growth of the POSCO does not Granger cause

6   Since the figure in 1973 is extremely different from other periods, we exclude that year from our sample. In addition, even though the real term of the first President Tae-Joon Park was 1968-1992, we include the 1993 and 1994 in the analysis of the Tae-Joon Park period. The reason is that these two years would have been affected by the management of the Tae-Joon Park.

the growth of the manufacturing production was rejected. This result indicates that the POSCO's performance made a significant contribution to the growth of the manufacturing production and would support the previous empirical result based on the input-output analysis to examine the front-back industry effect. That is, it is interpreted that the success of the POSCO was the success of the Korea steel industry and this led the growth of the manufacturing sector via the front-back industry effect.

[Table 11] Granger causality test for POSCO's sale growth and the growth of manufacturing sector

Items	1974–2014 (Whole Sample Period)			1974–1994 (TJP Term)		
Null Hypothesis	F-Stat	P-Value	Result	F-Stat	P-Value	Result
The sale growth of the POSCO does not Granger cause the growth of manufacturing production	4.216	0.009	Reject	4.844	0.028	Reject
The growth of Manufacturing production does not Granger cause the sale growth of the POSCO	4.523	0.006	Reject	4.121	0.042	Reject

Note: TJP Term denotes the term of the first President Tae-Joon Park.

In addition, we can test the reverse causality about whether the growth of the manufacturing sector contributed the sale growth of the POSCO. As the result of the test, the null hypothesis (4) that the growth of the manufacturing production does not Granger cause the sale growth of the POSCO was also rejected. This result implies that the growth of the manufacturing sector such as automobile, electronics, ship, and electricity, had a positive impact on the growth of the steel industry and thus contributed to the sale growth of the POSCO. In sum the results of the Granger causality test indicate that there have been a mutually organic relation between the steel industry and the automobile, electronics and ships industries and they made a positive structure each other via the front-back industry effect and thus contributed together to the Korea economic growth.

The second empirical analysis for the test of the Hypothesis 1 is the dummy variable approach to reflect the expansion period of the POSCO's factory. As described in previous section, if the POSCO's performance contributed to the Korea economic growth, we infer that the factory expansion of the POSCO increased the production capacity, the POSCO's performance and eventually contributed to the growth of the manufacturing sector. For the empirical analysis, we consider the following model:

$$y_t = (\beta_0 + \beta_d D_t) + \sum_{i=1}^{p} \beta_i y_{t-i} + \epsilon_t \,. \tag{5}$$

where D_t is the dummy variable where it is 1 in the completion year of the POSCO's factory expansion and the increase in the steel production capacity and otherwise it is zero. The Equation (5) is an AR model (autoregressive model) and if the completion of the steel factory expansion increased the steel production capacity and thus resulted in the high growth of the manufacturing production, the value of the estimated coefficient $\widehat{\beta}_d$ in the Equation (5) is expected to be positive and statistically significant at the conventional level.

We estimate the model (5) for two sample periods of the 1974 -2014 and the 1974-1994. The dummy variable, D_t, is set at 1 in the 1973, 1976, 1978, 1983, 1987, 1988, 1990, and 1992 when the four expansions of the Pohang steel mill and the four expansions of the Gwangyang steel mill were completed and is set at zero otherwise.

[Table 12] The effect of POSCO's expansion on the growth of manufacturing sector

Estimated Coefficient	1974-2014 (Whole Sample Period)			1974-1994 (TJP Term)		
	Estimates	t-Stat	Significance	Estimates	t-Stat	Significance
β_0	6.644 (1.680)	3.954	Significant (1%)	6.929 (2.832)	2.447	Significant (5%)
β_d	7.408 (2.574)	2.877	Significant (1%)	6.152 (2.708)	2.271	Significant (5%)
	0.175 (0.131)	1.335	Not Significant(10%)	0.254 (0.173)	1.468	Not Significant (10%)

Note : The parenthesis of the second and fifth columns denotes the standard error of the estimated coefficient and that of the fourth and seventh columns denotes the significance level for the hypothesis test of the estimated coefficient.

The estimation results are similar in the both samples. The values of the estimated coefficient on the constant dummy variable, $\hat{\beta}_d$, are all positive and statistically significant. The estimation results indicate that when the POSCO completed the expansion construction of the steel factory and increased the steel production capacity, the POSCO's performance increased and this resulted in the high growth of the manufacturing production. Especially, in the completion years of the expansions of the Pohang steel factory and the Gwangyang steel factory, the average growth of the manufacturing production was estimated to be higher by about 6% ~ 7% than other periods. Therefore, it is evaluated that the POSCO's performance contributed greatly to the growth of manufacturing sector and thus to the Korea economic growth.

In sum, the empirical results of the Granger causality test and the dummy variable approach appear to support the Hypothesis 1. That is, it is evaluated that the good performance of the POSCO to produce the rice of the industry led the growth of the manufacturing sector and had a positive impact on the heavy-chemistry industrialization and this made a significant contribution to the Korea economic growth.

The Hypothesis 2 suggests that various technology innovation and management innovation, and the firm culture in the POSCO resulted in the improvement of the POSCO's productivity and this eventually contributed to the Korea economic growth via the contribution to the development of the manufacturing sector and the productivity enhancement of the Korea economy. That is, this hypothesis indicates that in order to realize the education patriotism of the Tae-Joon Park that encouraged fostering the talented human resources to lead the future industry of the state, as the POSCO carried out the technology development, the technology innovation, R&D investment, the industry-academic cooperation, the education of the field workers, the workplace innovation via the firm-level self management, the positive relation between the development of the firm welfare and the surplus management, and the creation of the economic externality for Korea industrialization via the learning and the dissemination of the story of the POSCO's success, the POSCO supported the improvement of Korea economy's productivity and the accumulation of the human capital and consequently contributed to the growth of the Korea economy. To conduct the empirical analysis of the Hypothesis 2, we examine how the growth of the POSCO's productivity affected the growth of the productivity of Korea economy and consider the following regression model:

$$y_t = \beta_0 + \sum_{i=0}^{p} \beta_i x_{t-i} + \epsilon_t \, , \tag{6}$$

where y_t is the growth of the productivity of the Korea economy, and x_{t-i} is the growth of the per capita productivity of the POSCO. We incorporate the lags of the independent variables to consider that the change in the POSCO's productivity could affect the growth of the productivity of the Korea economy in the short run and in the long run. The sample period for the data availability is 1974-2003 and the estimation result is as follows:

$$y_t = \frac{5.835}{(0.953)} - \frac{0.030}{(0.038)} x_t - \frac{0.010}{(0.039)} x_{t-1} + \frac{0.028}{(0.038)} x_{t-2} + \frac{0.057}{(0.027)} x_{t-3} + \epsilon_t. \quad (7)$$

$$\overline{R}^2 = 0.180$$

According to the estimation results, the estimated coefficients from the contemporaneous coefficient to the second lagged coefficients, $\beta_0 - \hat{\beta_2}$ are not statistically significant but the value of the third lagged coefficient, $\hat{\beta_3}$, is 0.057 and statistically significant at the 5% level. That is, if the growth of the POSCO's productivity increases by 1%p, the growth of the productivity of the Korea economy increases by 0.06%p in the 3 years. We interpret that if the POSCO increases their productivity by carrying out various management innovation, the technology innovation, the firm welfare, the self-management, and the industry-academic cooperation, these efforts may be incorporated into the Korea economy and eventually, increase the productivity of the Korea economy 3 years later. Consequently, this empirical result supports the Hypothesis 2.

In sum, as the result of the empirical analysis on the Hypothesis 1 and Hypothesis 2, we evaluate that the increase in the POSCO's performance resulted in the increase in the growth of the manufacturing production and this had a positive impact on the Korea economic growth. Moreover, it is evaluated that the improvement of the POSCO's productivity resulting from various technology innovation, management innovation and the firm welfare brought about the increase in the productivity of the Korea economy over several years and the POSCO's effort to pursue the training, education, and industry-academic cooperation contributed to the accumulation of the human capital in the Korea economy.

IV. The growth of the POSCO and the role of Tae-Joon Park Leadership

So far, we tried to find that the growth of the POSCO made a significant contribution to the rapid and sustainable Korea economic growth via the study on the existing literature and the empirical analysis on the relation between the POSCO's performance and productivity, the growth of the manufacturing sector, the productivity of the Korea economy, and the Korea economic growth. As shown in the previous section, the POSCO accomplished remarkable success in management performance and high productivity through the role of the market-oriented national firm, technology and management innovations, the technology development and the training of the high-brain researchers via the industry-academic cooperation, and the welfare-oriented firm culture. We evaluate that the POSCO as the key driving firm of the steel industry, dedicated to the growth the manufacturing sector, the enhancement of the productivity of the Korea economy, the accumulation of the human capital, and eventually contributed deeply to the Korea economic growth. In a word, the POSCO is the model case for the firm to have led the Korea economic growth. If so, what are the key factors for the success of the POSCO? McKern and Malan (1992) state that the main reasons for the POSCO's success are the leadership of the Tae-Joon Park and the mission and the commitment of the POSCO's workers.

Lots of existing literature assure without any hesitation that the leadership of the first President Tae-Joon Park (hereafter TJP) from the foundation in 1968 to 1992, is the key factor for the POSCO's success. Even though the existing literature showed the decisive contribution of the TJP leadership to the POSCO's growth by using various methodologies, most literature focused on the key characteristics of the TJP leadership. The existing literature suggests the following factors of the management philosophy of the TJP leadership: the patriotism and the state organism (W. Kim 2012), the integrity leadership (M. Kim 2012), the compliance leadership (Park 2012), the management by great spirit (Baek 2012), the Tae-Joonism and the thought of the classical scholar (Song 2012a, 2012b), the self-management (Lee and Kim 2012), the view of the science and technology (Lim 2010), the hero leadership (Jun 2013), the mission of the martyr (Choi and Kim 2012), the undying patriotism (Choi 2013), the "Jae-Cheol-Bo-Gook" and faithfulness (Choi 2012), the education leadership (S. Lee 2012), the welfare idea and the firm development (Y. Lee 2012), and the spirit to defeat Japan (Hur 2013)[7]. Although there are other factors about the management philosophy of the TJP leadership, they appear to be similar with above main factors.

This study assumes the fundamental mechanism—the frontier TJP leadership $\Rightarrow$ the success of the POSCO $\Rightarrow$ The Korea economic growth—and focuses on the key factors of the TJP leadership for the Korea economic growth with synthesizing the various characteristics of the TJP leadership suggested in the existing literature. Especially, we take a different approach with the existing literature by deeply focusing on the role of the TJP leadership in terms of economics. After we outline the key characteristics of the TJP leadership which is supposed to have played an important role in the Korea economic growth, we will consider the re-examination of the existing literature and the empirical analysis.

---

7   Hur (2013) shows an excellent summary for the existing literature on the management philosophy of the TJP leadership.

1. The management performance over the term of the first President Tae-Joon Park

The Korea President Jung-Hee Park who supported the view that the steel industry is the national power, had a strong desire to build the construction of the synthetic steel mill from 1962 (Rhyu 2001). The President Jung-Hee Park insisted the state revivalism and dreamed the national prosperity and defense by accomplishing the national industrialization via the heavy-chemistry industrialization and the promotion of the defense industry. The President Jung-Hee Park realized that the steel industry is the national key industry and is the foundation of the heavy-chemistry industrialization and the promotion of the defense industry, and for this end, he designed the economic development plan. In this process, the first President of the POSCO, Tae-Joon Park, was affected by the strong national revivalism of the President Jung-Hee Park and recognized that the steel industry to produce the steel which would be the rice of the industrialization, should be the pillar of the national revivalism project. That is, Tae-Joon Park's idea was the realization of the "Jae-Cheol-Bo-Gook" which implied that the steel is the source for all industries and is the fertilizer of the industrialization to make the nation revive and be the wealth and power (W. Kim 2013).

The synthetic Pohang steel mill (renamed as the POSCO in 2002) was built on April 1, 1968, in order to realize the promotion of the steel industry for the national revivalism of the Korea President Jung-Hee Park and the spirit of the "Jae-Cheol-Bo-Gook" of the POSCO President Tae-Joon Park. The President Tae-Joon Park called the Center for Pohang Comprehensive Construction to be the cradle of the construction works as "the Rommel House" and managed the construction field works efficiently. He completed the construction of the first Pohang steel factory which had 1.03 million tons per year of the steel production capacity, on July 1973, one month ahead, with the full commitment to the mission to demonstrate "the Spirit of the Right Face" meaning that all workers should be drowned in the Pohang Sea if the construction project of the Pohang Steel Mill failed. Since then, as the POSCO completed the second, the third, and the fourth Pohang steel factory expansions, the POSCO had the 9.1 million tons per year of the steel production capacity in 1983 and ranked as the 12th steel company in the world. Furthermore, Tae-Joon Park started to build the first Gwangyang steel factory with successfully hosting the construction project for the second Korea synthetic steel mill in 1982 and made the POSCO have the 20.5 million tons per year of the steel production capacity with completing the fourth Gwangyang steel factory and be the 3rd steel company in the world in 1992.

Over his term from the operation of the Pohang steel factory in 1973 to 1992, the first President Tae-Joon Park accomplished the remarkable success in management performance as follows: the 34% of the annual average sale growth, the 71.3% of the annual average net profit growth, and the 2.3% of the ratio of the POSCO sale to the Korea GDP in 1992. The annual average productivity growth measured as the per capita steel production, was the 15% and the ratio of the POSCO's steel production to the Korea total steel production was the 71.3% and the localization ratio of the POSCO was the 63.1% in 1992. As the result of the remarkable performance, the world credit evaluation company, Standard and Poors (S&P) rated the credit rating of the POSCO as "A+" and this evaluation was the very good rating whereas the credit ratings of other main firms were low due to the threatening of the national security by the North Korea.

[Table 13] Management performance over the term of the
President Tae-Joon Park (1968~1992)

Items		1973	1992	Growth (%)	Year Avg. (%)
Sale & Profit	Sales(b KRW)	41.6	6,182.1	14,861	34.0
	Profit(b KRW)	4.6	185.2	40.3	71.3
	Sale/GDP(%)	0.8	2.3	287.5	8.0
Productivity	Production(1k ton)	449	20,012	4457.0	26.2
	Production / Person(ton)	106.6	848.0	8.0	14.9
	Ratio of Domestic Steel Production(%)	15.5	71.3	460	12.9
	Ratio of Domestic Production Facility(%)	12.5	63.1		
POSCO's Credit Rank			- S&P:A+ - Moody's :A2		
Ratio of Government Share Holding(%)		66.6	20.0		
Workers		2,581	23,599		
World Ranking		-	3rd	-	-

Source : POSCO (2004) and author's calculation

In addition, as the result of the Granger causality test for the
POSCO's sale growth and the growth of the manufacturing
production over the TJP term in the [Table 10] and [Table
11], we found that there was the bidirectional causal relation
between these two variables and that, as the result of the
dummy variable approach, the growth of the manufacturing

production was higher in the expansion year of the Pohang and Gwangyang steel factories than other years over the TJP term. Especially, the President Tae-Joon Park tried to make strong efforts on the promotion of the technicians and the productivity improvement via the technology development, the safety, the quality management, the self management, the firm welfare, the industry-academic cooperation, the training, and R&D investment in order to make the POSCO the world-class steel company. The preliminary empirical analysis for the efforts can be conducted based on the regression analysis between the growth of the POSCO's productivity and the growth of the Korea economy productivity over the TJP term as in the case of the whole sample in Section III and the estimation result is as follows:

$$y_t = \frac{6.924}{(0.992)} - \frac{0.046}{(0.033)}x_t - \frac{0.019}{(0.034)}x_{t-1} + \frac{0.018}{(0.033)}x_{t-2} + \frac{0.054}{(0.023)}x_{t-3} + \epsilon_t \quad (8)$$

$$\overline{R^2} = 0.372$$

According to the estimation result, the estimated coefficients on the contemporaneous and the second lagged growth of the POSCO productivity, $\beta_0 - \hat{\beta_2}$, are not statistically significant but the third lagged coefficient, $\hat{\beta}_3$, is 0.054 and statistically significant at the 5% level. That is, this result indicate that if the growth of the POSCO's productivity increases by 1%p in this year, the growth of the Korea economy productivity increases by 0.054%p in the 3 years. We infer that since the estimation result for the TJP term is very similar with that of the whole sample, the overall management performance of the POSCO appears to be based on that of the TJP term and this result is consistent with Kim and Choi (2011).

2. The essence and the role of the TJP leadership

What factors of the leadership did the President Tae-Joon Park make the POSCO be the exemplary icon of the Korea firm growth model? It is necessary to examine the essence and the role of the TJP leadership if ones investigate how the TJP leadership led the success of the POSCO and resulted in the Korea economic growth by contributing to the rapid industrialization of the Korea economy in terms of the economic growth and the firm performance. Most of existing literature, however, focus on the effect of the TJP leadership on the POSCO's performance and try to explain the essence and the characteristic of the TJP leadership.

In this study, we focus on the examination of the essence and the role of the TJP leadership in terms of macroeconomics view of the Korea economic growth. That is, we analyze the essences of the TJP leadership which could be related to the key factors of the Korea economic growth among various key factors in this chapter and address the channel through which these essences contributed to the Korea economic growth while we examined how the growth of the POSCO had an influence on the key factors of the Korea economic growth in the previous chapter.

A. The commitment to the rapid growth of the manufacturing sector and the rapid industrialization through the Taejoonism and the realization of the "Jae-Cheol-Bo-Gook"

The POSCO led the growth of the manufacturing sector with the pivot on the heavy-chemistry industry from the completion of the first Pohang steel factory construction and contributed to the rapid economic growth. If so, what are the absolute driving forces for POSCO to lead the industrialization standing on the front of the Korea heavy-chemistry industrialization only within the 6-7 years of the completion of the first Pohang steel factory construction? The key driving force was the "Jae-Cheol-Bo-Gook" spirit of the President Tae-Joon Park. The key idea of the "Jae-Cheol-Bo-Gook" spirit is that the steel is the base of the industrialization, the industrialization is the foundation for the national prosperity and defense and the national democratization is possible in the firm base of the national prosperity and defense. The core principle of the "Jae-Cheol-Bo-Gook" spirit is that the missions of the POSCO are to provide cheap but high-quality steel products for the nation, to increase the national wealth and to complete the social responsibility through the rational management.

The President Tae-Joon Park deeply felt the tragedy of the Korean modern history which included the Japanese colony, the division of the Korea into the South and North, and the severe poverty and strictly thought that the inability of the Korea ancestors should be blamed at the first. He had deep lamentation because Korea was not as strong as Japan and thus became the Japanese colony. Hence, Tae-Joon Park had a strong desire to defeat Japan by establishing the rich and strong state via the industrialization and the democratization, resolving his sorrow of Japanese colony and being a richer and stronger country than Japan (J. Choi 2013). The President Tae-Joon Park judged that to defeat Japan, which resulted in the tragedy in the Korea modern history, they should establish the driving force to enable the rapid economic development and the construction of the world-class Pohang steel mill was the core. He understood very well the modern industrialization that the steel would be the physical base and the driving force for the modern industrial civilization and the nation and decided to concentrate on the steel industry, insisting the "Jae-Chol-Bo-Gook" spirit that the construction of the integrated steel mill should be essential for the industrialization and the national prosperity and defense.

The "Jae-Chol-Bo-Gook" spirit of the President Tae-Joon Park was combined with the strong steel industry spirit of the Korea President Jung-Hee Park who led the developmental state system for the national revival in 1962 and was supported at the national level. The Korean President Jung-Hee Park recognized that the anticommunism and the national modernization should be the most imminent task for the national revival and for this end, the top priority task should be the rapid industrialization. The President Jung-Hee Park judged that the rapid development in the manufacturing sector should be necessary for the national industrialization and the key was to promote the heavy-chemistry industry with centering on the petroleum-chemistry, steel, ship, electricity and electronics, automobile, and machinery. Especially, he regarded that the steel industry was the key national industry for the building of the industrial country and pushed forward the promotion of the heavy-chemistry industry as the start of the construction of the Pohang integrated steel mill in the second 5-year economic development plan. Consequently, the "Jae-Chol-Bo-Gook" spirit of the Tae-Joon Park and the national revivalism of the Korea President Jung-Hee Park were realized in the economy field via the construction of the Pohang integrated steel mill and this has been a core driving force to lead the growth of the manufacturing sector, the rapid industrialization and thus the Korea economic growth.

In 1960s, however, the Korea economy did not have any capitals or social infra for the construction of the steel mill and there was a severe objection against the construction of the steel mill in the Korea political and economic world. In this situation, to make matters worse, the financial plan of the KISA (Korea International Steel Associates) which was composed of 7 steel companies in the USA and Europe, in order to carry out the construction of the steel mill via the loan of foreign capital, went to pieces completely (Rheu 2001). Tae-Joon Park considered the idea of the transfer of the Korea's property claims against Japan in Hawaii and for this end, he tried to have the support and the cooperation of the Japanese government and the Japanese steel association with his undying patriotism. Eventually, he began the construction of the first Pohang integrated steel mill in 1970 with busy himself about the realization of the idea (J. Choi 2013).

President Tae-Joon Park took a step forward from the sacrifice of the frontier in the construction of the Pohang steel mill and emphasized the sacrifice of martyr for the national prosperity and the descendant's welfare (J. Choi 2013). Tae-Joon Park insisted strong principle of life that since the Pohang steel mill was built by the precious money of the ancestor (taxpayer) which was called 'Korea's property claims against Japan', the construction should be successful. He thought of failure as equivalent to committing a crime, so, POSCO had to take an attitude to repay to the nation and the ancestors by successfully completing the construction of the steel mill with "the Spirit of the Right Face." Therefore, from the point of the view that since the POSCO was a national firm operated by the taxpayers' fund, the workers had to complete their responsibility as a civil servant and furthermore, from the point of the historical implication and the role of the POSCO, the great cause of the era that the POSCO had to be managed not simply as a profit-seeking firm but as a national firm at the national experience and knowledge level, still remained as the core management ideology of the POSCO (W. Kim 2013).

D. Lee (2004) describes the undying patriotism and the sacrifice of martyr of Tae-Joon Park as two mottos in his life: "My short life for my forever nation" and "There is no absolute despair." The first motto indicates the undying patriotism at the religious level that he would like to serve his nation as God and devote his short life to the nation. The second motto implies the positive willingness, the hope and the strong confidence, suggesting that whatever the desperate situation is, he cannot give up and can overcome the absolute despair (J. Choi 2013). B. Song (2012a) suggests "the Taejoonism" which is an integrated explanation framework by consistently unifying all events and factors of the Tae-Joon Park who made a great achievement by establishing the POSCO as a national firm beyond an excellent private firm. B. Song emphasizes that the Taejoon Park ideology can be summarized as the three sentences: "There is no absolute despair," "There is no absolute impossibility" and "There is no absolute self-interest." The Taejoonism can be the comprehensive spiritual force with which the President Tae-Joon Park realized the "Jae-Cheol-Bo-Gook" spirit by the construction of the POSCO and led the rapid industrialization of the Korea economy. B. Song (2012b) emphasizes that the Tae-Joon Park had a classical scholar spirit as the practice, the activity in the field, and the criterion of the behavior. However, the cores are different from the existing thought in terms of the strong willingness(knowledge), the rightness of communication (rightness), the lope of belief (integrity), and the deep movement and the joyfulness (love).

K. Baek (2013) calls the comprehensive idea as "the Management by Great Spirit (MBS)." The comprehensive idea is what the President Tae-Joon Park showed in the all periods from the foundation to the growth and includes both rationality and non-rationality and are realized by the ultra management values and management methodologies. The Management by Great Spirit means that the leader who has the spiritual affection for the nation produces the indomitable management value by melting the mission and that the management value is realized as the practical management system by the tempering such as the steelmaking or the smelting. Tae-Joon Park showed the consistent and unshakeable management value in all the periods from the foundation to the growth of the POSCO. According to the principle of the modern business administration, the funds, technology, human resources, and market are needed for the foundation and the management of the firm, and the foundation of the POSCO was possible due to the power of the Great Spirit to melt everything in the tough process in which the POSCO had to make the funds, technology, human resources, and market themselves and establish their business. The Management by Great Spirit of Tae-Joon Park was expressed in the five management values: the value of the frontier spirit, the value of the public priority, the value of the humanism, the value of integrity, and the value of creative innovation. The MBS was realized with the active thought of the practical force, strong active energy to look for challenges to the end with the inside force of the mission and focus on the right direction (K. Baek 2013). That is, the Tae-Joon Park's MBS based on the national spirit has been the driving force to make the world-class POSCO by melting all the limits when POSCO faced the national mission of revival of the steel industry (K. Baek 2013).

The characteristics of the TJP leadership which contributed to the growth of the manufacturing sector and the industrialization of the Korea economy are summarized as follows. The TJP leadership was combined with the developmental nationalism of the Kore President Jung-Hee Park and realized the "Jae-Cheol-Bo-Gook" spirit. This eventually contributed to the Korea economic growth. President Tae-Joon Park thought that the national prosperity and defense via the industrialization was to overcome the tragedy in the Korea modern history, and for this end, wholeheartedly committed himself to raising the steel industry as the rice of the industrialization. He carried out the construction of the Pohang steel mill with the courage of his convictions, his integrity, no self-interest, and the attitude that there was no absolute despair in order to overcome all objections and obstacles. In addition, he showed the undying patriotism and the sacrifice of martyr and led the growth of the POSCO via the Management by Great Spirit. The comprehensive ideology framework of the TJP leadership is the Taejoonism and is the overall spiritual driving force for the "Jae-Cheol-Bo-Gook sprit." spirit. Consequently, the aspect to contribute to the growth of the manufacturing sector and the industrialization in the characteristics of the TJP leadership can be summarized as the following flowchart: Taejoonism ⇒ The Management by

Great Spirit ⇒ Jae-Cheol-Bo-Gook spirit ⇒ The growth of the manufacturing sector ⇒ The rapid industrialization ⇒ The rapid Korea economic growth.

B. The commitment to the foreign-oriented trade policy via the pursuit of the world-class POSCO

As the import-substituting industrial policy was replaced by the export-leading foreign trade industrial policy in the early period of the Korea President Jung-Hee Park government in 1960s, the steel industry was reset as the government-leading key industry. In the foundation stage (1968 1973), the POSCO was owned by the nation and was the growth engine for the Korea economic growth in the Jung-Hee Park's government which tried to push forward the rapid industrialization and economic growth (Rhyu 2001). The Jung-Hee Park's government nominated the POSCO as the national key industry and the frontier of the heavy-chemistry industrialization and advocated the key body of the strategic industrial promotion policy through which the government carried out the national security and the export expansion strategically. The POSCO was totally supported by the government as the leading firm for the export-oriented foreign economic policy.

Tae-Joon Park deeply felt the national mission of the POSCO and dreamed the construction of the POSCO as the world-class steel company in order to realize the "Jae-Cheol-Bo-Gook Spirit." He recognized that the POSCO had to have the world competitiveness in order to be the world-class steel company and the world competitiveness could be supported by the lower production cost, high-quality product, the efficient management and the technology development for the sustainable growth and for this end, tried to push forward various efforts.

Tae-Joon Park had a strong willingness to build the competitive world-class steel company which could produce the cheap but high-quality steel product and tried to fulfill the ultra-rational management value in order for the POSCO to have the international competitiveness from the early periods of the foundation. He predicted not only the domestic demand for the steel product but also the international demand in the early period of the foundation and in line with his prediction, he tried to build the world-class integrated steel mill. Since the steel industry was the national key industry to have the economy of scale, he judged that the efficient promotion of the steel industry could be possible by the construction of the only integrated steel mill. Since the domestic demand for the steel product in Korea was higher at the early stage of the industrialization than the domestic supply and the POSCO was a national firm, it was considered normal for the POSCO to provide their all productions for the domestic firms. Tae-Joon Park, however, continuously exported the 20% ~ 30% of the POSCO's total steel productions and put his heart and soul into having the world competitiveness with insisting that the POSCO was the global steel company to compete with the foreign steel companies (D. Lee 2004).

Tae-Joon Park recognized that the POSCO had to reform the firm constitution fundamentally according to the growth stage in order to be the winner in the international competitiveness. Although it was important to successfully build the steel factory at the early stage of the factory construction and then to secure the cost advantage via the accumulation of the production technology, he thought that the only accumulation of the production technology could not guarantee the success if the POSCO wanted to be the global steel company, and tried to make the system to compete in the base of the efficient production management, the quality management, the technology innovation in the facility and the process, and the development of new product (Kim and Choi 2011). Tae-Joon Park strongly fulfilled the efficient management philosophy in the firm management in order to make the world-class POSCO such as the production cost reduction via the lower purchase of equipments and the lower cost of construction, the firm consciousness for the production cost and quality, the best level in the technology, safety, quality, and the production cost, the effort for the management and technology innovations, and the effort for the self management. K. Baek (2013) emphasizes that Tae-Joon Park consistently carried out the ultra-rational management values such as innovative management, compliant management, global management, quality management, creative management, and sustainable management in the construction, expansion, and the management frontier from the early foundation and this was the core management thought (Management by Great Spirit) to make the POSCO be the world-class steel company.

Tae-Joon Park tried to incorporate his life motto of "To be the world best whatsoever" into the technology. He emphasized that the securement of the international comparative advantage, the diversification of the market, and the creation of new demand depend on the level of technology power and that the technology development should be the core driving force for the firm development and continuously improved the existing technology level with devotion to the R&D. He also established the POSCO's independent R&D system and made an effort to continuously possess the dominating position in the world steel market by the technology development (Lim 2010, Park and Nam 2012).

The Tae-Joon Park's willingness to make the POSCO be the world-class steel company, can be the practical manifestation of the "Jae-Cheol-Bo-Gook Spirit." Tae-Joon Park tried to remind his undying mission that since the POSCO was a national firm to be built by the national precious fund, the POSCO had to contribute not only to the stability of the domestic price but also the enhancement of the international competitiveness of the domestic firms by providing the steel products for the domestic customers at the lower price than the international price via the efficient management and the continuous technology development and by the reduction of the production cost of the related industries and led their commitment by sharing it with all his workers. His pioneer leadership to realize the world-class POSCO, devoted greatly to the export-leading growth policy led by the Korea government via the leading role of the POSCO.

C. The strong commitment to the Korea government role
through the pursuit of the market-oriented national firm

Since the financial shares of the Ministry of Finance and the Korea Tungsten Company on the POSCO capital were 56.2% and 43.8% respectively in the foundation in 1968, the POSCO was completely the nation-owned national firm. On the one hand, the POSCO had to be controlled by various state interventions and regulations according to the "Steel Industry Promotion Act." On the other hand, the POSCO was the state within the state or the state agency with a lot of supports from the national institutes by the aggressive national strategy and the strategic industrial promotion policy (Rhyu 2001). In order to realize the "Jae-Cheol-Bo-Gook Spirit", Tae-Joon Park had undying patriotism and the mission of martyr without any self-interest and wanted to establish the POSCO as an exemplary national firm which should be the foundation of the industrialization for the Korea development in priority. At the same time, he regarded the market-oriented national firm as important because the POSCO was a national firm and had to pursue the aggressive and commercial firm strategy continuously in order to make the competitive advantage in the world market. With the economic point of the market-oriented view, he tried to seek continuously the firm strategy which supported that as the state-owned firm, the POSCO was within the state but had to grow as the independent global company (Rheu 2001). J. Choi (2013) describes that the POSCO was within the market but exceeding the market, meaning that the POSCO was the firm to serve the nation and the people, and Tae-Joon Park carried out the national mission of the POSCO with the point of the mutual views on relation between the state and the firm as the state view and the firm view.

Tae-Joon Park emphasized the important national mission of the POSCO from the foundation and clearly announced that the mission of the POSCO was to increase the national wealth by providing the cheap but high-quality steel products for the nation and to complete the social responsibility through the rational management. He continuously asked all workers to serve for the nation and the society and to have the strong mission as a civil servant because the POSCO was a national firm. He also emphasized that the steel company to produce the steel which was the rice of the industry in the industrialization strategy of the developmental state, had to have the responsibility to lead the manufacturing sector and the industrialization as a national firm. He thought that since the POSCO was the historical national firm established by the national blood and sweat, they had to pursue the mission of the national firm through the firm mission, the foundation spirit, and the shared value. This TJP leadership of the undying patriotism enabled the POSCO to have the close policy cooperation with the government from the early stage of the Korea industrialization, to be the frontier of the market and to be the driving force of the Korea economic growth with creating and raising the market. Consequently, the POSCO played a pioneer role in leading the government-leading economic growth with shaping the market-creative and mutual-cultivating government-firm relation to develop the national capitalism.

Tae-Joon Park recognized very well that if the POSCO, as a national firm, was managed based on the bureaucratic system of the national firm in the system of the authoritarian nation, the POSCO tended to be affected by the wave height of the competitive market with being restrained by the principle of the bureaucracy and could not survive in severely competitive world market. He thought with the point of the practical and industrial occupational view that the national firm had to cope with the market situation sensitively and pursue the market efficiency and growth in order to accommodate various profit-seeking desires of the market. He judged that the market-oriented producers had to have the intelligence in order to predict and cope with the response of the customers, and the firm manager needed to have the on the spot foresight to timely analyze, read, and cope with the market (W. Kim 2013). From this point of view, Tae-Joon Park was a complete marketeer. Tae-Joon Park started to export the steel product with targeting the international steel market from the beginning of the POSCO foundation and showed the prescience to transform the firm organization with deeply reading and predicting the long-term trend of the world steel market (W. Kim 2013). Moreover, he actively carried forward the introduction of new technology one step ahead, R&D, the expansion of the science and technology, and the industry-academic cooperation in order to increase the world competitiveness via the quality improvement of the POSCO's products and the reduction of the production costs.

These strong pursuits of the market-oriented national firm by Tae-Joon Park could lead the government-leading industrialization by supporting that the POSCO played a key role in carrying forward the heavy-chemistry industrialization domestically and play the leading role in pursuing the economic development strategy of the export-leading foreign trade policy by the government internationally. If he was a businessman to simply manage the national firm, the POSCO would not have become a world-class company and the government-leading economic development strategy would not have been successful due to inefficient heavy-chemistry industrialization.

D. The commitment to the productivity improvement and the accumulation of human capital through technology innovation, management innovation, education patriotism, and the pursuit of advanced firm culture

Tae-Joon Park had a strong desire to accomplish the education patriotism with carrying forward excellent education for long-term development of the industry and the nation as he tried to achieve the "Jae-Cheol-Bo-Gook Spirit" with the success of the POSCO (Lim 2010). He selected the manpower among fund, material, technology, and human resource needed for the firm management as the most important factor. He recognized that the high technology power, the mission and the good human resources were the driving forces in the process of the rapid economic growth. In 1970s, he realized that the education in the Korea engineering colleges was isolated from the industrial reality and thus was not realistic. He developed various company-own training programs via the POSCO Training Center and systematically established new field education model. Tae-Joon Park pushed ahead with steady activity of technology improvement through the oversea technology training and the company training and especially, he emphasized the technology improvement and innovation in the workplace and insisted that the arrangement and clearance in the workplace should be most fundamental. Tae-Joon Park introduced the master technician program in order to inspire the importance of the development of the field technology and prepared the compensating system for the technicians. The master technician program was to select skillful field workers with good personality and attitude and to make them competitive field workers who could be admired from all the workers due to both their high contribution and excellent technology (T. Park 1985).

In addition, Tae-Joon Park established the comprehensive research institute to support the R&D of each business unit at the basic and integrated science level in order to pursue the strong self-conscience for the technology and thorough technology self-reliance and built the research-oriented university, the POSTECH, as the innovative plan of the securement of the talented human resources which could cope with the demand for high brains. He designed the industry-academic cooperation framework in order to lead an innovation in the firm management and raise the high brains in terms of long-term view and for this end, established the organic triangle research cooperation system which was composed of the POSCO -the Institute of the Industry-, Science and Technology, and the POSTECH. It is evaluated that these efforts, with the cluster of high brains, contributed greatly not only to the consistent research from the basic research to the commercialization but also to the optimization of the research efficiency (Lim 2010). Tae-Joon Park set forth his management mind at the national level that the integration of the comprehensive research institute with the research-oriented university should be the foundation for building a large scale facility of the science and technology R&D.

Tae-Joon Park sought the continuous productivity improvement and the increase in the international competitiveness through the technology development and innovation and R&D investment. He regarded the technology development as the core of the sustainable firm development and thought that the technology should be the driving force for the firm development. Since the international comparative advantage, the diversification of the market, and the creation of new demand which the POSCO actively sought depended on the level of technology, he tried continuously to improve the level of the existing technology and commercialize their independent technology development in the international steel world (T. Park 1985). He made strong efforts in improving the strand casting technology to play a key role in increasing the productivity in the steel mill and planned new steel factory which was supposed to have the world hi-tech facility and to be called the "21-century steel mill", and consequently constructed another world-class steel factory in Gwangyang outside Pohang region. He always deeply felt that the POSCO could not survive in the international competitiveness of the steel industry without the independent technology development.

Tae-Joon Park tried to improve the productivity through the workplace innovation. The workplace innovation is the high-performance innovation in which the improvement activities by the participation of the field workers are crucial. Depending on how newly and efficiently the field workers reform their work places, the medium and long-term performance could be significantly different (Bae 2008). The self management originally was the terminology used to indicate the total improvement activity of the small group in the workplace with centering on the first frontier supervisor or worker of the field in the Japanese steel industry and Tae-Joon Park introduced the self management activity and carried forward the independent POSCO innovation system in the workplace. Tae-Joon Park regarded the self management as the management of the humanism because the good management system was to respect the human nature and dignity, help the self-realization, and to achieve the target of the firm management (Lee and Kim 2012). Tae-Joon Park tried to provide their workers with the opportunity to develop the independent spirit and the independent ability and this effort became the self management activity in the POSCO. The purpose of the self management of Tae-Joon Park was that the workers was supposed to analyze and resolve their self problems, experience the resolving process, increase their capacity and simultaneously stimulate the motivation with the management to respect human being. Lee and Kim (2001) show that the self management activity was energetically conducted and as a result, the POSCO's management performance such as the labor productivity improved when Tae-Joon Park had the religious confidence on the self management and led strongly the introduction and the growth of the self management.

Tae-Joon Park pursued the advanced firm culture and the firm welfare with the spirit of the civil servant and the belief for the ideology of the firm welfare and the building of the welfare society which were related to the "Jae-Cheol-Bo-Gook Spirit." He supported the strong ownership company and was confident with the inseparable relation between the life of the worker and the growth of the company. Then, he supported the welfare of the nation based on the achievement of the firm welfare and fulfilled the welfare system at the firm level. Tae-Joon Park established a typical firm welfare system which included the provision of the worker-ownership housing, the amplification of the living facility, the scholarship program and the perfection of the education facility, the asset accumulation by the stock-sharing plan for the employees, and the employee participating program by the selective welfare system (G. Lee 2012). It is evaluated that the welfare system by Tae-Joon Park could be a factor for POSCO to have the management surplus by leading the long-term years of labor and this consequently contributed to the improvement of the POSCO's labor productivity.

In sum, Tae-Joon Park put efforts on the continuous increase in the POSCO's productivity via the technology development and innovation, the enhancement of the international competitiveness through the R&D investment, the workplace innovation based on the effort of the self-management, and the pursuit of the firm welfare related to the "Jae-Cheol-Bo-Gook Spirit." We evaluate that his leadership based on these efforts contributed to the improvement in the Korea economy productivity and consequently devoted to the rapid and sustainable growth of the Korea economy.

3. The TJP leadership and the performance of the POSCO: Empirical analysis

A. Characteristics and quantification of the leadership

Before the empirical analysis on the relation between the leadership and the economic growth, we need to understand the concept of the leadership. The right concept of the leadership has not been defined clearly and is different according to the point of the researcher's view. The research on the leadership started from the study on the effect of the dictatorship and the democracy the early 1900 and developed from the discussion on who has a right to decide to the study of the leadership (Bass 1985). Stogdill (1974) shows that as the result of the examination of the leadership concept over 65 years from 1902 to 1967, there were the 75 types of the leadership but the common context was the process of exerting the social influence for the organization's target.

The leadership is generally classified as two different types of the leadership: the transactional leadership and the transformational leadership. The transactional leadership refers to the effective achievement of the organization target by transacting the common elements which the leader and the followers mutually need. That is, it is the transactional way in which the followers show the efforts to faithfully fulfill their allocated tasks and the leader provides the proper compensation for their efforts. Hence, in the transactional leadership, the followers obtain the compensation for their business ability and the leader gets the benefit as the achievement of the organization's target. Since there is an obligation to obey the regulation in the transactional leadership, the leader takes a priority not on the stimulation of the change but on the stability of the organization. However, the followers obey the regulation in order to obtain the compensation for their efforts but it is general for the leader not to generate the willingness of the followers for the organization target.

The transformational leadership started to criticize that all the existing theories of the leadership were the same kinds of the transactional leadership. J. Bruns (1978) recommended the transformational leadership at first and since then, Bass (1985) materialized it. The transformational leadership is about the power of the leadership with which the leader accomplishes the target through the reform of the followers' values and attitude as the leader suggests the expected common target to the followers and appeals the mutual efforts to achieve the target. The transformational leadership is to inspire the followers to put efforts in order to achieve the long-term vision which the leader suggests while the transactional leadership is the exchange transaction between the achievement of the target and the compensation. The followers show the reform process in which they change their sentiment, values, and standard of behavior motivated to confidently achieve the target.

Bruns (1978) defines that the transformational leadership is the process which requires both the leader and followers to have the higher level of moral. Hence, the leader does not use the lower standard of emotion such as the fear, hatred, greed, and jealousy as in the transactional leadership but encourages the followers to reform their consciousness for themselves and strive for the organization target by appealing to the high-level ideal and the moral values of the followers.

Bass (1985) integrated the transactional leadership, the transformational leadership of Bass (1978), and the charismatic leadership. According to Bass (1985), the transformational leadership is the influential power with which the leader satisfies the high-level desire in order to accomplish the performance more than expectation beyond the self interest, makes the followers recognize the work characteristic, importance, and values, and have their motivation.

Bass (1985) suggests that the leadership is divided into the transactional leadership and the transformational leadership and the transactional leadership is sorted as the contingent reward and the management-by-exception, and the transformational leadership is classified with the charismatic leadership, the intellectual stimulation, and the individualized consideration. This classification is summarized in [Table 14].

[Table 14] Types of leadership

Leadership		
Transactional Leadership	Contingent Reward	Contracts exchange of rewards for effort, promises rewards for good performance, recognizes accomplishments
	Management -By-Exception	Intervenes only if standards are not met
Transformational Leadership	Charismatic Leadership	Provides vision and sense of mission, instills pride, gains respect and trust
	Intellectual Simulation	Promotes intelligence, rationality, and careful problem solving
	Individualized Consideration	Gives personal attention, treats each employee individually, coaches, advises

Source: Bass (1985) reprinted

Allen et al. (2006) have a different approach on the transformational leadership with Bruns (1978) and Bass (1985) who regard the transformational leadership as the connection between the pioneer and the decision of the leader to the reform of the individual follower and emphasize with the expansion of the transformational leadership that the leadership is not a decision of the leader but the process of making mutual reform with the unification of a lot of people being within a system. This new concept of the leadership is called various names such as the shared, the participatory, the collective, the collaborative, the cooperative, the democratic, the fluid, the inclusive, and the relational leadership. The collective leadership emerges as the globalization, the variety of normal life, reform, the development speed of information technology, the complexity, the tension resulting from various values, the income inequality, and the demand for sustainable education increase. The main roles of this leadership are to create the environment to support the prosperity and the growth of the peaceful life quality, to leave the sustainable harmony with nature to next generation, and to generate the society that shares responsibility and mutual interest.

The scientific methodology to quantify the leadership is important for the empirical analysis on the effect of the leadership on the performance or the development of the organization. However, since the concept of the leadership is so abstract, it is very difficult process to quantify the leadership. The study on the methodology to quantify the leadership is Bass (1985). Bass (1985) designed the Multi-factor Leadership Questionnaire (MLQ) which reflects the 73 various factors for the military persons in order to quantify the five elements of the leadership. However, Bass (1985)'s MLQ had repeated and ambiguous questions, and so, Bycio, Hackett and Allen (1995) amended Bass (1985)'s MLQ. Bycio et al. (1995) set up individual detail item of the leadership from the MLQ as the independent variable and conducted the survey by selecting the related item. The respondents to the questionnaire were nurses (97% of female, 37 of average age) and they were supposed to answer the zero 4 levels according to the degree of how many times their boss showed the same action with the questionnaire. The dependent variables were the degree of the extra effort, the satisfaction with the leader, and the influential power of the leader. As the result of this study, the above independent variables had more positive impact on the dependent variable above in the case of the transformational leadership than in the transactional leadership and in the sub items, the variables of the management-by-exception had a negative impact on the dependent variables above. The variables of the charismatic leadership had the biggest positive impact on all the dependent variables.

B. The leadership and economic development

The study on the relation between the leadership and the regional economic development is Stimson et al. (2004). Stimson et al. (2004) maintain that the strong proactive leadership induces the vision of the future development and results in the reform of the organization and the institution with improving the regional capacity through the strategy and the plan. Furthermore, they insist that as the effective institution and infra system induced by this reform make the mechanism use the resource endowment and the market conditions work and generate the sustainable development, it is possible to have the regional economic development. Hence, the regional economic development (RED) can be expressed as the following functional form:

$$RED = f(REM \ mediated by \ (L, I, E)] \tag{9}$$

REM (Resource endowments and its ⟨fit⟩ vis-a-vis market conditions) is the resource endowment and the fit to the market conditions, L denotes the leadership, E is the Entrepreneurship and I is the institute or the organization which is the important social organization to provide the rule structures. Hence, the RED can be expressed as the function of the resource endowment and the fit to the market conditions which are composed of the leadership, institution, and the entrepreneurship.

Stimson et al. (2004) show the adequacy of the RED function

by using the case studies. They have the case studies for two American regions of Pittsburgh and Houston, two British regions of Birmingham and Liverpool, the French region of Rennes, and two Asian city states of Hong Kong and Singapore. Pittsburgh is the model case which showed that Pittsburgh experienced severe unemployment in the early 1980s due to the depression of the steel industry but the private and the public leaders revived the regional economic development with improving the education, culture and technology of the Pittsburgh. Huston achieved the rapid economic development with the compliant spirit of the firm but did not enjoy the benefit of the regional development due to the absence of the leader. The Rennes was known as the symbol of the city revitalization in 1980s. The Rennes could develop the successful strategy due to the regional capital and achieve the city revitalization with centrally the high-level service, the new technology firm, the improvement of the life quality, the high level of the research, and the employment structure. The committee for the regional economic development was made in Birmingham and the Birmingham was the model case focusing on the regional economic issues. Sir Richard Knowles supported the Economic Development Committee with the charismatic leadership. Although this leadership ended with failure by resulting in various economic issues, it attracted the public interest for the economic development. However, the Liverpool had the opposite result in contrast to Birmingham. The leader of the Liverpool did not have sufficient capability and the unemployment rate in the Liverpool only to depend on the port industry increased with the change in the trade center from the Western Europe to the North America. This situation has lasted over 20 years due to the absence of the leader but the Liverpool could make the city revitalization as the center of the regional economy with searching the idea of the diversification for the economic grounds of the city.

In spite of the rare natural resources, Hong Kong could develop the commercial center through the macroeconomic conditions, the policy combination, and the regional institution. Singapore, in spite of the absences of the agriculture, the natural resources, the industrial tradition, and the firm spirit, accomplish economic development through the introduction of the authoritative bureaucracy based on the competitive base for multinationals. Stimson et al. (2004) show using the case studies that the RED can be accomplished by the REM (Resource endowments and ⟨fit⟩ vis-a-vis market conditions) which is composed of the leadership, institute, and the entrepreneurship.

From the point of the microeconomics view, the channel through which the leadership has an impact on the economic growth could be used to examine how the leadership can affect the firm performance. Cho and Choi (1998) studied what impact the leadership type of the CEO had on the performance of the information and technology (IT) by using the survey data for 25 manufacturers of the Seoul metropolitan and the Kyungnam province. They considered the structure-oriented leadership and the consideration-oriented leadership of the CEO as the independent variables and measured it with Likert's 5 scores. The measures of the IT performance as a dependent variable were ① the degree of the use of the IT on the management decision (in terms of professionals) and ② the satisfaction of the user for the IT (in terms of user). As the result of the empirical study, they could identify that there were a positive correlation between both the structure-oriented leadership and the consideration-oriented leadership and the performance of the IT. However, they showed that the structure-oriented leadership had a stronger impact on the IT performance in terms of the user than the professional, while the consideration-oriented leadership had a stronger impact to the professional than the user.

[Table 15] Leader's behavior for group performance

Leader Behavior		
Task-focused Leadership : understanding task requirements, operating procedures, and acq-uiring task information	Transactional	praises, rewards or avoids punishing a subordinate who fulfills expectations
	Initiating Structure	minimizes role ambiguity and conflict
	Boundary Spanning	increases the resources and the amount/variety of information available to the team
Person-focused Leadership: facilitating the beha-vioral interactions, cognitive structures, and attitudes that	Transformational	focuses on transforming followers' motivational state and vision via meaningful and creative exchanges
	Consideration	creates and preserves team cohesion.
	Empowerment	develops self-management and self-leadership skills of subordinates
	Motivation	creates continuous team effort, especially under difficult circumstances.

Source: Burke et al. (2006)

If so, what characteristic of the leadership contributes greatly to the firm performance? Burke et al. (2006) explain that the leader's behaviors in the [Table 15] can contribute greatly to the term performance outcomes. Burke et al.(2006) had an empirical study on how much each task-focused leadership and person-focused leadership contributed to the team performance. The comprehensive meta-analysis was used for the data analysis and the team performance for the dependent variable was set as the three types; the perceived team effectiveness, the team productivity per quantity, and the team learning. As the result of the empirical study, they found that both the task-focused leadership and the person-focused leadership had a positive correlation with the team efficiency, the team productivity and the team learning.

C. The role of the TJP leadership: An empirical analysis

The method to quantify the TJP leadership as described in the previous section is rare and the existing quantifying method does not reach to the objective estimation of the effect of the leadership based on the econometric model. When, however, it comes to several existing literature, M. Lee (2012) analyzes how the TJP transformational leadership had an impact on the market-oriented attitude of the organization via the deep interview with the key directors who had worked with TJP in one of the market-oriented management team. As a result, it is shown that the TJP leadership had a positive impact on the market-orientation and the management performance. Kim and Lee (2012) show that the factors of the verbal and psychological aspects in the TJP's speech had a significant relation with the important events to affect the POSCO. It is found out that as there were more important events where TJP had an impact on the team in charge, TJP more frequently used both positive and negative emotional words in the speech which was a main communication means with the team members.

K. Baek (2012) selected the 31 critical events related to TJP from various literature and as the result of the event analysis, he outlined the 14 key factors of the TJP leadership; the strategic foresight, the importance of economic view, the pursuit of the scientific perfection, the national mission, the humanism, the belief of integrity, the aggressively strategic choice, the behavior of the performance pressure, the initiative and sacrificing behavior, the support of the worker's improvement, the thorough field management, the adhesion of principle, persuasion and understanding, and strategic bargaining power and designed the comprehensive TJP leadership model based on these factors. He emphasizes that the most influential factor among 14 factors is the national mission.

D. Choi (2012) analyzed the quotations of the TJP based on the Herman's (2003) seven characteristics of the leader and found that the main characteristics of the TJP leadership were shown in the fields of 'the humanism and belief', 'the comprehensive complexity for resolving the problem,' and 'the priority for task achievement.' He emphasizes that the reason POSCO could become the world-class steel company in such a short period was that TJP not only put emphasis on the technology research and the self management based on the mutual belief with the workers but also established virtuous circle of setting the targets and achieving them. Kim and Kim (2012) analyze the 18 speeches in the beginning of new year, the 21 speeches in the anniversary of the company foundation, and the 13 speeches in the end of the year and find that as TJP had more realistic and optimistic communications with the workers, there were the significant increases in the amounts of sailing out, the steel production, the profit/ the sales, the total sale profits, the sales, the amounts of the sale, and the business profit.

In this study, we use the idea of the newspaper reports in Kim and Choi (2011) in order to quantify the TJP leadership.

Kim and Choi (2011) analyze the direct and indirect effects of the POSCO on the Korea economy by using the POSCO reports in the specific Korea newspaper. That is, their idea is that if the POSCO's direct and indirect impacts on the Korea economy were important, the main channel of disseminating the effects was through the press. They choose the specific daily newspaper of the "Jung-Ang Daily Newspapers" and selected 1,679 times reports about the POSCO from 1966 to 1992 and finally selected 1,674 cases with some adjustments. In this study, we re-select the reports about the TJP leadership from the Kim and Choi (2011) reports. The main contents of the selected reports are the pride, the technology support, the workers' welfare, the efficient management, the R&D, and the first President TJP. We produce the annual time-series number of the reports by integrating above leadership-related reports and examine whether the number of the leadership-related reports were significantly related to the management performance and the productivity of the POSCO. We model the following equation:

$$y_t = \beta_0 + \sum_{i=1}^{p} \beta_i x_{t-i} + \epsilon_t ,$$ (10)

where y_t is the sale growth or the productivity growth of the POSCO to reflect the management performance and x_{t-i} is the number of the TJP leadership-related reports at $t-i$ year.

We include the lagged independent variables in order to reflect that the leadership may have an impact on the management performance and the productivity in the short run and in the long run. The estimation result based on the ordinary least squares is as follows:

⟨ y_t : the sale growth of the POSCO⟩

$$y_t = \frac{-36.92}{(25.03)} + \frac{0.799}{(0.998)} x_t + \frac{2.083}{(1.195)} x_{t-1} + \frac{1.380}{(1.139)} x_{t-2} + \frac{2.556}{(1.148)} x_{t-3} + \epsilon_t$$ (11)

$$\overline{R^2} = 0.208$$

⟨ y_t : The growth rate of the per capita productivity⟩

$$y_t = \frac{-38.93}{(18.99)} + \frac{1.245}{(0.758)} x_t + \frac{0.951}{(0.907)} x_{t-1} - \frac{0.775}{(0.864)} x_{t-2} + \frac{3.795}{(0.871)} x_{t-3} + \epsilon_t$$ (12)

$$\overline{R^2} = 0.573$$

[Table 16] Times and contents of reports which are related to TJP leadership in the newspaper

Item\Year	Pride	Tech Support	Employee Welfare	Efficient Manage-ment	R&D	TJP	Total
1973	7	1					8
1974	4						4
1975	7	4					11
1976	21				1		22
1977	5		1		1		7
1978	11				2		13
1979	8		2		2		12
1980	5						5
1981	11				1		12
1982	3			1		1	5
1983	3				2	3	8
1984	4				1		5
1985	2			4	4	1	11
1986	4			3	4		11
1987	1			1	1	1	4
1988	6		2	1		1	10
1989	5			1	1	1	8
1990	6		3	1		4	14
1991	1		2	1	4	1	9
1992	9					12	21

Source : Author's reproduction based on the Kim and Choi (2011)

As the estimation result, in the case of the sale growth of the POSCO as a dependent variable, the estimated coefficients on the number of the TJP leadership-related reports are positive but not statistically significant except one case. The estimated coefficient on the 3-year lagged number of the TJP leadership-related reports is positive and statistically significant. This result indicates that when the TJP leadership activity was more frequent, the POSCO had the better performance in 3 years later and thus we infer that more active TJP leadership had more positive impacts on the POSCO performance.

In the case the growth of the per capita productivity as a dependent variable, the estimated coefficients on the number of the TJP leadership-related reports are positive except the two-year lagged reports (x_{t-2}) and especially, the estimated coefficient on the 3-year lagged number of the TJP leadership-related reports is positive and statistically significant. Hence, in the case per capita productivity of the POSCO, we infer that when the TJP leadership activity was larger, the POSCO had higher productivity in the three years and thus the TJP leadership contributed to the improvement of the POSCO's productivity.

The empirical analysis result on the TJP leadership can be

summarized as follows. The various TJP leadership activities over the his term such as the technology development and technology innovation, the management innovation, the field innovation via the self management, the training and the workplace learning, the industry-academic cooperation, and the company welfare, contributed to the improvement of the POSCO's per capita productivity and these resulted in the successive POSCO's management performance. The productivity improvement and the good management performance contributed greatly to the improvement of the Korea economy productivity and the sustainable Korea economic growth.

V. Application of TJP leadership to the economic development of developing countries

1. The TJP leadership and the POSCO's successful model

In this study, we examined the key factors for the rapid Korea industrialization and economic growth and investigated using the review of the existing literature and the empirical analysis how the growth of the POSCO had an impact on these factors. Moreover, we identify what were key roles of the TJP who contributed critically to the growth of the POSCO through the review of the literature and the empirical studies. In the modern world economic society, the developing countries which try to pursue the rapid economic growth have strong learning desire to carry forward the economic development of their own countries through learning of the Korea economic growth and for this end, actively considering the institutional introduction. Nowadays, the Korea is looking for various supports in order to help the economic development of the developing countries and this study would like to suggest the application plan of the POSCO's growth model for the strategy of the economic development of the developing countries.

We integrate the analysis results on the main causal relations between the role of the TJP leadership, the POSCO's success and the Korea economic development and stylize the POSCO's growth model. This typical growth model of the POSCO can be transmitted to the developing countries very well and contribute to the pursuit of the successful economic development. That is, when we focus on a few important firms such as the POSCO by analyzing the successful cases and developing them into the driving force for the economic growth based on the learning, application and dissemination of the role firm model, this strategy can be important starting point to stimulate the economic growth of the developing countries (Kim and Choi 2011).

What does the POSCO's growth model suggest in this study? The key points can be summarized as five aspects. First of all, the government tries to raise the market-oriented national firm and carries forward the government-leading economic development. Since the economic infra is very poor in the early stage of the economic development, the driving force based on the economic development strategy by the private sector leadership appears to be weak. In this environment, it is necessary to have the strong government leadership in order for the government to raise a national firm and fulfill the industrialization and such leadership can be much stronger in the case of the national firm than the private sector. However, the only promotion of the national firm may result in an inefficient firm performance due to the bureaucratic management and decrease the international competitiveness of the firm. Hence, in order to actively introduce the efficient and competitive elements of the market system and increase the world competitiveness, the government has to raise the market-oriented national firm.

Secondly, the government has to foster a world-class national firm which can lead the strategic foreign trade policy for economic development. The lesson learned from the world economic history is that the countries which pursued the foreign trade policy for economic development had higher average economic growth than other countries. The foreign trade strategy tends to increase the international competitiveness through the tough price and quality competition and these results in the improvement in the efficiency and the productivity of the firm. In this process, the surviving firm tends to be the world-class company. In this context, the POSCO could be the model case of the Korea firms by pursuing the world-class company through the openness and competition.

Thirdly, it is to raise the leading firm which can be the foundation for national industrialization and modernization. The steel company such as the POSCO produces the steel products which is the rice of the industrialization and can have an important impact on the national key industries such as electronics, electricity, shipping, automobile, and the heavy-chemistry industry. The steel company can provide the cheap and high-quality steel products for these industries and consequently can contribute to the increase in the international competitiveness of these industries. Hence, (the steel industry as the leading industry does not need to be but it is important to raise the leading industry and firm which can lead the national industrialization, even if it is not steel industry.)

Fourthly, it is important to carry forward continuous efforts on the productivity improvement and the accumulation of human capital through the technology innovation, management innovation, R&D, and industry-academic cooperation. The story of the POSCO's success implies that the key factors to leading the sustainable growth of the firm are endless technology innovation and the technology development. Moreover, the high-brains lead the national and industrial development. The POSCO put very active and various efforts for the productivity improvement and the accumulation of human capital. Especially, the technology development by the accumulation of human capital and the productivity improvement are very important in the countries, such as Korea, which has very few natural resources. In the countries which are similar environment with Korea, it is necessary to keep in mind this point.

Fifthly, it is necessary to raise a CEO who pursues undying patriotism, the market-oriented and rational attitude, and the management by great spirit. The successful case of the POSCO assures that the ideology and the point of economic view of the CEO are very important. As shown the TJP leadership, it is very important for the CEO of the national firm to abandon his or her self interest and to have undying patriotism in order to inspire the public interest and the self participation of the workers. The national firm to be the foundation of the industrialization can be another state beyond the simple firm aspect. Therefore, in order to accomplish the mission of the national prosperity and defense with national spirit, it is essential to have a CEO who carries forward practical management such as the first President Tae-Joon Park in the POSCO.

2. The application plan of the TJP leadership: The role of the POSCO

How well do the developing countries utilize the POSCO-type growth model? This study shows how important role the POSCO and the TJP leadership played in the Korea economic growth and provides an implication for the application plan to the developing countries based on this study. The application plan can be supported in terms of the role of the POSCO and the role of the government in the developing countries. What roles does the POSCO play in helping the developing countries learn the POSCO-type growth model and establish and carry forward their economic development strategy? Nowadays, the POSCO changed from the national firm to the private company but continuously pursues their social responsibility activity and the creative sharing value activity via the main activities of the POSCO TJ Park Foundation. Of course, this activity originates from the wish of the founder Tae-Joon Park. Therefore, the POSCO needs to disseminate the TJP leadership to the developing countries and find out the cooperation plan in order for the POSCO to help these countries effectively learn and apply the leadership to the economic development strategy at best. The cooperative plan needs to develop in terms of two aspects.

First of all, the POSCO try to build the center for the TJP leadership and run and support the international leadership program in order to help the developing countries raise their potential leaders. The center helps the potential leaders learn the key factors of the TJP leadership and systematically educates the strategy for the firm growth and the national economic growth. This education should be done in the very professional dimension and thus should be the way for them to have the opportunity of the practical and professional training. Especially, as the center runs the program for the economic policymakers in the developing countries, the POSCO can not only contribute to the establishment of the economic development plan but also significantly dedicate to the future growth of the POSCO by having the opportunity to develop mutually economic cooperation relation with the developing countries. Moreover, as the center helps the potential leaders learn how the TJP leadership developed from the foundation of the POSCO to the world-class POSCO and provides the practical education program through the field training in the POSCO steel mill or steel museum, it is necessary for the POSCO to stimulate their desire for the economic development.

Furthermore, the POSCO has to continuously support the research in order to systematically find out the key factors of the TJP leadership and develop the application plan for the developing countries. As the POSCO supports the scholarship and the research fund for the researchers of the economic development strategy in the developing countries and provides the opportunity to study and apply the key factors of the TJP leadership to the economic development plan, the POSCO would help the establishment of the economic development strategy and contribute to the succession of the undying patriotism of TJP.

Secondly, the POSCO needs to conduct the broad and various corporate social activities in order to carry forward their social responsibility at the international level. Nowadays, as the global firm is more popular across the international border, there is a limit to the promotion of the global leaders for the nation with focusing only on the education of the professional leadership in the leadership center. The reason is that the most important key factor of the TJP leadership is the undying patriotism and in the modern world, the undying patriotism is related to the social responsibility to contribute to the neighbor and the community across the international border. In order to succeed the wish of the first President Tae-Joon Park and to inculcate potential leaders in the developing countries about his undying patriotism, the POSCO should integrate the leadership center with the corporate social responsibility and support the social responsibility at the broader level and conduct various activities.

For this end, the POSCO needs to support the social responsibilities for the economic development in the developing countries with religion to the POSCO's responsibility and provide strong supports for the management of the TJP leadership program at the more extensive level. For example, each year, the Korea Press Foundation invites the press reporters of the countries which dispatched troops to Korea in the Korea War in the early 1950s and successfully runs the learning program which introduces the development process of various sectors such as Korea economy, politics, and culture. The POSCO needs to develop and launch various programs which benchmarks the program of the Korea Press Foundation and can practically contribute to the economic development in the developing countries by inspiring the leadership learning and the social responsibilities.

Nowadays, the POSCO is the world-class steel company living up to the President Tae-Joon Park's expectation. However, in the harsh international market in which the large company could not keep its sustainable growth in the endless international competition and crumbled away before long, the way for the POSCO to stay at the world-class company is to continuously remind and share the TJP leadership at the firm level. As one of ways, it is necessary for the POSCO to have in mind that the professional leadership training and the extensive social responsibilities are at least the necessary condition for the world-class POSCO.

3. Application plan for the TJP leadership: The role of the government in the developing countries

This study emphasizes that the strong Korea government leadership played a key role in the Korea economic development. In line with this point, the government of the developing countries to pursue economic development needs to be deeply interested in the POSCO-type growth model and actively utilize it in the establishment of their own economic development strategy. In detail, what roles and plans does the government of the developing countries carry forward?

First of all, the governments of the developing countries need to develop a cooperation program with the POSCO and run the training program to learn the Korea economic development model, the TJP leadership, the POSCO's management, and the POSCO's culture. In the situation where the developing countries did not experience their own countries' economic growth in the past, in order to draw a blue print for the fruit of the future economic growth and to have the practical wish, it would be helpful for the government of the developing countries to have the opportunity to learn the exemplary case of the Korea economy and the indirect experience. For this end, the government should try to develop the close cooperation relation with the POSCO and actively participate in the various international leadership training programs which the POSCO provides.

Secondly, the government of the developing country should host the leadership program supported by the POSCO and do their best in discovering and raising the potential leaders such as Tae-Joon Park by actively utilizing the scholarship and the research supporting programs. When the Japan walked into the industrialization earlier than other Asian countries and Korea was colonized by Japan, the first President Tae-Joon Park had an experience to build his point of the practical economic view through the insightful learning of the Japanese economic development. From this point of view, the learning and the training of the potential leaders in the developing countries about the Korea's case would have a very positive impact on the inspiration for their economic development.

Thirdly, the developing countries' governments need to develop the close network with the Korea government and the POSCO. In the foundation period of the POSCO, they did not have their own technology and tried to learn the technologies from the Japanese steel industry and developed them into their own technologies. The developing countries in the initial stage of the economic development are similar. In this situation where the technology level is low and the accumulation of human capital for the industrialization is weak, it is necessary for the government to raise their firms and industries by having the strong supports from the POSCO and the Korea government and for this end, the developing countries' government actively should pursue the establishment of the close cooperative relation with the Korea government and the POSCO. For example, the developing country's government could try to develop the strategical cooperative relationship with the Korea government and the POSCO in order to launch the training program to support the technology development and the promotion of technicians.

VI. Conclusion

As Korea achieved the remarkable annual average economic growth at 4.5% over 40 years, the Korea economic development is recognized as the exemplary case for the world economic growth history. In the early stage of the economic development, Korea had the economic aids from the Western developed countries but nowadays, Korea changes to the supporting country for the economic development in developing countries. Moreover, as the result of high economic growth, the status of the Korea economy becomes higher and higher in the world economy and the world society needs more contributions of Korea economy. In the perspective of developing countries, what are most necessary needs from the experience of Korea successful economic growth? The starting point for this question is learning of the strategy useful in order to build the industrial infra that plays an important role at the initial stage of economic development and the establishment of the world competitive firm. From this point of view, how Korea economy has built the industrial infra and has fostered several world-class companies such as POSCO, Samsung Electronics, and Hyundai automobile company?

The purpose of this research was to develop a POSCO-type growth model by deeply analyzing the background of Korea high and rapid economic growth and the role of the POSCO as the key growth engine and to seek an application plan which Asian developing countries such as Vietnam and India can use as an important strategy in pursuing their own economic development. Especially, we tried to deeply investigate the contributions of the POSCO in Korea economic development which have been the foundation for the establishment of Korea key industries and thoroughly examined what were key factors of TJP leadership which have been greatly contributed to the world-class POSCO and how these factors have worked in order to lead Korea economic development. Furthermore, we tried to standardize a POSCO-type growth model with focusing on the TJP leadership and developed an application plan which is useful for providing efficient economic development strategy for developing countries actively seeking efficient economic growth such as the case of Korea economy.

The key factors of Korea economic growth can be summarized in four aspects. First of all, Korea economy has pursued the substantial growth of manufacturing sector and flexible foreign trade policy. Secondly, Korea government has showed strong leadership in establishing and propelling the economic development strategies. Thirdly, Korea economy has smoothly rooted the market economy system and continuously fulfilled the efficient resource allocations. Fourthly, Korea economy made a positive relationship between education and economy based on the strong education spirit and accumulated optimal human capital and tried to achieve high and sustainable economic growth by enhancing productivity through technology developments and management innovations. Among above four key factors, two most important factors can be the government strong leadership and human capital.

In terms of four key factors of the Korea economic growth, the POSCO contributed to the development of Korea economy as follows. First of all, the POSCO has played an important role in leading the heavy-chemical industrialization and the growth and manufacturing sectors through the industrial development. The steel is the seed of industrialization and the steel industry is a large equipment industry, so the industrial relation effect tends to be very high because the steel industry demands a lot of goods of other industries and provides the steel products as intermediate goods for other main industries. As the result of empirical study on the analysis of the front-back industrial effect, the POSCO ranked the top or the second top and we evaluate that the POSCO made a significant contribution to Korea's industrialization and growth of manufacturing sector.

Secondly, the POSCO contributed the government-leading industrialization through a market-oriented national firm. In the initial stage of the economic development, since the capital accumulation tends to be poor and the social infra is weak, it is almost impossible for the private sector to lead effective economic growth. In order to realize the historical mission of Korea government under this situation, the POSCO took the lead of the government-leading industrialization with the economic philosophy of "Jae-Cheol-Bo-Gook" and the frontier of the heavy-chemical industrialization and faithfully, fulfilling the role of the market-oriented national firm which pursued strong international competitiveness in order to be a world-class steel company.

Thirdly, the POSCO has made a significant commitment to

the enhancement of national productivity and the accumulation of human capital through technology development, R&D investment, industry-academic cooperation and firm welfare. According to the TJP's mission of the POSCO, the envision of the "Jae-Cheol-Bo-Gook" and the education patriotism, indicating that the POSCO should develop human resources in order to lead national future industries, the POSCO has tried to achieve national industrialization and create the positive external effect with technology development and innovation, R&D investment, industry-academic cooperation, the training of field workers, the field innovation via company-wide own management, the positive relationship between the development of firm welfare and the surplus management, and learning and dissemination of the POSCO's success and consequently. All such actions have been dedicated to the enhancement of national productivity and the accumulation of human capital and thus the POSCO has contributed to the Korea economic growth.

As the result of the empirical analysis on the relationship between the success of the POSCO and Korea economic growth, we found that the sale growth of the POSCO had a positive impact on the growth of manufacturing sector.

Especially, the growth of manufacturing sector has been significantly higher in the expansion year of the POSCO's steel factory than other years. In addition, the growth of the POSCO's productivity had a positive impact on the growth of Korea national productivity with 3 years lags.

As the exemplary case of the model firm to lead the Korea economic growth, what are key factors of the POSCO's success? Lots of existing literature emphasizes the TJP leadership. Based on the mechanism which is the initiative TJP leadership ⇒ the success of the POSCO ⇒ Korea economic growth, this study considered all characteristics of TJP leadership and tried to analyze the key made a critical contribution to Korea economic growth.

First of all, TJP has made a contribution to significant growth of manufacturing sector and rapid Korea industrialization by the Taejoonism and the realization of the "Jae-Cheol-Bo-Gook spirit." TJP has kept his own confidence, integrity, no self-interest, and no absolute impossibility which were useful for overcoming all interruptions and obstacles, has tried to build the POSCO with undying patriotism and sacrifice of martyr and has led to the development of the POSCO with the "management by great spirit." The comprehensive integrated system of the TJP leadership which has committed to Korea economic growth through the great achievement of the world-class POSCO is the "Taejoonism" and this is the overall spiritual engine of the "Jae-Cheol-Bo-Gook."

Secondly, TJP has committed to the flexible foreign trade policy through the pursuit of world-class POSCO. TJP has felt that the mission of the POSCO for Korea would be realization of the "Jae-Cheol-Bo-Gook" and has dreamed of building the world-class POSCO. In order to achieve the mission, TJP has tried to accomplish global competitiveness of the POSCO and for this end, he has put various efforts such as the reduction of production costs, the improvement of product quality, the efficient management, and technology development for sustainable growth of the POSCO. The initiative TJP leadership for the realization of the world-class POSCO has been important contribution for Korea government to lead the growth policy of foreign trade-oriented exports by making the POSCO play a frontier role in the exports policy.

Thirdly, TJP has played an important role in achieving Korea government-leading economic development through the pursuit of the market-oriented national firm. TJP has shared the important mission of the POSCO for Korea economy with all workers at the beginning of the POSCO and has tried to fulfill the responsibility, as the national firm, that they should lead to the growth of manufacturing sector and national industrialization. In addition, TJP has focused on the reduction of production costs and the improvement of product quality in order to enhance the international competitiveness and has pursued the market-oriented management such as a one-step ahead introduction of new technology, R&D, expansion of science and technology and industry-academic cooperation. All these activities have made the POSCO play a key firm role in the heavy-chemistry industrialization and in the government-leading industrialization in the domestic context and a leading role in the realization of Korea development strategy by pursuing the government-leading foreign trade exports policy in the international context.

Fourthly, TJP has contributed to the enhancement of productivity and the accumulation of human capital through technology innovation, management innovation, educational patriotism and the pursuit of advanced firm culture. TJP has realized the necessity of education for industrialization and national development and has respected the educational patriotism. TJP has put great emphasis on training of industrial workers and the education of high-brain manpower through the training of field workers and the establishment of the industry-academic research cooperation system. TJP has continuously enhanced the POSCO's productivity and thus contributed to the enhancement of national productivity, through technology development and innovation, management innovation, self-management and field innovation, and advanced firm welfare. The empirical analysis has shown that TJP's suggestive leadership for management has had a positive impact on the POSCO's performance and productivity.

As the result of the main causality analysis between TJP leadership, the success of the POSCO, and Korea economic development, this study suggests following points for the application of developing countries. First of all, it is the learning of the POSCO-type growth model. The key aspects of the POSCO-type growth model are ① to pursue the government-leading economic development based on the establishment of the market-oriented national firm, ② to foster a world-class national firm which can lead the strategy of foreign trade policy for economic development, ③ to promote a leading firm which can be a foundation for national industrialization and modernization, ④ to pursue continuous efforts on the productivity improvement and the accumulation of human capital such as technology innovation, management innovation, R&D, and industry-academic cooperation, and ⑤ to foster a CEO who pursues undying patriotism, market-oriented and rational attitude and management by great spirit.

Secondly, the POSCO should build the center for TJP leadership in order to pursue learning, education and research for leadership development and to cultivate the potential leaders in the developing countries and to host the training session for them. In addition, the POSCO has to contribute to fostering potential leaders by providing the scholarship and the research funds for developing countries and has to run a leadership program for the policymakers of developing countries. Furthermore, the POSCO has to develop a program for its social responsibility and support the corporate philanthropic activity for the developing countries and provide active supports for the management of TJP leadership program.

Thirdly, the government of the developing countries has to develop a cooperative program with the POSCO and plan a training program for the learning of TJP leadership, POSCO's management, and POSCO's firm culture. In addition, the government has to host a leadership program supported by the POSCO, scholarship, and the research funds in order to raise their potential leaders and build a systematic cooperative relationship with the Korea government and the POSCO.

The purpose of this study is to contribute to the establishment and the pursuit of the economic development strategy by effectively providing the key factors of TJP leadership for developing countries. In addition, we hope that this study is utilized as the important reference for integrating the growth model of the newly re-leaping POSCO into the long-term plan of Korea economy and for keeping the sustainable relationship between the POSCO and the long-term development of Korea economy.

Acknowledgement :

This research is supported by the POSTECH. The author thanks Director Kwang-woong Choi (Tae-Joon Park Institute), Dr. Ki-Jun Jung and Dae-Hwan Lee for their constructive comments. The author also thanks Sun-Young Ahn, Jae-Young Moon, Eui-Hwan Park for their excellent research assistance.

References

Korean references

Ahn, Sang Hoon, and Ki Ho, Kim (2005). "Market structure and productivity: With the micro data of the Korea manufacturing sector" *The research on the financial economics*, Vol. 233, Bank of Korea Economic Research Institute.

Bae, Jong-Tae et al., (2012), 『The management ideology of Tae-Joon Park 2』, Book Asia Publisher.

Bae, Jin-Han, (2008), "Korea's Economic Development in Terms of Labor Market and Human Resource Development", *Economy and Management Review*, Vol. 31, No.2 1-32

Bae, Kyu Shik, (2008), "How do we carry forward the workplace innovation?: Workplace innovation and promotion policy", *International labor Brief* Vol. 6, No 11, KLI, 1-3.

Baik, Ki Bok, (2012), "The leadership of Cheongam Tae-Joon Park: The evidence theory and the derivation of the comprehensive model based on the critical events" 『The Tae-Joon Park's leadership』, Book Asia.

Baik, Ki Bok, (2013), "Management by Great Spirit of Tae-Joon Park", 『The ideology of the Tae-Joon Park brings about the future』, Book Aisa.

Baik, Ki Bok,(2012), 『The Tae-Joon Park leadership』, Book Asia.

Bank of Korea, Economic Statistics System http://ecos.bok.or.kr/

Byun, Hyung-Yoon,(2012) 『History of Korean Economy Development』, Knowledge Industry Publisher.

Cho, Jung-Ho, Choi, Soo-Hyung, (1998) "An Empirical Study on the Impact of Ceo's Leadership Style on Information Technology Success.", *Review of Business and Economics*, Vol. 11, No.3, 239-252

Choi, Dong-Joo, (2012), "The study on the Tae-Joon Park's value system based on the quotation analysis: With Herman's Leadership Trait Assessment," 「Taejoonism」, Book Asia.

Choi, Dong Yong, (2007), "Inter-Industry Analysis on Steel Industry," *POSRI Management Review*, Vol. 7, No.1 29-45

Choi, Jin Duk, (2013), "The tragedy in the Korea modern history and the undying patriotism of the Tae-Joon Park," 「The ideology of the Tae-Joon Park brings about the future」, Book Aisa Publisher.

Choi, Jin Duk, and Hyong Hyo, Kim (2012), "The sacrifice of martyr for the nation and the firm: The philosophical review for Tae-Joon Park and the existing reflection," 「The ideology of Tae-Joon Park」, Book Asia.

Han, Jae-Ho et al., (1988), 「POSCO and National Industrial Economy」, RIST

Heavy and Chemical Industry Promotion Council (1973). 「The promotion plan of the heavy-chemistry industry」.

Heavy and Chemical Industry Promotion Council (1979). 「The practical status of the heavy-chemistry industry」.

Hur, Nam Jeong (2013), Revisiting Park Tae-Joon's leadership : attributes of Japanese culture & practical application, Hanyang University GSIS Ph.D Dissertation.

Im, Gyeong Soon, (2010), "Park Tae-Joon and Science & Technology," *Journal of Science & Technology Studies* Vol.10 No.2. 37-76

Jun, Sang-In, (2013), "Theory of the hero Tae-Joon Park: Modern political ideology of the 'Jae-cheol-ib-gook'," 「The ideology of the Tae-Joon Park brings about the future」, Book Aisa Publisher.

Jun, Sang-In, (2012), "Tae-Joon Park and region, firm, city: the co-existence and integration" 「Taejoonism」, Book Asia.

Jung, Koon-Oh, Lim, Eung-Soon, (2008), "Role of the Korea Steel Industry in the National Economy Analysis" *KAIS Review*, Vol. 9, No.3, 831-839

Kang, Kwang-Ha, et al. (2008). 「The policy decision system in the high economic growth era」, KDI.

KIET (1997), Study on the Development History of POSCO.

Kim, Byung-Yeon, and Sang-Oh Choi (2011), "POSCO and Korean Economy Analysis Based on Bibliographical and Empirical Method" *The Journal of Korea Business History*, Vol. 26 No. 2, 5-49.

Kim, Dohoon (2007), "History of Iron and Steel Production : Development of Modern Civilizations with Iron and Steel Production Technology Improvement(1)", *"Material Yard"*, Vol. 20 No. 4, 68-77.

Kim, Dong Heon, Lee, Manjong, Lee, Hongshik and Han, Chirok (2011), "The establishment of the Korea economic growth model and its application plan to the developing countries," Korea National Assembly Research Service.

Kim, Kwang Seok, and Jun Kyung Kim (1979). 『The Reasons of the high Korea economic growth』, KDI.

Kim, Min Jeong, (2012), "The integrity leadership based on the individual factor analysis," 『The Tae-Joon Park leadership』, Book Asia Publisher.

Kim, Myoung-On, Kim, Ye-Ji (2012). "Classification of Realistic Optimism Revealed in the Words of CEO and Its Effect", 『The management ideology of Tae-Joon Park 1』, Book Asia Publisher

Kim, Myoung-On et al. (2012). 『The management ideology of Tae-Joon Park 1』, Book Asia Publisher

Kim, Myoung-On, Lee Ji-Young(2012). "Relationships between Organizational Context and CEO's Use of Psychological Words in Speeches: Based on K-LIWC Analysis", 『The Tae-Joon Park leadership』, Book Asia Publisher

Kim, Nak Nyeon (1999). "Korea's Economic Growth in 1960s and the Role of the Government", *"The Journal of Korea Economic History"* Vol. 27 No.1 115-150

Kim, Sang-Kyu, Lee, Jae-Sang, Lee Eun-Young and Yun, Young-Kyun(1998), 『POSCO and Korean Economy Analysis Based on Inter-Industry Model』, POSRI

Kim, Si Dong, (1987). 「The process of promotion of the industrial rationalization in 1980s and the policy direction」, KIET.

Kim, Wang-Bae, (2012), "The developmental state and the national revivalism: The study on the Tae-Joon Park's patriotism in terms of the sociology of knowledge" 「Taejoonism」, Book Asia Publisher.

Kim, Wang-Bae, (2013), "The national and social view of Tae-Joon Park," 「The ideology of the Tae-Joon Park brings about the future」, Book Aisa Publisher.

Kim, Won Kyu et al (2000). 「The productivity analysis of the Korea industry」, KIET.

KITA (2010). Main Trade Indicators.

KOSTAT(1995). 「The Korea footpath via statistic」.

Korea Steel and Metal News(1996), Basic Knowledge of Steel, Korea Steel and Metal News

Korean Educational Development Institute(2008). 「2007 Education Statistics - Statistical Summary」.

Kwak, Gang Soo, Dae Jung Kim and Tae Young Kang (2012), "How to Measure Steel Company's Performance : Use of Factor Analysis Method", 「The management philosophy of the Tae-Joon Park 2」, Book Asia Publisher.

Kwak, Sang-Kyung et al. (1992), 「The POSCO and the Korea economy」, Su Jung Dang Publisher.

Kwon, Young Min, (2002). "Labor Endowments and Economic Growth : A New Growth Approach", *The Korea Journal of Economic Studies* Vol. 50 No.3. 271-305

Lee, Dae Hwan, (2004), 「The Steel King Tae-Joon Park」, Heyonamsa Publisher.

Lee, Do-Hwa, and Chang-Ho Kim (2012), "CEO Leadership and the workplace innovation: The case of the POSCO's self management QSS", 「The Tae-Joon Park's leadership」, Book Asia.

Lee, Myong-Sik, (2012), "The Effects of Top Management Leadership on Market-Orientation and Business Performance in Industrial Market: Focusing on Conger-Kanungo Model" 『The Tae-Joon Park's leadership』, Book Asia.

Lee, Sang Oh, (2012), "The study on the Tae-Joon Park's educational leadership", 『The Tae-Joon Park's leadership』, Book Asia.

Lee, Yong-Gab, (2012), "The welfare ideology of CEO and the firm welfare development: The study on the POSCO's welfare development," 『Taejoonism』, Book Asia.

Lim, Eung-Soon, (2010), "Economic Effects of the Korean Steel Industry," *POSRI Management Review*, Vol. 10, No.2, 5-27

Park, Chul Soon, and Yoon Sung, Nam (2012), "The POSCO legend and Cheongam: Servant manager and firm competitiveness" 『The management ideology of Tae-Joon Park 2』, Book Asia Publisher.

Park, Hun Joon, (2012), "The influence of the founder CEO on the positive organization compliance: Value consistency and mediator effect" 『The management ideology of Tae-Joon Park 1』, Book Asia.

Park, Tae-Joon, (1985), 『The wish of the Jae-Cheol-Bo-Gook: The quotations of the Tae-Joon Park』, POSCO.

Park, Tae-Joon, (1987), 『New Kind of Separated Families』, POSCO.

Park, Young Goo, (1999). "Foreign dependence and economic structure: The empirical study on the heavy-chemistry industry and the foreign dependence in 1970s" The Journal of Korea International Economics Association.

Park, Young Goo, (2001). "Government vs market?: The efficiency and implication since the adjustment of the heavy-chemistry in 1980s" The Journal of Korea International Economics Association.

Rhyu, Sang Young, (2001), "The political economy on the growth of the POSCO: Government-firm relation, continuous controversial, pursuit of the rent" The Journal of Korea Political Science Association, Vol. 34, No.2 67-87

RIST (1990), Development of Inter-Industry Model of POSCO.

Seo, Jeong-Heon, (1991), 『Development of Inter-Industry Model of POSCO(II): Based on Supply-Side Inter-Industry Model』, RIST

Seo, Kab Kyung, (2011), 『The management history of the steel King Tae-Joon Park』, translated by Dong Jin Yoon, Haneon Press

Shin, Taeyoung (2004). 『The contribution of the R&D investment to economic development』, Policy reference 2004-03, STEPI.

Social Science Research Institute at SNU (1987), 『The study on the POSCO's contribution to national economy and on the firm culture』, Social Science Research Institute at SNU.

Social Science Research Institute at SNU (1991), 『The study on the firm ideology of the POSCO and the firm culture』, Social Science Research Institute at SNU.

Song, Bok, (2012a), "The study on Taejoonism as a speciality", 『Taejoonism』, Book Asia.

Song, Bok, (2012b), "The Classical Scholar ideology of the typical scholar Tae-Joon Park" 『The ideology of the Tae-Joon Park brings about the future』, Book Asia Publisher.

The Compilation Committee of "35-year History of POSCO" (2004), 『35-year History of POSCO』

The Compilation Committee of "40-year History of POSCO" (2009), 『40-year History of POSCO』

The Compilation Committee of "The Korean Economy : Six Decades of Growth and Development" (2011) Sixty-year History of the Korean Economy.

Allen, K.E., Bordas J., Hickman G., Matusak L.R., Sorenson G., and Witmire K. (2006), *Leadership in the Twenty-First Century*.

Barro, R.J., and J.W. Lee (1993), "International comparisons of educational attainment," *Journal of Monetary Economics* 32, 363-394.

Barro, R.J., and J.W. Lee (1996), "International measures of schooling years and schooling quality," *American Economic Review* 86, 218-223.

Barro, R.J., and J.W. Lee (2001), "International data on educational attainment: updates and implications," *Oxford Economic Papers* 53(3).

Barro, R.J., and J.W. Lee (2013). A New Data Set of Educational Attainment in the World, 1950-2010," *Journal of Development Economics* 104, 184-198.

Bass, Bernard M. (1985), "Leadership: Good, Better, Best," *Leadership and Performance Beyond Expectations*, The Free Press.

Borenzenstein E., De Gregorio and J. W. Lee (1998). How Does Foreign Direct Investment Affect Growth?, *Journal of International Economics*, Vol 45, pp 115-35

Bruns, J. M. (1978), *Leadership*, New York: Harper & Row.

Burket, C.S., K.C. Stagl, C. Klein, G.F. Goodwin, E. Salas, and S.M. Halpin (2006), "What type of leadership behaviors are functional in teams? a meta-analysis," *The Leadership Quarterly* 17, 288-307.

Bycio, P., R.D. Hackett, and J.S. Allen (1995), "Further Assessments of Bass's (1985) Conceptualization of Transactional and Transformational Leadership," *Journal of Applied Psychology* V.80, No. 4, 468-478.

Coe and Helpman, (1995). International R&D Spillovers, *European Economic Review* 39 No.5, 859-887.

Collier, P., and D. Dollar (2001). *Can the world cut poverty in half? How Policy reform and international aid can meet international development goals*, World Development.

Davila, T. Epstein, M. & Shelton, R., 2006, *Making innovation work*, Wharton School Publishing.

Deininger and Squire (1996). "A New Data Set Measuring Income Inequality," *World Bank Economic Review, Vol.* 10. No.3.

Easterly, W. (2005). "National Policies and Economic Growth: A Reappraisal," *Handbook of Economic Growth,* edition 1, volume 1, 1015-1059.

Frankel, J. A., and D. Romer, (1999), "Does Trade Cause Growth?" *American Economic Review* 89(3), 379-399.

Grossman, G. M. and Helpman, E. (1991) Endogenous Product Cycles, *Economic Journal* Vol.101.

Hauseman, R., and D. Rodrik (2002). "Economic development as self-discovery," NBER Working paper No. 8952.

Hermann, M.G. (2003), "Assessing Leadership Style: Trait Analysis in Post", J.M., *The Psychological Assessment of Political Leaders: With Profiles of Saddam Hussein and Bill Clinton,* University of Michigan Press.

Im, G.S. (1999), "The Birth of the Postech: The Building of a Research University in Korea," in Kim, Yung sik and Bray, Francesca eds., *Current Perspectives in the History of Science in East Asia,* 238-242, Seoul: Seoul National University.

Kelley, T. (2001), *The art of innovation,* Currency Doubleday.

Kim, Chulsu, (2005). "Chapter 73 Korea," The World Trade Organization: Legal, Economic and Political Analysis.

Krugman, Paul (1994). The Myth of Asia's Miracle, Foreign Affairs.

McKern, B., and R. Malan (1992), POSCO's Strategy in the Development of Korea, Stanford Business School Case, 1992

Mukand, S., and D. Rodrik (2005). "In search of the Holy Grail: Policy convergence, experimentation, and economic performance," *American Economic Review* 95, 374-383.

OECD (1999). *Trade, Investment and Development*

Frankel and Romer (1999) "Does Trade Cause Growth?", *The American Economic Review,* 89(3), pp. 379-399.

Rodrik, D. (1996). "Understanding economic policy reform," *Journal of Economic Literature* 34, 9-41.

Rodrik, D. (2003). "Growth Strategies", NBER Working Paper No. 10050

Stern, N. (2001). "A Strategy for development," ABCDE Keynote Address, Washington DC, World Bank

Stimson, R.J., R.R. Stough, and M. Salazar, (2005), "Leadership and institutional factors in endogenous regional economic development," *Investigaciones Regionales* Vol. 7, 23 52.

Stogdill, R.M. (1974), *Handbook of Leadership,* New York: Press.

Williamson, J. (1990), "What Washington means by policy reform, Latin American Adjustment: How much has happened? *Institute for International Economics,* Washington.

World Bank (1993), "The East Asian Miracles: Economic Growth and Public Policy" *A world Bank Policy Research Report,* Oxford University Press.

World Bank (2001), *Global Development Finance.*

World Steel (2014), *Crude Steel Production Statistics*

청암 박태준 연구서 8

한국 경제성장에서 박태준 리더십의 역할과
개발도상국 적용방안에 대한 연구

발행일	2015년 10월 22일
펴낸이	김재범
펴낸곳	(주)아시아
지은이	김동헌
편집	정수인 김형욱 윤단비
관리	박신영
출판등록	2006년 1월 27일 제406-2006-000004호
인쇄	AP프린팅
제책	대원바인더리
종이	한솔 PNS
디자인	박종민

전화	02-821-5055
팩스	02-821-5057
주소	서울시 동작구 서달로 161-1 3층
이메일	bookasia@hanmail.net
홈페이지	www.bookasia.org

ISBN	979-11-5662-176-8 94080
	978-89-94006-39-0 (set)

이 도서의 국립중앙도서관 출판도서목록(CIP)은 서지정보유통지원시스템 홈페이지(http://seoji.nl.go.kr)와
국가자료공동목록시스템(http://www.nl.go.kr/kolisner)에서 이용하실 수 있습니다.
(CIP제어번호: CIP2015027375)